ZAPOTEC

PUEBLA

Puebla

Tehuacan

Olmec Land

Tuxtepec

Upper Mixteca

Nochistlán

Ixtlán de Juárez

SIERRA DE JUÁREZ

Tilantongo

Etla

Yalalag

Achiutla

Guelatao

Oaxaca

ZEMPOALTEPEC MTS.

Monte Albán

Teotitlán
del Valle

GUERRERO

Zaachila

Mitla

Lower Mixteca

Zimatlán

Tlacolula

O

A

Ocotlán

X

INTER-AMERICAN HIGHWAY

RIO VERDE

Miahuatlán

Jututepec

PACIFIC

Pochutla

GULF OF CAMPECHE

Alvarado Bay

PALOÁPAM R.

PLAYA VICENTE R.

SAN JUAN R.

C R U Z

Puerto México

TABASCO

U. S.

MEXICO

GULF OF MEXICO

PACIFIC OCEAN

Chimalapa

UNEXPLORED

C H I A P A S

C A

Juchitan

INTER-AMERICAN HIGHWAY

LAGOONS

Tehuantepec

Salina Cruz

palacios

OCEAN

BOOKS BY HELEN AUGUR

ZAPOTEC

TALL SHIPS TO CATHAY

PASSAGE TO GLORY

HELEN AUGUR

ZAPOTEC

DOUBLEDAY & COMPANY, INC.

GARDEN CITY, N.Y., 1954

LIBRARY OF CONGRESS CATALOG CARD NUMBER 54-5174

COPYRIGHT, 1954, BY HELEN AUGUR
ALL RIGHTS RESERVED
PRINTED IN THE UNITED STATES
AT THE COUNTRY LIFE PRESS, GARDEN CITY, N.Y.
FIRST EDITION

For the Gilberts—Sue, Ben, and Susan

CONTENTS

9

Contents

LIST OF ILLUSTRATIONS (*following page 126*)

PRONUNCIATION OF NAMES

Except for Indian place names, which follow various rules, readers familiar with Spanish do not need this table. For those who do not speak Spanish, the important thing is to pronounce the vowels distinctly; they always have the same sound: a, *ah;* e, *ay* (as in *day*); i, *ee;* o, *oh;* u, *u* (as in *bull*). The consonants which give trouble are: j, pronounced like *h;* ll, like *y;* ñ, like *ny,* and x, which may have a z or *h* sound, depending on the origin of the word. Place names ending in *an* or *al* are usually accented on the last syllable.

cacique,	kah-SEE-kay
campesino,	kahm-pay-SEEN-oh
Chiapas,	chee-AH-pahs
Cocijo,	koh-SEE-hoh
Cocijoeza,	koh-see-hoh-AY-zah
Guelatao,	guel-ah-TAH-oh
Huave,	whoo-AH-vay
huipil,	whoo-ee-PEEL
istmeño,	eest-MAYN-yoh
Ixtlán de Juárez,	eest-LAHN day who-AHR-ĕz
Juchitán,	hooch-ee-TAHN
Miahuatlan,	mee-ah-hoo-out-LAN
Mitla,	MEET-lah
Mixe,	MEE-hay
Mixtec,	MEEZ-teck
Monte Albán,	mohn-tay ahl-BAHN
Oaxaca,	wah-HAH-kah
Oaxaqueño,	wah-hah-KAYN-yo

Pronunciation of Names

Papaloápan,	papa-loh-AH-pahn
Quetzalcoatl,	KWET-zahl-coh-ahtl
Tajín,	tah-HEEN
tehuana,	tay-HOOAN-ah
Tehuantepec,	tay-hooan-tay-PECK
Tenochtitlán,	ten-oak-teet-LAHN
Teotihuacán,	tay-oh-tee-whah-KAHN
Teotitlán del Valle,	tay-oh-teet-LAHN del VAL-yay
vallista,	vai-YEES-tah
Xaquia,	sah-KEE-ah
Xipe Totec,	SHEEP-ay toh-TECK
Xochicalco,	soch-ee-CAHL-coh
Yalalag,	yah-LA-la
zapote,	zah-POH-tay
Zapotec,	ZAH-poh-teck
Zempoaltepec,	zem-poh-AHL-tay-peck

PART ONE

I

SO TEMPERATE AN AIR

In the center of Oaxaca there are three great valleys that flow together below the pyramids of Monte Albán. For beauty it is hard to choose among them; whichever one you happen to see first will capture you in its own way. You are never prepared for your first moments in this land, because it has been described to you in visual terms, and its first impact is on other senses.

If you happen to arrive by plane you will come down from a wilderness of mountains into the Valley of Oaxaca. With your first breath you realize that the air is fragrant; breathing is like drinking Rhine wine. On either side the fields stretch unbroken to purple ranges of the Sierra Madre del Sur, but you are not yet registering a mental picture. The forgotten pleasure of breathing is followed by one even rarer in this crowded world—the recognition that you are in a landscape with the right dimensions. A valley must be of certain proportions or one feels hemmed in. This one is so balanced that it opens out and out like the gateway to the Promised Land, and indeed it leads to the sumptuous Isthmus and the Pacific.

These first sensations, of air delicious on the palate and the skin, and of a land perfectly scaled to people, are a good introduction to Oaxaca and to the Oaxaqueños themselves. They too have a light, cool touch and an ingrained sense of proportion. Two centuries ago Thomas Gage traveled through Guatemala and all Mexico, only to write:

Zapotec

"Oaxaca is of so temperate an air, so abounding in fruits, and all provision requisite for man's life, so commodiously situated between the North and South Sea—that no place I so much desired to live in whilst I was in those parts as Oaxaca."

Perhaps he meant by "all provision requisite for man's life" something more than corn and fruits, for in the Valley of Oaxaca among the Zapotecs one begins to learn in what their daily bread consists. They are perhaps the oldest people of gentle breeding on this continent, a marvel of survival, and it is worth while to learn what things they have chosen to keep, and what has kept them whole, through three millenniums in this valley.

THE LITTLE PRAYERS

We were to spend New Year's Eve in Mitla, at the far end of the valley, and we started out in the late afternoon, when the mountains are an intense purple and a blue mist lies along their base. For this alone I would have come back to Oaxaca, to see that blue smoke roll along the valley's edge.

Near the city the plain is broad and pastoral. Fields of castor bean, corn, alfalfa ripple past; the villages lie well off the Inter-American Highway, islands of dense verdure with the twin towers of an old Dominican church just topping the trees. Oxen pulling tall-sided carts heaped with bamboo drowse along the Camino Real that skirts the Highway, and a little *campesino* drives his animals home from pasture, goats, burros, sheep, and cows all herded together.

Gradually a note of fantasy comes into this pastoral quiet. The mountains draw closer, sending out spurs and grotesque peaks, every one with its name and legend. The plain is broken by odd cone-shaped hills, some of them not hills at all but the muffled shapes of pyramids which once bore the palaces and temples of Zapotec kings. A lake covered the valley floor then, and the monarchs were rowed from their seat in Teotitlán del Valle to the festivals on Monte Albán.

This valley has always been the great artery of Zapotec life, running from the sacred mountain of Albán to the holy city of Mitla, the entrance to the underworld where the dead go to join their gods. Mitla lies in a region of limestone caves, many of them enchanted still, and as among most old peoples, caves mean the beginning and the end of life. Mitla was the supreme cavern, and under its exquisite temples kings and high priests were buried in the centuries before the Conquest.

There is a cave in a hillside not far away which may belong to a more ancient time when the Zapotecs worshiped the earth jaguar and a cave meant his open mouth from which mankind sprang and into which all men returned at death. When the Dominican missionaries arrived this hillside cave was an important shrine in which the people sacrificed turkeys amid clouds of copal incense. With their policy of preserving pagan sites and changing only the objects of worship, the friars erected a cross before the magic cave. The Zapotecs tore it down, and the friars set up a second cross farther down the slope. This was allowed to remain, and those Indians who prayed to it found their prayers answered. They began to revere it as miraculous and named it the Cross of Petitions.

Possibly it is still thought that the power of this hillside stems from the cave, for in recent times the Zapotecs moved it, so to speak, down to the cross. They built a small circular chapel around it with the whole front open, so that the rood appears to stand in the mouth of a cavern. And possibly there is a memory of the jaguar mouth as the greatest Zapotec symbol, the year sign, for all the people of the region come to the Cross of Petitions to make their New Year prayers.

By ten on New Year's Eve the young moon has set and the sky is powdered white with stars, more stars than one dreamed existed. On the dark slope below the enchanted cave fires are strewn like warmer stars, hundreds of fires, each one with a family sitting in a circle around it. And around them all, holding them all within a fiery circle, there is a rim of burning brush, a great round of golden light.

In the center is the chapel with its cross, and tonight it is a luminous cave, trembling with the light of many candles. The stone cross wears a gauzy white streamer and a garland of flowers, and beside it are two young men, not priests, who receive the offerings of the worshipers. The quiet people press into the chapel, holding candles and yellow flowers and a bit of paper with a picture of the cross, to place later on their home altars.

Each in turn, they give these things to be blessed. The young man presses the paper against the center of the cross at the front, then at the back. He sprinkles candles and flowers with holy water and gives them back to the petitioner, who then blows incense in the four sacred quarters of the earth and goes to his fire to build his prayer.

The prayer is visible. Whatever it is that the petitioner most desires—a house, a rich field, a yoke of oxen—he makes in miniature, as a little prayer. His family are all there, praying together around their fire for what they want most. This is the country of the best maguey, which provides fiery *mezcal* and fiber for ropes and bags, so many of the prayers are fields of maguey made from the pale green inner spikes of the plant itself, stuck one by one into the ground and neatly spaced, as in a real field. Houses are built of twigs or stones, and a tiny candle burns inside so that it looks warm and lived in.

One young bachelor, building a home for some sweetheart back in the mountains, was praying for a fine tile roof. He finished the walls, set the rafters of maguey spikes, and then with light and tender hands he tiled the roof with rounded bits of sugar cane laid one overlapping the other.

The family next to him wanted everything. They had built a complete farm, with a house, a corncrib, fruit trees in bloom, and a garden green with vegetables. The man tethered his burros with blades of grass, and a round corral was waiting for the sheep and goats. As we passed, the woman was playing a solemn game of magic, flipping pebbles to make them come alive, and calling "Sheep" so the stones would be sheep.

Within the wide fiery circle many, many circles around the fires, family by family building their prayers, talking quietly together, now and then tossing small firecrackers from one group to the next, brief flashes of flame linking the families. All is subdued, quite unlike a fiesta, and the people speak only their soft liquid Zapotec. Many of them have come from far away, and their oxen and tall country carts stand on the outer edges of the throng. They began coming yesterday, and the roads are full of worshipers just now arriving. But all will remain on the hillside through the night beside their prayers. By making the prayer to the earth, of its clay and plants and stones, the earth will bless them in the coming year. For tonight, at least, they possess thriving fields and fat cattle and fruit trees in early bloom.

WEDDING IN JUCHITÁN

When we heard the tootling band that Sunday morning we hurried to track down the wedding fiesta. In the Isthmus of Tehuantepec all comers are welcome at marriage celebrations, and the whole community rejoices; its Venus cult is, after all, one of propriety.

The isthmus women, *tehuanas*, are said to be the most beautiful in the world, and of all the women in this small area along the Pacific those of Juchitán are the loveliest nowadays. Its rival, Tehuantepec, always more polyglot and easygoing, has been sliding downhill of late years, and the true tehuana is now to be found in the towns of pure, or nearly pure, Zapotec blood. Juchitán presents the anomaly of a tropical town which is neither slack nor disorganized, and the same discipline has made its women queenly. Not all have perfect features, but all possess beauty. Proud bearing and grace of movement are universal and are learned the hard way, walking barefoot with burdens on the head.

The golden Aphrodites, as women of firm Zapotec character, have mastered all the feminine arts: how to wear the most becoming clothes women ever devised, how to keep fastidiously clean even if their River of Dogs is dry most of the year, how to sit in silence and be alluring. All this has turned their men into poets and composers, so that the isthmus arts are often those of the troubadour—the *sandunga*, a dance-song-poem of many versions, each one a languorous sigh; the delicate carnality of the marimba; the flowery rituals of courtship. But the crowning art of Wedding is, as everywhere, the business of women.

We caught this bridal fiesta in the lull before its formal opening. By high noon it would start in the pavilion newly built before the groom's house, and it would end two or three days later when everybody had had enough. Juan the bridegroom's modest house sat in a scramble of dwellings in the inside of a block, a communal back yard where dogs and pigs and naked tots roamed at will.

The fiesta pavilion was a bower of bamboo, fresh and green, supported at the sides and through the center with stout saplings entwined with flowers. From the roof of broad banana leaves hung green coconuts and banners of the delicate paper cutwork in which the isthmus excels. Around two sides were ranged the chairs and benches for the members of the wedding, with new hand-woven bedspreads stretched behind to form walls. In the opposite corner the band played at random, and now and then a couple of Juan's elderly aunts would come out of the house and primly dance a *son*, for at fiestas the old people are allowed to have most of the fun and drink as much as they like, while the young people must be dignified.

At the moment the groom's section of the wedding party were in his house, resting and preening. The day had already been strenuous, and it was the culmination of months of family ritual—formal pourparlers, an endless exchange of calls and gifts between the families, long speeches by the go-betweens, the choice of god-parents, *madrina* and *padrino*, to take charge of the wedding, and, in short, a rigmarole delightful to the elders and excruciating to the young couple, who are kept strictly in the background.

All this in a tropical climate where the girls are deliberately trained in allurement and the men are handsome and lively, where the wind in the tamarind trees is the whisper of lace ruffles against little red slippers. . . . But the isthmus, they say, is the place where the men allow the women to think they rule. Those competent matrons who control the market, which is the social and economic heart of the town, and in their homes weave the intricate patterns of family ritual know what they are about. Their daughters are properly married, and the fiesta is the lavish reward for their patience. Even when lovers elope, as they often do nowadays, they only come back to ask their parents to give them a wedding.

The morning after the bridal is still marked by a bow to the old rite of demonstrating to the whole community that the bride came spotless to her husband. Nowadays the proofs of her virginity are not carried in triumph about the town, and the simple, chivalrous declaration by the groom that all is well is followed by the popping of firecrackers to signify that the fiesta can go on.

This particular wedding did not follow an elopement; Juan and Maria had suffered the months of parental negotiation, gone through the civil wedding and its fiesta, waited several weeks for the church wedding, and gotten up before dawn today.

While it was still dark the bridesmaids in fiesta attire had come to his house to fetch the groom and escorted him to the home of Maria's madrina, the real power behind the ceremonies. After the six o'clock wedding in the church Maria returned to her madrina's house and the rest of the party—Juan with his padrino and six groomsmen, the six bridesmaids, and a bevy of Maria's girl friends —crowded into the little house beside the pavilion. Like actors, they kept offstage until it was time for the curtain to go up for the next act.

23

Zapotec

In the pavilion hordes of children hovered, restless for the excitement to begin. A huge sow lumbered in, chose a quiet spot, and nursed her six piglets long and thoroughly. The town drunks, who never miss fiestas, rambled about, making speeches. Two solid citizens set up a table near the entrance, arranged bottles of mezcal and plates of cigarettes on it, and proceeded with the common-sense isthmus practice of allowing guests to contribute to the fiesta. We paid over our pesos and were given a pretty paper flag as receipt, and the men were offered a drink and a cigarette.

Within the open door of Juan's house the bridesmaids were preening. They wore the gala costume, a matching skirt and straight sleeveless blouse, *huipil*, of velvet, solidly embroidered in silken flowers in all the colors of the tropics. Around the bottom of the skirt was a wide fluted ruffle of starched white lace to match the famous "head-huipil" which is the halo for tehuana beauty. This is a baffling affair, a complete child's dress of thin silk with a wide flounce and neck ruffle of starched white lace.

The tehuanas have two ways of wearing the head-huipil. For church the neck ruffle of the little dress is worn close around the face, and the rest of it makes a modest cover for the shoulders. For fiestas the dress is turned upside down and the wide flounce forms a halo framing the hair. Why and how this bit of frippery evolved nobody knows, but it is exquisitely becoming. Tehuanas spend small fortunes on their clothes and their necklaces and earrings of pure gold coins, but since they pay for them out of their own market earnings nobody is hurt.

All over Oaxaca the women like to braid bright wools or ribbons into their hair and to groom it carefully. Often, even in Tehuantepec, the braids are left hanging down the back. But no Juchitán woman would leave her house without performing that final act of her toilet which makes her so queenly: crowning herself with her own shining hair. The thick braids are crossed high at the front, leaving the back of the head flat to accentuate the straight line of backbone and neck. The bridesmaids now groomed their coronets of hair entwined with soft wide ribbons that matched some flower in their gowns, and then with innumerable bobby pins anchored the frail head-huipiles to withstand the strong isthmus winds.

Meanwhile Juan and his groomsmen were slicking down their own hair before a cloudy little mirror. They were as incongruous beside the girls as crows, dressed in stiff black suits and heavy store shoes, exactly as they dress for a funeral. This lamentable getup snuffed out the virile good looks of which isthmus men have their due share when they wear their easy white field clothes.

Finally the girls picked up their bouquets of larkspur, took the arms of the groomsmen, and followed the band, now tootling violently, for the march to the madrina's house. The entire floating population tagged along, rejoicing, and some of us managed to crowd into the madrina's house after the wedding party.

The madrina was an important person in the town, a doctor's wife with a big house. To the left of the entrance, in the doctor's waiting room, all the male relatives sat stiffly on hard chairs set against the walls. In the main room was the family altar with flowers, candles, pictures of saints, and the doctor's house sign in colored glass just under the crucifix. Chairs were ranged on either side for the maids and grooms, who sat facing each other in utter silence.

The madrina, resplendent in an ample velvet costume, swept in and instantly took command of the hangers-on—gringos, naked urchins, little girls carrying fat brown babies, and other undisciplined folk. She made us welcome; she instilled a sense of order by her social aplomb and signified that her female guests might follow her back to the patio.

There a group of opulently fat and impressive matrons were giving the final touches to the refreshments they would carry on their heads to the fiesta. Great calabashes lacquered in brilliant colors were piled with sandwiches wrapped in white paper, with tiny frosted cakes, and bonbons of every hue. Cases of beer, soft drinks, and mezcal were being loaded on an oxcart standing at a rear door.

At last we saw the bride. She was in her madrina's bedroom, surrounded by a flock of women who were making the final adjustments to her veil. Her dress was white satin with the starched lace flounce, and her net veil was caught with artificial orange blossoms (though real ones were growing just outside the windows). Maria was not as pretty as some of her bridesmaids, and her semi-modern gown could not compete with tehuana glory, but she was playing her part with fortitude.

When she came into the main room, escorted by her madrina, and sat down beside Juan there were no smiles, no whispered words. All these youngsters were as solemn as the Plume Dancers, dignified, hieratic. They waited, stiff in their chairs, while the matrons readied themselves for the great moment—the procession to Juan's house, where the bride would now stay forever.

At high noon the pageant moved down the street in a blaze of color. First the band, then Juan and Maria arm in arm, Maria carrying her bridal bouquet of fresh tuberoses, behind them the madrina and padrino, the grooms and maids and a bevy of girls in tehuana costume, the matrons bearing on their heads the calabashes of festive foods, then the male relatives, and finally the hordes of spectators.

It was a gorgeous parade. The sun poured down and turned the embroideries into jewels; the wind caught at the lace halos and made them quiver with white light. Down the broken sidewalks the people ran to catch up with the procession, heads popped out of windows, dogs barked, chickens and children and pigs scurried, and the cause of all the excitement, Juan and Maria, walked like obedient puppets in their conventional black and white, with no expression whatever on their faces.

At the edge of the market there was another riot of color, the women in their Sunday huipiles of red and yellow, the men with pink and orange shirts, massed in a thick crowd, watching the parade as it came close to them and then wheeled left toward Juan's house.

There in the green bower was the loveliest picture of all, the wedding party seated along the two far sides like ibises and flamingos and quetzal birds, and around the central pillars the young girls dressed in rainbows. The sun was straight overhead and came down through the green roof in motes of gold, touching the dark braids with their ribbons of cerise, yellow, bougainvillaea, peacock, emerald, the chains of thin gold coins, the golden earrings. The whole airy bower shimmered.

The tootling band had done its part, and now the marimba, cool as sherbet, began a *danzón*. The wedding party rose and moved gravely in the subtle rhythms. These young people danced far better than the Latins of the cities; their movements were sophisticated, understated. It was hard to believe that they were dancing on rough ground that yesterday was barnyard dust for scratching hens. They danced as on a floor of gold, which it was at this noonday moment.

In their midst, still solemn, were Juan and Maria, and the back of Juan's collar was ruffed up, as it had been for the last hour. But his bride had never whispered to him, "Do straighten down your collar, my heart." She was not yet acting like a wife. Whether they were wildly happy under their calm bearing it was impossible to guess. They were simply the center of a glorious festival in which all Juchitán partook, the black-and-white core in a delirium of color.

GENERAL STRIKE

On Sunday nights in the city of Oaxaca everybody comes to the Zócalo to listen to the band. The townspeople stroll under the dense Indian laurels, clad in their Sunday best, the cement benches are full of families, and even the little bootblacks and the foraging dogs take time out. All Oaxaqueños have a passion for music, and during the week a marimba orchestra alternates with the famous band, which on Sunday gives two concerts.

The Zócalo is a byword in Mexico because it concentrates the delightful essence of Oaxaca. Its central garden is beautifully tended, and the *portales* which surround the entire square are considered the finest in the republic. At the foot is the Government Palace with its deep arcades, and along the other sides are hotels, shops, newsstands and candy stalls, and tables where tourists and bourgeois citizens sit hour after hour, watching the life of the Zócalo.

Here is the heart of the entire state, the shifting pattern of its interests, endless as a Chinese play. The morning stage draws the most colorful crowds, the country people bound for the great market below the Zócalo—mountain Zapotecs driving burros laden with charcoal, Mixe bent under huge sacks of chiles, valley women bearing on their heads a pile of hand-woven rebozos, or two live chickens, or a bunch of garlic worn like a round hat. Black-clad Spanish women hurry to church; fat politicos amble to the palace, where a delegation of campesinos waits its turn with the powers. Students stop on their way to the Institute of Arts and Sciences to tease the señoritas with blue-black hair and eighteen-inch waists, and in the arcade of the tourist hotel Susanna appears with a wicker tray of carnations on her head.

Sunday evenings everybody drops these serious pursuits and preserves the reputation of Oaxaca as the home of delightful leisure. Most Oaxaqueños work steadily from dawn to dark, but they carry their labor and chronic poverty with grace, and they always have time to listen to music.

On the twenty-third of March the Sunday-evening crowd paced under the laurels, trying to act as if the band were there as usual, as if everything were normal. It was one of the bravest acts of the general strike, now ending its third tense day. The strike had begun on Friday, the birthday of Benito Juárez, the mountain Zapotec who became the Lincoln of Mexico, and it was part of the unending fight he had led against corruption and oppression.

The people of the state, from bankers to charcoal burners, were striking against a regime they had not chosen, since only the slate of Mexico's ruling party had been offered at election time. The shutdown proved how united the people were; it was complete voluntary paralysis. The market, the stores great and small, the gas stations and soft-drink stands were boarded up; busses, taxis, private cars vanished from the streets; householders padlocked the iron grilles across their doorways. Only the hospitals and the churches were open, and their offices were needed.

For things had gone amiss on Friday night, and the governor's private bodyguards had fired round after round into the mob of feckless youths who had appointed themselves in a Halloween spirit to break the windows of unpopular buildings. The hospitals were crowded, and today the city had buried its dead, and from almost every house black crape fluttered in sign of the general mourning.

An uglier crisis was building up, for the governor had imported an army of mercenaries and quartered them in barracks outside of town. When they were drunk enough they would be turned loose among the thousands of country people who had come afoot to Oaxaca to help along the strike. The official hope was that a civil war would start, obscuring the real issue: the resignation of the governor.

The strike committee of substantial citizens and law students was taking turns at a loud-speaker on an Institute balcony, explaining the crisis to the campesinos massed in the plaza below, urging calm and prudence on men who seemed incapable of violence. A block away in the Zócalo other civic leaders paced quietly among the country women with their babies warm-wrapped within their rebozos. It was a gallant promenade; they were walking on a powder mine.

All around the pleasant square, like a profanation, were tanks, gray tanks with machine guns at the ready, gray jeeps with field guns manned by green-gray soldiers in battle dress and steel helmets. Mexico's only motorized division had arrived from the capital, as if to announce that the war had begun.

In the barricaded hotel the Americans wrung their hands. What could be done against such evil? Had these soldiers come from Mexico City to fire on women and babies?

It was better in the Zócalo, even in its ring of steel. One still hated these soldiers with a bitter, helpless hatred, but the unity of Oaxaca was an elixir. At this moment, and in all the troubled weeks and months that followed, there was never a doubt that a geographical area with people ranging from semi-barbarians of unknown race to intellectuals of pure Spanish blood had long since been welded into a spiritual unit. *El Pueblo*, the Oaxaca People, meant far more than a state acting like a small nation.

The invasion of the alien tanks had the quality of outrage, as if an army of robots—robots with the power to kill—had entered a free and peaceful country. In the dim light the soldiers had no faces; they were metal men, part of their machines, as motionless.

The people were busy with their strike. Every now and then a ragged truck would come in from a valley town, from Tlacolula or Mitla or Ocotlán, bearing a defiant streamer, "Food for the Strike," and circle the Zócalo to the side called Portal of the Flowers. There a long line of townswomen crouched over their charcoal fires. The truck would stop alongside, and the men would hand down cuts of meat and baskets of carefully washed vegetables, which the women would seize and plunge into their bubbling earthenware pots.

In good time the women ladled out bowls of stew and gave them, with stacks of warm tortillas, to the weary country people who had walked many miles to Oaxaca to help along the strike. Under the very shadows of the hateful tanks the women fed their allies.

How it began nobody knows. Perhaps one of the cooks looked up into the tank nearest her and saw a face under the helmet, the face of a hungry lad who had had nothing to eat all day long. However it started, in a few minutes the ring of steel had become a circle of tired, hungry men enjoying food offered with Oaxaca hospitality.

There were bad moments in the next days, but the soldiers were men of order, like the Oaxaqueños, and once the tension eased they began to act like Oaxaca boys. They lolled in the bandstand, calling out endearments to the señoritas and practicing their "Allo, goo-by" on the tourists. They were polite, or robustly ribald, with a due appreciation of which reaction fitted the moment.

Everybody waved them a friendly farewell when they went back to Mexico City.

II

LAND AND PEOPLE

The Azompa potters near the capital often scratch a motto on their green glazed plates: *Viva Oaxaca, no hay otro*. It is one of those clichés which is profoundly true; Oaxaca is unique. The first step to understanding it is to detach it from our popular notions about Indians and Mexico; and this despite the fact that it is the most Indian state in the country and has always been important in national life.

It is well to scuttle these popular notions because, right or wrong, they apply to Northern Mexico. Once across the Oaxaca border, you are in another country altogether: Middle America, which includes Southern Mexico and Central America. All this region was once a cultural unit, the home of an ancient and marvelous civilization we have scarcely begun to study; and in Oaxaca the tang of antiquity is still sharp.

The high cultures of Middle America began, it is believed, in the region centering in Oaxaca and radiated out until finally they touched Peru in the south and the Ohio and Mississippi valleys in the north. In the twelfth century the Toltecs and other highly civilized peoples living in the area around the modern Mexico City were driven out by a succession of barbarian tribes coming down from the north. The most aggressive of these tribes were the Aztecs, who sponged up much of the older culture, which they combined with their own contributions—mass human sacrifice and imperialism.

33

Zapotec

We get our ideas of the Aztecs from the Spanish chroniclers, who wrote Mexican history upside down and incorrectly and whose errors were immortalized by our own gifted and unsuspecting William Prescott. We cannot deal with Oaxaca until we set the Aztecs in their right place, a very late and direful chapter in Mexican history. The Aztecs are often credited with founding Mexican culture, inventing the calendar and picture writing and other marvels. The truth is that they were the Johnny-come-latelys of the country; they got the calendar from the Zapotecs, who had developed it more than two thousand years earlier, and picture writing and many arts from the Mixtecs, a second great Oaxaca tribe.

Modern excavation and study of ancient sites in Middle America will mean the rewriting of our histories. In another generation we should have the story of the North American continent, right side up, and far more fascinating than Prescott's. It is already clear that the Maya, the only pre-Conquest people besides the Aztecs whose name is familiar to every high school pupil, are not the isolated marvel we believed them to be. They were one of several great races who belonged to the earliest days of Middle America.

At the moment experts are apt to name the Zapotecs and Maya as the pioneers, if not the creators, of Middle American culture, with other old Oaxaca tribes somewhere in the dim picture. Owing to its central position, Oaxaca has always been the clearinghouse for the arts and ideas of Middle America, and its people still show their cosmopolitan heritage. Because of its valleys Oaxaca was the first great cultural crossroads of the continent, and because of its mountains the atmosphere of the classic days has been preserved.

Physically, the world of Oaxaca is extremely varied. You can hardly name a climate, a mineral, or a plant which is not found somewhere in its 36,000 square miles. The state has a long stretch of the Pacific, and from its highest peaks you can see both Pacific and Gulf at once, for here the continent reaches its narrowest width north of Panama. And here, too, North America swerves sharply eastward at a right angle so that the Pacific lies south, not west, of the land.

It is amazing that this region, the most mountainous in the Americas, can feed its million and a half people; from the air it is a labyrinth of peaks. The Sierra Madre del Sur runs northwest along the Pacific as a single system until it enters Oaxaca, where it surges into the heights of Zempoaltepec and explodes in all directions. Eventually it is resolved into the mother ranges of south, west, and east, but meanwhile Oaxaca is a chaos of chains, highlands, and isolated peaks, and between them old volcanoes have somehow found room to build their cones. There are no active volcanoes in the state, but it lies in an earthquake belt and now and then runs up a high score on the seismographs.

The mountains nourish rivers, the larger ones emptying into the Gulf, linking Oaxaca from time immemorial with Vera Cruz and its coastal cultures. There is the mighty Coatzacoalcos, "Sanctuary of the Serpent," whose coastal basin was the legendary home of the god Quetzalcoatl; the San Juan and the Playa Vicente, and the great Papaloápam, "River of Butterflies," in more practical terms the river of sugar plantations, irrigation projects, and murderous floods.

Nothing goes to waste in Oaxaca, and the mountains provide more than spectacular scenery. They create the climates that make it possible to grow everything from papayas to apples, they shelter wild game and timid peoples, and they still hold rich stands of valuable timber. But in the thickly settled regions centuries of charcoal making and burning off slopes for cornfields have squandered the forest heritage and led to erosion and the diminishing of rivers.

The richest resources of the mountains lie underground, as Cortés well knew when he chose the major part of Oaxaca as his own marquisate. He coveted the gold and silver, which fairly brims out of the sierras, but there is more treasure which remains almost untouched—iron, lead, coal, mercury, and vast deposits of mica. Indians who would not believe television if they saw it are busily producing mica for TV sets, just as their valley brothers grow castor beans for the fine oil required by implausible objects called jet planes. But the Oaxaqueños detest working in mines or factories; they much prefer to get their living out of the soil and to make everything they use by hand, and thus have everything about them beautiful.

There are seven distinct regions of Oaxaca, each with its special products. But for its mountains the state would be altogether tropical, for its southern tip is only fifteen degrees from the equator. Its coastal plains and lower mountain slopes facing the Pacific or the Gulf are rich in the fruits and fibers of the tropics, but it is the central valleys that define Oaxaca's real endowment. This is the *"tierra del sol,"* the temperate tropics of Mexico. The spacious valleys—Etla, running northwest of the capital, Zaachila-Zimatlán south, and Oaxaca-Tlacolula southeast—lie five thousand feet above sea level, and the combination of high altitude and low latitude creates a climate in which almost anything can grow. The mean temperature is an ideal 72° Fahrenheit, altering only slightly from winter to summer; the important shift is from the dry to the rainy season. From November to late March not a drop of rain falls, then the daily showers begin, and the whole landscape, even the colors of the mountains, is transformed.

These rich valleys have an extraordinary range of products, whatever you might find on a big Wisconsin farm, from livestock to honey, but growing right along with the familiar vegetables and flowers are warm-country exotics. Pomegranates and coconut palms border rows of cauliflower and plump short carrots; frangi-pangi and hibiscus are at home with old-fashioned pinks and mari-golds. At all seasons there is an abundance of fruits, vegetables, and flowers, but the long dry winters when cows and sheep walk miles in search of something worth the cropping result in meats that are tough and juiceless, and in any case atrociously butchered.

After all, meat is a comparative novelty to the Indians, for livestock came in with the Spanish. To many Indians meat and even poultry are luxuries limited to fiestas.

There is no corner of the state which fails to produce the great Indian staples: corn, beans, chiles, and squashes. This has meant that people could settle down anywhere, even in an isolated mountain pocket, and be self-sufficient. Since the Zapotecs long ago moved into the central valleys, the isthmus, and the kinder mountain areas, the fourteen other Oaxaca tribes have less desirable homes. But they cling to the *tierra* of their fathers, no matter how poor their birthright. The Huave survive somehow on their parched Pacific lagoons; the Mixtecs refuse to leave the Upper Mixteca with its beautiful, baleful orange and crimson earths of complete erosion. The Chinantecs endure the miasmas of their dripping rain forest because it is their home, as it is the home of the jaguar and the almost extinct quetzal bird. The Mixe stay put in mountain fogs that almost never lift, perhaps comforting themselves with tales of people still more wretched who live like cave men in the bleakest mountain areas which have never been explored, timorous refugees from the human race.

In the sierras far from the cheerful Zapotec towns there are families and whole villages which are almost completely insulated from outside contacts. They live without markets, priests, doctors, or schoolmasters, jealously guarding their isolation from a world whose terrors did not vanish with the Conquistadores. The Indians never drank to excess before the Conquest, but in the lonely regions they are often besotted; corn makes a variety of solaces. These are the "closed" people, as the Zapotec traders, who penetrate everywhere, call them. The *cerrados* are intoxicated with homebrew and self-willed loneliness; they are unable to desire change.

Many Oaxaqueños are lonely not from choice but from sheer inaccessibility. They must live far from the towns and from each other because soil pockets are so few and far between. They have footpaths but no roads; chasms are crossed by narrow suspension bridges of vine. In these regions horses and burros are useless, so they have none. If they are bitten by certain flies blindness will follow unless a simple operation is performed—but the scanty health services of the state run on wheels, so there are villages where almost everyone is blind. They beg for schools—but if the state built a network of roads around a school the distances would still be too great for the children to travel every day, and so there are no schools. Three fourths of the Oaxaqueños are illiterate, the saddest statistic in Mexico, because so many of them have quick and eager minds.

More roads would help. The communications of the whole state are sketchy, and the only good highways have been built to attract tourists. There is adequate air service, used almost entirely by tourists and officialdom. There is an antiquated railroad across the isthmus and a renovated one leading to Mexico City. The only long paved road is the Inter-American Highway, which crosses the state in a southeast direction. From the Highway there is a spur into the heart of the Upper Mixteca, and another branch is being built down the southern valley to the Pacific. This road is designed to connect with another which may be built someday, a tourist coast road along the Pacific to Acapulco.

Aside from the excellent Highway, Oaxaca roads are dusty in winter, sometimes impassable during the summer rains, and always trying to the motorist. But during the few years since the Highway opened, the regions near it have become motor-conscious, and busses now run on lanes never intended for machines. The busses are mostly ancient relics with the determination of burros, and their drivers need all the help the amulets and holy pictures over the windshield can offer. But they do somehow run, and they are crammed.

The valley people still use oxcarts and burros for loads too large to tie on the roofs of busses or wedge inside, but they have sublime faith in the freightage capacity of the camions. Zaachila folk will come to the Oaxaca market in a feeble old bus whose roof sags under bales of alfalfa, bleating goats, and huge hampers of fruit and vegetables, and whose interior is packed solid with families carrying babies, small pigs and turkeys, with sacks of potatoes and grain, cases of empty soft-drink bottles, and long planks bearing a pretty array of cheeses or pastries. Everybody is jostled and bumped and scraped by the round market baskets the women carry, dust comes up through cracks in the floor in dense clouds, irritated turkeys peck at bare legs; there is much strangled coughing from the dust, but never a word of complaint, and always a lap ready for the nearest child.

The valley people, who have always been cosmopolitan, welcome the Highway and the motor age. And yet they share with all Oaxaqueños an independence of the rest of the world that does not stem entirely from the barriers created by their mountains or from scanty communications. They are not a backwash, but a proud and vigorous people who have good reasons for remaining themselves.

The early maps of Oaxaca made by the Spanish friars showed fifteen different tribes, most of them old peoples who had lived in the same area so long that they believed they had sprung from its rocks and trees. Today there are still these fifteen tribes, which have shifted little in place or in character.

This tenacity would seem to suggest that Oaxaca has remained strongly Indian because its people are backward. The reverse is nearer the truth. The Oaxaca Indians have held their own since the Conquest not because they are primitive but because they are, in their own way, highly civilized—and they prefer their own way. The first Indians to vanish after the Spanish invasion were those of Northern Mexico, the comparatively new arrivals from Northeast Asia who were nomadic or partly so and who possessed no strong cultures. Their roots in the country were shallow, and they had no long traditions to hold them together. Even the Aztecs, who had

39

reduced most of Middle America to vassalage, have virtually melted away as a separate race.

The peoples who belonged to the great Middle American culture still preserve their racial identities, languages, and old traditions. Some of them are greatly diminished, and others—the weaker fringe tribes of Maya and Zapotec civilization—fled the Conquistadores and hid in the mountains of Chiapas and Oaxaca, where their descendants live a hand-to-mouth existence today. But strangely enough, the oldest races like the Zapotecs, who might have been expected to die out after perhaps three thousand years on the soil of Oaxaca, still show tremendous vitality.

The 1950 census gives Oaxaca 1,445,000 inhabitants, and at least 70 per cent of them, or about a million, are Indian. No census of this mosaic of peoples can be complete, or accurate about racial origins. For one thing, an Indian who has learned Spanish in addition to his native tongue will often tell the census taker that he is non-Indian.

One day I asked my laundress what her race was.

"Why, pure Spanish, señora." Then she added negligently, "When I was little, I spoke only Zapotec. But then I learned Spanish, so I'm not Zapotec any more."

That is typical. There was no sense of racial inferiority in Candelaria's reply, but there were probably other things—a sort of tact, of keeping things simple, and a defensive instinct. To these Oaxaca people, learning Spanish often means a capitulation to a regime they secretly distrust and dislike. When you consider that in Mexico you cannot go to school or read a newspaper or travel far without knowing Spanish, it is significant that more than half the Oaxaca Indians speak no Spanish whatever.

This is true of all Southern Mexico (except Yucatan, where about a third of the Maya speak no Spanish), where the Indian population is densest. These seven states are all in the old sphere of Middle American influence, preserving the remnants of Maya, Zapotec, Mixteca-Puebla, Totonac, and Toltec cultures. But in the northern state of Sonora, whose tribes still rate as primitive, three fourths of the Indians speak Spanish.

It is clearly false to connect this language picture with backwardness, or even with isolation and poverty. There is no doubt that lack of opportunity, of schools and easy communications, has kept thousands of southern Mexicans from learning the official tongue. But another factor is at work. In the Valley of Oaxaca, where one would expect to hear Spanish on all sides, Zapotec is the prevailing language. Here are intelligent, prosperous people living near the capital, with good roads, many churches and schools, and the most frequent contacts with Spanish-speaking mestizos and travelers. But in many villages only half a dozen people know anything but Zapotec. Even Teotitlán del Valle, whose serapes are famous all over Mexico, was two-thirds monolingual at the last survey.

This valley is the reservoir of the oldest and proudest traditions of the race, and its people hold to their language as part of their subtle resistance to an alien culture. Oddly enough, Zapotecs often must resort to Spanish to make themselves understood by Zapotecs of other regions, for branches of the race have stayed put so long that they have developed five major dialects, with shadings between. A Teotitlán trader has some language difficulties when he crosses the valley to Tlacolula, and if he runs into a fellow Zapotec from the isthmus, from the mountains, or from the Miahuatlán area, he is at a loss unless they both know a little Spanish.

Of the fifteen tribes the Spanish found in Oaxaca, eight are now too small to be important; none has over 5,000 members in the state. The Chochos, Popolocas, and Zoque are very old tribes who now live mostly in bordering states, and the others play minor roles: Amuzgos, Aztecs, Chontal, Huave, and Trique. The Zapotecs are the largest race, and together with the Chinantecs and Chatinos, who belong to the same language group (believed the oldest tongue in America), they may number 600,000. The Mixtecs are the second great tribe, and though they spill over into Puebla and Guerrero, there are 166,000 in the state. With them are allied in language the Mazatecs and the Cuicatecs. Last of the seven main tribes are the Mixe, mountain people in the east of the state.

Much fascinating history and foggy prehistory lie behind the Oaxaca nations, and the people living today carry on hints of the old picture, including the feud between Zapotecs and Mixtecs. The tribes have intermarried little among themselves or with the Spanish; each language group has kept pretty much to itself.

For this reason it is necessary to glimpse them first as separate peoples and then see what holds them together as Oaxaqueños and gives the mosaic a pattern in time as well as space. For Oaxaca is a unity, *no hay otro*. And if this unity is based largely on Zapotec predominance, it has been won not so much by conquest as by the Zapotecs' gifts as moderators.

ISTHMUS PEOPLES

About two centuries before the Spanish came, the Zapotecs expanded into the Isthmus of Tehuantepec region and drove out three tribes living there: Zoque, Huave, and Chontal. This was not a peaceful expansion, but it was a reversal of Zapotec habit, and the displaced tribes had never belonged, and do not belong today, to the prevailing culture of Oaxaca. The Zoque are a primitive mountain people whose retreat took them to the inhospitable southeast corner of the state, where no surveyor has yet ventured. Enterprising souls among them gradually slipped across into Chiapas, where their tribe now thrives, and all that is left in Oaxaca is two slatternly villages, whose old men tell tales of the *binquizacs*, sons of the devil, who turned themselves into demi-animals to escape the Conquistadores and still live nearby.

The Huave fled from the rich coastal plains to the long, treeless sandspits which create lagoons near the city of Tehuantepec. These mysterious people probably drifted up from Peru as refugees who have remained primitive. They are a brave people, and bitter, and their five towns are blasted by sandstorms and the northers which sweep down the coast, by floods, droughts, invasions of insects, every misery. They are fishermen, selling their catch in the isthmus markets. But they will not injure the alligators, who are their totems, and are careful to throw them fish after a catch. (The alligator is also the totem of certain Zapotec fishermen of the region.)

Nominally the Huave are Catholics, and a story is told about the first church they built on the lagoons to serve the four towns then existing. A man from each town volunteered to be immured alive in the foundations so that the church would belong to all the Huave. They lay down on their backs, one on each wall, and the masons covered their legs with cement, then their bodies and arms, until only their heads were free. While the women wailed, the four men were given a last bit of food, and then the cement was poured over their heads.

This may be pure legend, but the intrepid innocence of the Huave comes out in a true incident of the Mexican war with the French. When President Benito Juárez appealed to his native Oaxaca for help, the Huave sent him thirty dollars and the promise that when the French fleet attacked their coast they would man their canoes and drive the enemy away.

The Chontal, who were driven farther up the Pacific coast, were described by the Spanish friars as fierce cave men wearing only skins, ferocious fighters who roasted and devoured their captives. It is possible that the Chontal represent a primitive migration, that of the Australoids who somehow made their way to both Americas at an extremely early period. Their language is said to be related to that of island groups across the Pacific.

Their name, "Chontal," means simply "stranger," and this race lives very much to itself in a pocket of mountain villages and wild coast. They make contact with their old neighbors, the Huave, selling them the most exotic product of all Oaxaca, the caracol-dyed thread of veritable Tyrian purple. The tiny sea snail from which this gorgeous color comes appears to be of the same family as the murex, which made the dye sold in the fairs of Tyre for the royal robes of the Mediterranean nations. Once or twice a year when the moon is right the Chontal wade out to the rocks where the tiny snails cling, and squeeze their excretion on hanks of yarn. This precious thread is becoming scarcer, and though the Huave women keep back a little to weave into their fiesta blouses, most of it is resold at stiff prices to the Zapotec tehuanas who never heard of Tyre or Rome but know imperial purple when they see it.

MOUNTAIN PEOPLES

The northern corner of the state, bordering on Puebla and Vera Cruz, is the traditional home of several of the nations which joined in creating the first high culture of America. It is part of the "Olmec Land" mentioned by the friars, which is legendary only in the sense that it stretches back far into prehistory. Because of its easy mountain passes and valleys it was the funnel through which early people poured: Maya, Zapotec, Mixtec, Totonac, and tribes now altogether vanished. By medieval times the main trade road from Mexico's central plateau entered Olmec Land and there divided into branches along the Gulf and Pacific coasts. The Inter-American Highway follows part of this venerable road but has not progressed as far, for its Pacific branch connected with Peru.

Among all the tantalizing buried sites of Oaxaca, those of Olmec Land may someday supply the missing first chapter of Mexican history. But its living people are almost as neglected as their ancestors; they are not the "closed ones" but the lonely and forgotten ones: Chinantec, Cuicatec, Mazatec, Chatino, with a sprinkling of highland Zapotec and fringe tribes. Of late the state powers have taken to bringing groups of Mazatecs to the capital for political or religious fiestas, for the austere beauty of their women is a fresh sensation in an afternoon of regional dances and provides a foil to the glowing carnality of the tehuanas. If it were possible to insult these Mazatecs, or indeed any Indians, this official exploitation would amount to an affront. They need every modern service: roads, schools, clinics, better farming methods; but even the poorest Indian is expected to contribute his vote, his mite to the tax collector, and his "quaintness" to a fiesta.

Mazatec dignity absorbs this shoddy patronage and creates quite another picture in the Dance Plaza beside the Church of Soledad in Oaxaca. Since so few observers venture into Olmec Land itself, we must see what we can make of this little delegation who have come to perform a *danza típica* in honor of the Virgin of Soledad, beloved protectress of the state. (These "typical" or folk dances are post-Conquest, but no matter.)

The setting is superb. The Dance Plaza is the highest of three which lie before the exquisite church, and from the tiered seats you look down on its rich façade and the fountains and broad steps shaded by Indian laurels and the jacarandas which will soon spread their fans of azure-lavender. The plaza is massed with groups of dancers waiting their turns, a phantasmagoria of color which becomes more and more improbable as the sun drops lower over Monte Albán.

We are looking at the line of Mazatec women standing beyond the row of seated girls from the isthmus, finding something, in that quiet line that makes a stillness in the heart as Monte Albán does when you see its patient pyramids against the gold curtain of sunset. The quality of endurance, of having-been-and-being, the Indian Time of Oaxaca. How can women standing in a long line suggest an abstraction containing them, and the pyramids, and the Virgin of Solitude by the Cross? But you know that it is there and that you are still outside. And this strange sense comes directly from them, not from something in your own mind, for until later you do not know who these women are or anything about them. They are simply creatures of a classic age who have somehow appeared.

In Oaxaca it is always the women who can evoke unfamiliar regions and periods, for the men look and dress alike in the standard white cotton field clothes to which modernity has reduced them. Sometimes they may add a gay red sash or wear a pink or orange shirt, but the men, like their clothes, seem cut from the same pattern. They are vigorous, small-boned, wiry; they have as a rule well-cut features and always wear a modest mustache and have their hair neatly trimmed at a barbershop.

Bernal Díaz del Castillo remarked that of all Mexican peoples the Oaxaqueños were the most beautifully dressed, and that applied also to the men. The women, especially of the highlands, have managed to hold onto their pre-Conquest finery, which is simply two lengths of cloth decorated and worn in styles belonging to a region or sometimes a single town. One length, the *falda*, is folded around the hips and held at the waist with a crimson or magenta belt; the other length, the *huipil*, makes the blouse. The highland women wear their huipiles very long, falling in straight folds almost to the ankle. They are decorated with inwoven or embroidered colors on the homespun white, in designs and color combinations which vary according to local traditions.

The Mazatec women, standing so serenely in their line, wore faldas of very heavy white cotton embroidered around the hem in cinnamon wool with little figures of men, women, and animals. Their long huipiles were sheer finery, alternating horizontal bands of thin silk ribbon and lace and needlework. This could have amounted to feminine frippery, but something gave all these highland women the souls of artists. The Mazatecas had chosen as leitmotif a burning violet silk for horizontal bands so spaced as to make their huipiles quiver with beauty. The women themselves had a finished, almost oriental smoothness of feature, and when after their dance one of them addressed the archbishop, who was sharing honors with the Virgin, the Mazatec language, too, sug-

Land and People

gested the Chinese, the voice rising before pauses instead of falling. Who the Mazatecs and their neighbors are nobody knows,
but they have lived in their mountains too long to be defined as
anything but classic Americans.

An air of old tragedy clings to them; people so alive and
vehement should not be mere survivors of a greater day. But five
hundred years ago the wide trade road through Olmec Land became the thoroughfare of conquest from the north, and as the most
northern of the Oaxaca nations the highland people bore the first
furies of Aztec and Spaniard. What happened to the Chinantecs
is recorded in grim detail. The Aztecs despoiled them of movable
riches, including many thousands of prisoners, who were marched
up to Tenochtitlán to become an offering of so many grilled
hearts for the insatiable Aztec gods. Their survivors were put
under tribute to supply the Moctezumas with cotton and rubber
and fruits, with jewels, gold, quetzal feathers, balsam, and with
their labor and their prayers. The Chinantecs were made to climb
their towerlike temples, which had a hundred steps on each side,
and pray to their own gods for the Aztecs. For 140 days of the
year the men were required to fast and leave their wives while
they toiled for the Aztecs, chewing rubber to still their hunger.

Still there was something left for the Spanish. They found the
people living in fine wooden houses and the women dressed as now
in huipiles of white, almost solidly embroidered in geometrical
designs in red and blue, and grooming their hair as now with
fragrant oil of mammee. They had lost their treasure and their
princes, but their warriors were so redoubtable that Cortés sent
for two thousand of them to aid him in a major engagement elsewhere, armed with lances headed with double-edged flint. Meanwhile the padres did their work so well that today the Chinantecs,
almost alone in Oaxaca, have forgotten the old pagan and magic
practices.

Of the shy and charming remnant of the old Chinantecs, blindness and the *pinto* disease, which covers the skin with blotches of

47

blue, take their toll, but the nation is increasing in numbers as it slowly loses its skills and happiness. They used to make fine baskets but no longer do, and only in a few villages are the old exquisite weaving and embroidery alive. They used to dance and sing, but now they dance not at all and sing only when drunk, which is too often. They have the ancient six-noted flute, the *chirimía*, whose voice you can hear all over Oaxaca, lovely and sad, and the drum and conch shell for relaying messages from one mountain to the next, and these, too, you can hear almost anywhere in the state.

Their isolation from the world and from each other is profound. Most of them live on the mountain slopes facing the Gulf, in dense, flowery rain forests which never know a dry season, jungles where monkeys, tapirs, brilliant birds and butterflies and wild orchids abound. Here they raise cotton, bananas, and the excellent coffee which draws the Zapotec trader, often their sole contact with the outside, for they themselves do not travel and have even dropped markets. This is a bad sign, for markets are the lifeblood of people living on the Indian level. The Chinantecs appear to be a retrograde folk, suffocated in their lush forests and perhaps weary now of having lived so long, and so long ago, as one of the great peoples of Olmec Land.

The Mixe to the southeast are quite unlike the other highland nations. If they had a past in the historical sense it was somewhere else, probably in the lowlands of the Gulf, where they have distant relatives. They have never adjusted to their neighbors or to their own region, which was surely not intended for human habitation. In the Mixe country the cruel, heavily forested Sierra Madre rises to the heights of Zempoaltepec, over eleven thousand feet, and the whole region is blanketed in clouds that never seem to lift. Since no stronger nation covets their land, the Mixe are at least safe and left alone, which appears to be what they most want. Of all cerrados, they are the most closed and surly; they avoid all strangers and do not even like to live close to one another.

48

Land and People

One often hears the Mixe described wholly in negative terms. For months on end many villages never see the sun; if the rain is not pouring down there is a drizzle or a cold fog. They are enveloped in clouds and misery and superstition; they are personally unattractive and dirty; they seem to possess no spark of ambition which would lift them out of their wretchedness, no sense of style, no hunger for the order and richness and close community life which have made the Zapotecs a great race. Nobody ever goes near them but a few Mitla traders, and missionaries who find them worshiping idols.

Most of these negatives apply to the Mixe buried deep in the mountains, where their semi-barbarity and lack of grace are unrelieved. But the Mixe govern themselves soberly and work hard in their fields, which are always on a steep pitch of land. Those near Zapotec country have opened up to a degree, and you can always find Mixe with their chiles in the Saturday market in Oaxaca, and at big fiestas there is a sprinkling of swarthy men and their wives in lumpy green homespun faldas and huipiles. A young American botanist who went to live among the Mixe with the idea of introducing them to new food plants reports that once you get to know them the Mixe are like everybody else. No doubt much of their unpopularity stems from the days when they raided Zapotec lands. For the rest, the Mixe temperament grates on the Zapotecs, who like everybody to be open and easy as they are.

THE MIXTECS

If ever a race was destroyed by sheer restlessness, it is the Mixtecs. They are still alive and still restless, but their old culture is dead. A deep gulf separates them from a glamorous past, when they were the consummate jewelers and potters of Mexico, when with their neighbors they migrated to the central plateau and created the distinctive culture called Mixteca-Puebla. They were the only people of either America to write their history (the

49

Maya recorded only dates and religious matters), and their eight brightly painted codices, which are all that the Spanish spared, trace Mixtec dynasties and major events for a thousand uninterrupted years ending after the Conquest.

Of this brilliant past which forms an important part of the Oaxaca story, almost nothing seems to remain in the people today. In an exhibition of Oaxaca's regional arts some of the crudest pottery and weavings come from the Mixteca, and yet a few centuries ago these people were making incomparable polychrome ceramics and the jewels of Tomb Seven, discovered on Monte Albán.

Nothing human can be explained by the first obvious factors which come to mind, but the creative exhaustion of the Mixtecs recalls the "mystery" of the Old Maya about which there has been a great to-do. Why, in the century beginning in A.D. 630, did the Maya abandon all their marvelous cities and move en masse to the jungles of Yucatan? For dramatic effect popular writers will still speculate about plagues, a shift of climate, or wars, of which there is no evidence, and then admit that there was no real mystery in this migration. The Old Maya had to leave their land because it could no longer feed them. But two other things are not so easy to explain: the strange restlessness in the Maya make-up which was always leading to violent change and disruption, and the fact that though they built a "New Empire" in Yucatan they never recaptured the glories of their earlier arts.

These three factors of exhausted soil, a rather neurotic instability expressed in sudden shifts and chronic internal discords, and a rapid petering out of creative vitality are also plain in the Mixtec story, but in a different pattern. The Mixtecs originated in Olmec Land, probably in the rubber country along the Gulf, and after shadowy migrations moved to the central plateau of Mexico, where for centuries they built up the northern fringe of Middle American culture. Barbarian invasions finally drove them out, and they scattered far and wide. Most of them returned to their ancestral home of Oaxaca, where they spread down the broad western valley, splitting into two kingdoms constantly at war with each other, rather in the fashion of the Maya clans and leagues.

Restless still, they invaded the rich heart of the Zapotec kingdom and captured the sacred city of Monte Albán, where for a brief time their arts flourished. After the Conquest they were confined to their Mixteca, and their land became eroded. Now they have no place to which they care to migrate, and they satisfy their hunger and their restlessness by working as itinerants in other regions but almost never in Zapotec territory. The bitter wars between Zapotecs and Mixtecs have not been forgotten by either side.

Today the Mixtecs are so poor that many of them cannot afford chiles to spread on their few tortillas. But most artists are poor; and why the Mixtecs are no longer even middling artists is something of a mystery. Again, there is an obvious explanation that does not quite explain: the Mixtecs are blighted like their land, exhausted by malaria, enteritis, intestinal parasites, malnutrition.

"The Mixtecs are just too poor to be well," said Dr. Luis Gonzales Piñon, the stocky, dynamic epidemiologist of the state. "If they were better fed, if they had more schools to teach them hygiene—for we give every schoolmaster who can come to the city a two months' course in public health—if they had more roads, so we could reach them . . ."

Such sentences are never finished; they end with a little gesture outlining the vicious circle in which so much of Mexico is cramped. Dr. Piñon and his devoted staff are fighting for public health in a big state with an equipment of twenty-one little medical stations, four trucks, one jeep, and three hospitals. When there is a bad epidemic they organize mobile brigades of doctors and nurses and sometimes hire planes to reach spots far from the roads. With this pitiful equipment they have somehow eliminated smallpox and dramatically reduced infant mortality.

Zapotec

The Mixtecs get major attention because they are in the greatest need. Everybody is worried about the Mixtecs. By superhuman effort state and federal agencies have nearly cured one of their worst diseases—the straw-hat industry. For years those Mixtecs who do not work as migrants and whose farms cannot possibly feed them have gathered a local palm and made straw hats. They are sound, marketable hats, but they sell so cheaply that these weavers are reduced to an economic level below that of the poorest natives of India or China. Still they have to be browbeaten into dropping this suicidal industry.

The migrants fare better. They spend the winter far afield and come home with enough cash to feed their families through the year. Many girls go into domestic service in the cities; thousands of men work on the coffee and sugar plantations of Vera Cruz or in factories in Puebla cities. The dreariest sight I saw in Oaxaca was at its richest gold-and-silver mine, La Natividad, where a crowd of very drunk Mixtecs were spending a Sunday afternoon in a drenching rain. Loud-speakers rigged to cantina juke boxes blared all around the muddy plaza. These miners seemed loutish and degraded, but in a kinder setting the Mixtecs are amiable enough.

The Upper Mixteca is familiar to motorists, for the Inter-American Highway runs down its entire length from the Puebla border to the city of Oaxaca. It is a strangely empty land, for its people live hidden back in the mountains, and its eroded soils create weird effects. Terraces of burning orange or henna reds are set off against the arsenic-green patches of grass, and along the horizon the mountains change with the hours from purple to sapphire to cloudy blue. This is the home of one of Oaxaca's most dramatic legends and of the "Mixtec Song," which all Mexicans love.

Here, after all their wanderings, the Mixtecs have taken root in poverty and discouragement, which they love as aging people love their ailments. They do have a choice: they could move farther south in their own Mixteca where good farmland is abundant. But that would mean changing from a mountain people to a tropical people. Probably it is too late for them to make such a drastic mutation.

The Lower Mixteca, like many regions along the Pacific, is a half-wild jungle with a strong mixture of Negro blood in its people. As children of nature who are lavishly fed and quite undisciplined, they are happy and carefree. So far, they have torn down schools as fast as they are built—which is not very fast—and ignore such formalities as marriage. The coast Negroes practice bride-stealing, escaping the boredom of getting family consent to a betrothal. "Only the blind are beggars," they say.

There are parts of the Mixteca where criminal gangs operate, something in the spirit of Lafitte's men in the bayous of the Mississippi. Nowhere is there the propriety and industry so evident in the Isthmus region, which has the same climate. On the Mixtec coast tropical ease and fun have their way. The women, who are often beautiful, go about naked above the waist; there are noisy all-night fandangos around a giant ceiba tree; sometimes the coast artists produce clay figures or dance masks which are vivid and amusing; sometimes their arts are merely juvenile. Nature is indulgent, providing fruit, nuts, chocolate, tobacco, cotton, and loofas of every size, from those the Oaxaqueños use as dish mops to the tremendously long ones which become snubbers for ships.

The best way to arrive at a picture of Oaxaca as a whole is to describe it as a country still living in a medieval system of production and exchange. This system not only works well but gives Oaxaca its rich variety and charm, for here is the greatest array of popular arts in all Mexico. The machine is absent, with its noise and drive; instead you see a whole country of people working silently and busily away making something sound and attractive to use and to sell.

Zapotec

That sums up Oaxaca economy: to produce food and everything else needed for life by working in the home dooryard and fields, each family by itself. The family is the producing unit; it feeds itself and works at the village specialty. Each handicraft—weaving cloth or baskets, making pottery or gold filigree earrings, working deerskins into garments or cowhide into saddles—is a village specialty, but there is no community factory, simply a collection of busy homes which turn out the local product. Then these products are exchanged between villages in the classic way at markets and fairs.

To the visitor this system presents an unending series of pictures which are deeply satisfying because they have belonged to human history for thousands of years. The husbandman driving his animals home at sunset; the potter shaping his clay; the woman at her spinning wheel; the child plaiting a basket; and finally the market, where everybody buys what somebody else has made, after he has sold his own basket of beans or pile of ollas. All these pictures are natural and relaxed and fill us with envy, because for us the instinctive satisfactions which go along with making things with our own hands vanished with the machine.

Classic America never had a guild system or factories of any kind. The basis of life was land, and each family had its share. But since Classic America was highly civilized, an intricate system grew up of specialization and interchange among villages. This has hardly altered today; through wars and colonial exploitation and the rush of modernity, Teotitlán has continued to make its serapes and Ocotlán its beige pottery. Since each town has its traditional designs and methods and materials, even a tourist soon recognizes that green glazed plates mean Azompa, and a finely etched steel knife comes not only from the city of Oaxaca but from the crude forge of Austroberto Aragon and his sons. Black pottery means Coyotepec, and one knows that the suavest ollas and the liveliest mermaids strumming guitars are the handiwork of Rosa and Juventino.

Land and People

In the city the potters, who turn out mountains of jars and dishes, use the potter's wheel, though they work it by a foot pedal, not by electricity. But Rosa and Juventino and their whole village still use the pre-Conquest technique. They squat comfortably in their own dooryard, shape the piece by hand, and then, if it is an olla, rotate it on two saucers, the bottom one inverted, until the jar is round. Then, instead of using a kiln, they make a fire once a week in a deep pit dug into a slope, with a grate and a draft at the bottom. They may even follow the methods of the great potters who turned out the Polished Black of Monte Albán, as the ceramists call it, by burnishing the fired piece with an agate, as was done twenty-five centuries ago.

There are other very ancient methods used all over Oaxaca. The primitive clay spinning whorl and the saddleback loom are familiar sights. The loom is simply a narrow warp frame tied at one end to a pole or a favorite tree and at the other to a strap which the woman slips around her hips. As she works she can keep moving into the shade. Visitors to Mitla can glance into any dooryard and find the women using this antique loom to make their famous rebozos and wool girdles.

Men's clothes are usually bought ready-made at a weekly market, and one suspects this is because the women, who like to make each garment an original creation, cannot be bothered to turn out the nondescript white cotton "pajamas" which are the male uniform of rural Mexico. Unless he is very poor, a man will own a store suit and perhaps a pair of machine-made shoes. But he lives in the good handmade huaraches from Tlacolula, he keeps warm in a Teotitlán serape, and his straw sombrero never knew a factory.

The women, particularly in the remoter parts of Oaxaca, make the clothes for themselves and their small daughters as they have for long ages, with the old implements and using the old gorgeous dyes. They embroider fiesta garments with a needle now instead of a maguey thorn, but the designs they use are classic.

55

Zapotec

Lately the women have begun to buy factory-made cloth, lace, and ribbons, which they will always find in a section of the market. But there are few textile factories in Oaxaca itself; like the mines, they may be opened, but they are soon abandoned. Factories break up family life, which is far more important than cash wages.

Another innovation is the new tourist market now opening up. The Spanish-blood Oaxaqueños still consider Indian objects beneath them and fill their houses with furniture and dishes made in northern factories. But the American tourists are so enchanted with the soundly made and often beautiful Oaxaca handiwork that they range the valleys for the staggered weekly markets: Saturday, Oaxaca; Sunday, Tlacolula; Monday, Zaachila, and so on around the week. Indirectly this buying, made without knowledge of village standards and traditional taste, may have an evil effect upon both; and it is fortunate that the Oaxaca Indians are stubborn about changing their ingrained habits.

Many ties hold the Oaxaca peoples in their mosaic, but the Zapotecs are the matrix. Their secret of leadership amounts to a complex art, somewhere between the Chinese gift for accommodation and the American impulse of democracy. There is no regimentation in Oaxaca; the Zapotecs themselves are divided into three distinct branches which live in such different climates that they vary widely from each other: the valley, sierra, and isthmus divisions. But no two towns, even in the same valley, are alike; Tehuantepec and Juchitán have never agreed about anything from politics to coiffures, and both differ from their close isthmus neighbor, Ixtepec. As for the *serranos*, the mountain Zapotecs, each village is a rule to itself.

Yet there is a common denominator for the Zapotecs and for all Oaxaca; these brilliant colors and shadings make a composition.

III

VALLEY TOWN

Teotitlán del Valle has its big fiesta in mid-January, and tourists often drive out from the city on the first day, when the famous Plume Dancers present the entire story of the Conquest. The costumes are spectacular, the natural setting is exquisite, but after an hour or two the ritual battle between Indians and Spaniards palls, and the visitors hurry away with no suspicion that they have been in a town which has been interesting for twenty-five centuries.

It is better to go to Teotitlán on a quiet day when all the men are weaving serapes and to come back many times so that the town opens up gradually. Even when you have struck up an acquaintance with Jorge and Victoriano and Jesús and the other Teotitlán men who come into the city with a stack of serapes on one shoulder, it is another matter getting to know them at home. As salesmen they are affable and incessant; their technique is a barrier to getting behind the commercial amenities. Zapotecs are born merchants, and it is interesting that the only other people who succeed in Oaxaca as storekeepers, bank tellers, and traveling salesmen are Syrians and Lebanese, who are coming into the state in great numbers and blend easily into the general picture.

What they sell makes the difference between these newcomers and the Zapotecs. The Middle Easterners embody the machine age; they are the final retailers of manufactured goods: dress materials, ribbons, laces. Behind them is a complicated mechanism of factories, wholesalers, jobbers, sample cases, trains, hotels, telephones and typewriters, expense accounts, and sales reports. There is nothing behind the Teotitlán man but his own home.

Don Leopoldo Torres makes the serape with his own hands and sells it direct to the customer. He is identified with his serapes, and the serapes are identified with Teotitlán, and this has always been so. Teotitlán is a weaving town which makes only serapes, just as Coyotepec in the next valley is a pottery town which makes only black pottery. Except for the Middle Easterners and their pretty goods which tempt the women, the machine and the mechanism of commerce do not enter the Oaxaca picture.

Don Leopoldo's ancestors, in the day when Teotitlán was the old Zapotec capital, wove fine mantles for kings and high priests, and when they tired of weaving they took the mountain road down into Central America to a certain great religious fair, where the weavings of their town were in great demand. Nothing has essentially changed; Don Leopoldo has made this very journey over the secret mountain road; a pilgrimage as well as a business trip, though the name of the god presiding over the fair has been altered.

The Zapotecs, especially those of the Valley of Oaxaca, are great cosmopolitans. One of the Torres boys has been in New York City, another spent a year in Los Angeles, but these experiences have dulled rather than increased the Zapotec gift for getting along easily with strangers. Don Leopoldo, whose travels have been only over the ancient routes, is more spontaneous in enjoying novelties. He loves nothing better than a lift in a fine American car, and if you stop at the edge of the village near his house he will be sure to invent some errand in the center of town so that he can sit back luxuriously against the cushions, puff a good American cigarette, and lean out to shout at passing friends.

The point is that Americans and their cars and gadgets are new and fascinating, and their arrival in Oaxaca is a great joke. Don

Leopoldo is highly amused at the picture of himself riding in a shiny car. He accepts neither car nor owner as having much to do with him personally, not at first. The valley people regard strangers with a quizzical, half-mocking air. They are courteous but reserved; the stranger is under the scrutiny of a judgment highly sensitive to nuances of attitude and character. If one passes muster simply as a human being, the sun comes out, and the Zapotec is his warm, demonstrative self.

The American captain had given Don Leopoldo many a lift in his fine car, and they had collaborated on several practical jokes over which Teotitlán is still chuckling. When the captain finally started home to Colorado, Don Leopoldo made a special trip to the city to say good-by. There was the *abrazo*, the perfunctory male embrace, the beautiful "Go with God," which is also routine manners, and the captain and his wife drove away. Don Leopoldo stood there watching the car out of sight. "My friend," he said, explaining the tears raining down his face. "He is my friend."

Because he is shrewd and yet impulsive, charming and accessible, but with a reserve fund of ancient experience and pagan fidelities which he would not dream of revealing to an alien, Don Leopoldo (whose name is not the one used here) will do well enough as a typical valley man—different from his neighbors in Mitla or Tlacolula because these towns are of another stamp, but still a good sample *vallista*.

He is five feet four or five, stockily built, but as lean and fit as his sons. (Only the isthmus people get fat as they age, and they do this on purpose, as a sign of their prosperity.) He has a strong, merry face, brilliant dark eyes set well apart, and a finely cut nose and mouth. One hesitates to call the Zapotec features "sculptured" because this calls up a picture of cold marble, and the Zapotecs have the warm gold-to-bronze skins of people who live in the sun. Their features are classic in the Southern Mexican sense, the patrician lines of nose and lips subtly smoothed down so that all the planes can be expressed in curves. The Oaxaqueños reveal their long ancestry, too, in their small, well-shaped hands and feet. Don Leopoldo at home wears the usual pajama-style white cottons and thrusts his bare feet into huaraches. When he dresses up he tucks in his shirt and wears a dark wool coat and black store shoes.

It is best not to speak of Don Leopoldo's wife but simply of the women of his house. Not that he has a harem, but among the women who gather in the kitchen—grandmother, various daughters-in-law, and perhaps cousins and sisters—there seem to be two who may be Don Leopoldo's wives—"an old one to cook, a young one to have the children," as the saying goes. It is valley etiquette, if a man has more than one wife, to keep them in different villages, but the Torres household is large and harmonious, and one never quite sorts it out.

All valley people have plenty of room. Their villages straggle out from the center, so that each family has a spacious dooryard and its own fields for corn and the fat spineless cactus they boil and eat. The cactus is rather a Teotitlán specialty, for as the whole valley floor rises from the old level when it was a lake, the soil is getting drier in the town, and cactus does better than corn. One Sunday I saw young Matías Torres and his wife in the Tlacolula market, and they explained that they had crossed the valley to buy flowers, for of late years Teotitlán has been too dry in the winter to grow flowers. Luckily this increasing drought does not affect its fences of tall organ cactus, which are the style all over this valley and give the towns one of their chief charms.

The Torres home is fenced from the dusty lane by a living green wall, and the side of the house giving on the lane is windowless, so that one must open the gate to get any idea of what is inside. The house of adobe blocks roofed with red tiles is L-shaped, forming two sides of the big patio, and has a wide veranda where the spinning and weaving can be done comfortably, outdoors but shaded from the sun.

As they work the family look across the tidy, well-swept dooryard to the abrupt crag of Xaquia, which springs from the range

enclosing the north side of the valley. Teotitlán is built just under
the mountain, and its Zapotec name means "foot of the rock."
Here the Bird of the Sun used to come, giving oracles to the priest
within the crag; and they say these rumbling oracles still come
from the rock when no strangers are listening. His son, the Bird
of Heaven, is everywhere; he is the *guacamayo*, the brilliant macaw
you will see in every valley dooryard.

The house is an almost empty shell around the patio, for
Teotitlán people are not citified enough to clutter their homes
with beds and bureaus. They hang their everyday clothes on pegs
and fold their fiesta finery away in a chest; at night they unroll
their straw *petates* and sleep on the floor. There is a weaving room
for the rainy season and the main room for the family altar, where
a table draped with an embroidered white cloth stands under an
arch of bamboo hung with colored glass globes. On the altar table
are chromo pictures of the Virgin of Guadalupe, and of Soledad,
patron of Oaxaca, set amid beeswax candles and bouquets of flowers. Before it on the floor is a heap of finished serapes, set there
to be blessed. There are a few rough unpainted chairs such as the
nearby serranos make, bunches of garlic and chiles and corn hang
from the rafters, and the walls are garish with big advertising
calendars cherished for their bright colors alone, since they are
long out of date.

The kitchen is a dirt-floored hut with a charcoal brazier or two
set on the ground, metates for grinding corn, and earthenware
pots of every size and shape. It has no tables or chairs because a
valley woman would be unable to work sitting up at a table. She
sits on the earth, and everything she uses is of the earth: whittled
wooden spoons, gourds and coconut shells with delicate carving
on the sides, ollas and casseroles of the tested ware made near the
city, plain terra cotta with a green glaze on the inside. Bowls for
serving soups or stews come from several different towns and are
gaily painted with flowers or animals or spiral motifs. But the
comal on which Luz Torres tosses her tortillas to bake can come

from no village but tiny San Marcos across the valley; it is a great flat plate of unadorned earthenware and a thing of beauty.

As dinnertime approaches, the women and children are gathered in the heart of the house. Grandmother Torres bends her handsome white head over a stew of tripe and vegetables. Luz, next in age to Grandmother, is patting tortillas with that expert rhythm which makes them perfectly round and of uniform thickness. Francesca is grinding chiles in a small mortar, Carla fans the charcoal fire under the tortillas, Carmen nurses her baby. They are talking Zapotec, a language of natural sounds like wind or water or the drowsy clucking of birds.

The women have been working all morning at their part of the serape craft, preparing the wool for the looms. Several nearby villages make a specialty of raising sheep for Teotitlán and deliver the fleeces fresh from the shearing. The women wash the wool, card it with homemade wooden combs, and spin it into skeins for dyeing. Then they wind the dyed thread onto bobbins, and the men take over. No woman ever attempts serape weaving; the serape is a male garment and must be woven by men.

The Teotitlán craft is a transition from Indian to European methods and has scarcely changed since the Conquest, for no part of the craft is mechanical. The Spanish introduced the sheep, the horizontal loom, and the newly discovered spinning wheel. Teotitlán men dropped the saddleback loom and the primitive spinning whorl and devised very simple editions of the European tools, which they make at home. Of late years they have stopped dyeing with plant juices and buy their dyes in the Oaxaca market, which means that chemical as well as vegetable colors are used.

But the Teotitlán palette is conservative, and only a few families have transgressed tradition by turning out gaudy-colored serapes for the *turistas*. The Torres family sticks to the old ways; their blankets are of soft gray, black, and white, with contrasting stripes at either end, a central motif of a stylized flower or a lozenge. Since the man wears the serape poncho-fashion, this middle part comes over his shoulders, so the design extends shoulder-width with a flower, or perhaps a small deer, woven in red or green, to give the garment an air.

Don Leopoldo, like all his fellow weavers, has accepted one innovation in design and makes some serapes with the "Greek fret" copied from ancient stones in the Mitla temples and in Teotitlán itself. This *grecque* motif has been at home in Oaxaca for many centuries for a codex drawing of an ancient temple at Tilantongo in the Mixteca shows it plainly carved over the central façade. So it is an innovation only in its use in serapes, and since a stepped pattern is ideal for weaving, the "Mitla design" serape has probably come to stay.

The one English phrase which Teotitlán men are bound to know is "Mitla design," which echoes down the arcade of the tourist hotel on days when the weavers come into the city. Don Leopoldo and his sons speak fair Spanish, but their women leave home so seldom that there is no need for them to know anything but Zapotec. That is true of most of the Valley of Oaxaca women, but those of Mitla are an exception. Women weave for women, and the Mitla matrons take the rebozos and wool sashes they make on the archaic saddleback loom into the city to sell, which involves knowing at least a patter of Spanish.

The Mitla women are rather like those of the isthmus: shrewd, capable, worldly, often beautiful, and always clothes-conscious. They set the style for the valley, an evolution from the classic wrap-around falda and straight huipil, which may, depending on the wearer, look dumpy or arrive at distinction. The valley skirt is full, like the isthmus, but has a local variation, a flounce of the same printed, machine-made cotton, decorated at the top with a zigzag line of narrow machine embroidery or rickrack braid. If the valley women would wear a straight huipil with this skirt their movements would have the grace of their isthmus sisters. Instead, they wear a full, square-necked blouse of contrasting material and tuck it in at the waist. The flowing classic line is thus lost in a baggy effect, but the vallistas cherish their belts, their one legacy from distant days. The *cinchón* is a long sash of supple hand-woven wool, and the best ones are dyed with cochineal, that burning magenta-red which is the soul of Mexico. Only the bougainvillaea and the cochineal insect achieve the true color; and Oaxaca, which has the imperial purple of the Chontal, also produces a little of the cochineal which used to be one of its chief sources of revenue.

The Torres women are barefoot, like all Oaxaqueñas except the mountain women, whose feet must be protected against stony paths. In the old days the vallistas went naked above the waist, but the padres made them cover their breasts, and so the rebozo was contrived. The Valley of Oaxaca women have hit on the smartest way to wear the rebozo. Like their isthmus sisters, they wind brightness into their braids—wools for every day, thin satin ribbons for best—and wind their braids around their heads. Then they bring the dark blue rebozo forward around the head, give it one twist at the front, and let an end fall in front over one shoulder and the other end drop down the back. There is a true art in this wrapping, and the effect is charming. If they must sit in the sun they bring up the loose ends to make a turban, which also has an air. There are many variations of utility; a woman with a baby will make a hammock of the rebozo to carry the infant against her breast, or a sling to carry the child on her back and leave her hands free. Or she makes a round pad of it on top of her head to support a tall heavy basket.

In this fecund land the rebozo becomes a maternal symbol, for the infant is always held warm and close to the mother and leaves the rebozo only to be held with equal tenderness by its father. Thus the Zapotec baby begins his life in a physical security almost as profound as the womb, and he is allowed to grow by the laws of growth within him, sheltered, watched, loved, but not forced to be anything but what he is. Babies are never denied the breast, and little children are never denied anything within reason and are greatly indulged as to sweets or whatever they ask for. They are not scolded or punished, because their parents do not get at cross-purposes with them.

If one concludes that Zapotecs grow up without neuroses, it is only another way of saying that in these people the primitive forces of life are so strong that they produce peace and happiness. The parental instinct is a pure force; the Zapotecs are enchanted with their children. Once in the Oaxaca market I saw a tiny girl pick up some fresh carrot tops and arrange them in a bouquet. She admired them so much that she turned to her mother and offered them in one of those delightful gestures of all childhood. Her mother gravely accepted the gift, then she was quite overcome and snatched up the baby and covered her face with kisses. This is a picture you can see wherever parents truly love and enjoy their children, but in Oaxaca the frame is different.

It is different because in Oaxaca almost all the people are working at home, not on complicated tasks which are far above the children's heads, but on crafts like weaving or pottery making which appeal to a child and in which he can play some simple part. The point is that he is *allowed* to participate, to be useful, so that his education as a child is not a matter of learning, through contrived tasks and games, skills which he will later apply to real life, but learning to clean wool or pat clay as an actual part of the family industry. Zapotec children will romp and play like children anywhere, but what really fascinates them is work, and they are allowed to work as much as they like.

Children whose mothers always sit on the ground as children do and make something pretty can hardly develop neuroses. They are not excluded from the adult world, and there is no strict dividing line between parents and children. The children, too, are parents, for as each new baby arrives the second youngest becomes the responsibility of an older brother or sister, and this is a definite assignment which lasts through the waking hours. Little boys have no notion that baby tending is a girl's work; on the whole, they are more vigilant and indulgent to their charge than their sisters. Thus the Zapotec family lives close together in a natural arrangement that makes them all parents and all children.

Watching the Torres youngsters come in and out of the odorous kitchen, one is struck by the sense that they are acting as complete human beings who do not need to be told what to do or not do. Little Miguel happens to be hungry, so the aunt nearest the tamale pot takes out the pat of corn meal with its filling of meat and chile, puts it on an oiled banana leaf, and gives it to him. Lolita happens not to be hungry, but she feels maternal, and since there is no baby available, she brings in a young pullet from the patio and sits with the big mothers, making a hammock of her tiny rebozo with those two twists she has already learned and rocks the pullet to sleep.

"If there is any justice to be found anywhere, it is among these people," an early Spanish chronicler wrote of the Zapotecs. "From the time a child is born he seems to obey the laws."

Teotitlán is a larger Torres family in which each member has his place and his own responsibility. It is not merely long tradition that makes the family and the town so orderly and harmonious, it is the Zapotec temperament. They enjoy living close together in a village. You will find no isolated farms in the valleys; the farmer prefers to trudge behind his oxen even to a distant field and come home at sunset to be among his fellows. Even in the mountains where the soil is poor the Zapotecs belong to a town, and though they may build a hut on a holding far from the center and live in it while they raise a crop of corn, they do not abandon their citizenship or fail to respond when their town calls on them for unpaid labor on a road or a public building. The pride and the social instincts of the Zapotecs are bound up in their town. This is a great contrast to those temperamental hermits, the Mixe, or worn-out folk like many Mixtecs or Maya fringe tribes next door in Chiapas, who so dislike town life that they will build a civic center in which nobody lives all year long and which is used only for an annual ceremonial in which the neighborhood drops its cherished isolation.

Town living has made the Zapotecs civilized and has preserved the race traditions. Old codices and maps of the days before the Conquest show the valley towns just where they are today and holding virtually the same lands which stretch miles to the next settlement. These are the "old towns," and some of them, like Mitla and Teotitlán and Tlacolula at the east end of the Valley of Oaxaca, are very ancient indeed. "New towns" have grown up as suburbs of the old communities to provide for surplus population, for there is a limit to the number of people a village can feed from its surrounding fields.

Despite the Revolution of 1910, which centered landownership in the towns, Oaxaca is going back to the old system of private ownership. From the earliest days this was a democratic arrangement; there were no big feudal lords who owned the lands and used the people as serfs; and under the Spanish the hacienda system was always breaking down. The Zapotecs had worked out a sound regime which kept everybody fed and in his own fields, and the system is again flourishing.

The land around the villages is divided into equal lots, *milpas*, and each family is assigned its own share. In time some of these holdings lapse as a family dies out or moves away, and thus some families have their original inherited milpa plus others they have acquired. Don Leopoldo is living on a milpa which some remote ancestor was given after all the villagers co-operated in clearing the land, and the Torres family also own tracts scattered here and there around Teotitlán. The village owns only the poor land roundabout, and anybody is free to work it. Landless newcomers may rent land which belongs to the citizens of Teotitlán, but they cannot buy it outright.

In its municipal government Teotitlán has managed to preserve the ancient system, against formidable pressure. The political party

67

which rules Mexico has managed to install a mayor (*presidente*) and secretary in many communities, but in Teotitlán there is a civic order in which graft and abuse are impossible, since nobody is paid. Holding office is a great honor, and only those worthy of honor are selected as town fathers. Every two years, on the first of January, there is a solemn transfer of office, in which the retiring presidente hands his gold-headed staff of office to his successor. The presidente is assisted by five councilors and by *topiles*, or constables, young men who take turns serving for a few weeks with no pay. The Zapotecs have a way of going into public problems with great thoroughness, and if the elders make a policy decision or settle a private dispute, their word is accepted without question. It is significant that the presidente of Teotitlán speaks not a word of Spanish.

The schoolmaster is the only evangel of the new order who has been accepted as part of the town. A priest arrives to celebrate Mass every fortnight; the people themselves keep the church in perfect order. There is no doctor in this town of twenty-five hundred people, who keep well by the ministrations of the *curandera* with her ancient mixture of magic and herbs, and by the *temescal*, the little sweat-oven you see in every dooryard, used especially by women after childbirth. However, the valley people are beginning to take ailing children to the doctors in the city. As a rule the vallistas are in robust health because they have an abundant and varied diet and have developed immunities to most diseases which mow down comparative newcomers like the Mixtecs. Cleanliness and sunshine do the rest.

On an ordinary day Teotitlán has the appearance of being almost deserted, for each family is hidden behind its hedge of organ cactus, busy at loom and spinning wheel. In the center of town, at the *cabildo*, three old men sit on a bench outside the municipal offices and the jail—which is literally empty as a rule. A cluster of women lingers in the triangle of shade before the small market, which is over by noon. Down the street an opulently pregnant

68

young woman moves homeward with a basket of crimson roses on her head, past the school with its hum of boys' voices reciting the oceans and the continents, conning over the dimensions of the globe. A bas-relief of a jaguar, carved centuries before Christ, drowses in a yellow wall as the rattling bus comes in from Oaxaca. Up the magnificent double flight of stone stairs leading to the church a mother moves with her small son, who is clutching a bouquet to offer a beloved saint. Above the quiet town the crag of Xaquia stands, the crag where the Bird of the Sun came to give oracles to his people, and comes still, they say, when no strangers are there to listen.

On January 15, the day of San Esquipulas, the town is early astir. Everything is in readiness: the costumes of the Plume Dancers have been refurbished, the church and atrium decorated, and the ceremonial gifts of boiled corn meal and chocolate prepared for the patron of the fiesta. The prosperous citizen chosen as *mayordomo* foots the bill for the celebration and receives the first homage of the day. A little procession headed by the inevitable band moves down the streets to his house, bearing a huge calabash of chocolate-flavored *pozole* and bouquets of yellow flowers.

Just before ten the Plume Dancers form in the lane outside the Torres house, where several young men of the family and their friends have been dressing for the Dance of the Conquest. This group will play the part of the Indians, and they are arrayed in splendor. Another group, gathering in another street, are small boys hideously dressed in blue uniforms and caps to burlesque the Spanish soldiers. Their leaders, Hernán Cortés and Pedro de Alvarado, are allowed fine plumed hats, but the Spanish make a sorry picture and are meant to do so.

As for the *Plumados*, they are brilliant guacamayos, descendants of the Bird of the Sun. Everything about them glitters. They wear silk shirts of all the sun colors and pantaloons of Chinese brocade in gold-fringed tiers. Their breastplates and stomachers are a mail of old Spanish dollars to suggest sun disks. Their famous headdresses are solar disks about three feet in diameter, made of alternating sectors of down feathers dyed scarlet, orange, green, yellow, purple, and amid this rainbow are mirrors which repeat and sharpen the colors. This plumage is borne on a gilt casque, and its hues are reflected in the silk kerchiefs tied around the arms and in embroidered sandals. The Plumados carry a rattle in the right hand and a stylized three-pronged spear in the left.

The band escorts the dancers through the town and up to the church. As in other valley towns, it is large and fine, set in a huge fenced churchyard with a patriarchal Indian laurel shading the entire façade. The weavers of Teotitlán have a fiesta art of winding bamboo and reeds into arches decorated with flowers, and of making elaborate branched candlesticks, a filigree of cherubs and delicate wheels of golden beeswax set off with bits of metal paper in gold and silver and magenta. These candelabra and lavish bunches of fresh flowers decorate all the altars. A white cloth covers the Madonna on the high altar, and an image of Esquipulas has the place of honor.

The Plumados take off their sun disks and enter the church. They kiss the image of San Esquipulas and make the rounds of the altars, kneeling and kissing an edge of the altar cloth. From this time they become ritual dancers set apart from the villagers and with grave dignity perform their roles.

The band, sitting under the laurel tree, announces the first of the many simple tunes which accompany the long story of the Conquest. It begins with the Indians in possession of their land, and the Plumados dance alone, going through the native figures: the dancers make a small spring forward, then whirl completely around, crouch on one knee and turn, then make another forward leap. Teotitlán dancers begin their training as small boys, for the movements must be executed with grace, and even with two alternating teams the Conquest dance requires memorizing sequences which go on for hours. For this reason the *campo*, or leader, is always a veteran who has spent a lifetime mastering the intricacies of the dance.

At critical points of the story the campo recites passages of narrative: the arrival of Cortés, the alerting of the Indians under Moctezuma, the battle for the land, and the final submission of the Indians to the Cross. The drama increases with the arrival of the absurd little Spanish soldiers. At first they dance alone at some distance from the Plumados; gradually the two bands come closer until finally they are fighting, crossing in oblique lines, each Indian clashing his three-pronged spear against the broadsword of the soldier. Cortés carries a sword in his right hand, a cross in his left.

Two little girls figure in the dance. Cortés, of course, has his Malinche, the Indian who deserted her people for love of the Conquistador, but Moctezuma, too, has a bedizened little girl, his daughter. The solemnity and growing tragedy of the dance are overenlivened by two clowns, small boys wearing pig masks with a piece of fresh pork impaled on one tusk. Like all jesters, they are allowed any japery that strikes their fancy, and these pigs squeal and grunt and caper at will.

Toward noon there is a stir, and the spectators get to their feet to welcome the presidente and councilmen, who are ushered to the coolest seats under the tree. At the first pause in the dance the mayordomo produces bottles of mezcal and little glasses. The presidente drinks the first *copita*, then the councilmen and all the male spectators follow suit. One after the other the dancers come up and kiss the hands of the town elders—a courtesy accorded them by all the townspeople whenever they appear on the streets. The elders sit watching the dance all afternoon, and copitas are poured at frequent intervals. Tomorrow there will be no dance, but the fiery mezcal of the valley will still be poured.

It is hard to discover what this fiesta means, and far too easy to read meanings into it. But there is no doubt that the real significance lies below the surface, for the Indian does not live in the surface of time; he lives in vertical time, in which each moment contains past and present. This is not an abstract idea but a way of experiencing so natural to the Zapotecs that their old religion was based on it. Teotitlán is having its annual fiesta, as all towns do on their saint's day. But why this tragic story of the Conquest? The finest young men of the town, arrayed like the sun, are telling the story of Indian defeat and despoilment. This much is on the surface, and it explains nothing.

The dance is being held below the crag of Xaquia, on the site of the pagan temple which the Dominicans tore down to build their church. Fortunately they preserved some of the ancient stones carved with bas-reliefs of jaguars and strange Semitic-looking men or with the grecque designs such as adorn the temples of Mitla. The squared spirals of these motifs are thought to represent Quetzalcoatl, the winged serpent.

All about are the grass-covered pyramids of the day when Teotitlán, then called Xaquia, was the first Zapotec capital, and their secrets are still inviolate. But some years ago, when Monte Albán was excavated, a small clay model of the Xaquia temple was found in a tomb. In it was a guacamayo, the Bird of the Sun, and the top of this little temple was open, as if to allow the bird to come and go. Are the Plumados, so plainly guacamayos, rehearsing rites to their sun god? They are, on the surface, paying homage to San Esquipulas, a Christian saint. Is there a connection, or is this fiesta merely a jumble of ceremonials old and new, in which copitas are the real point?

We go into the beautiful church to try to discover what Esquipulas means. We know what he is, a miraculous image in the town named for him, where Guatemala, Honduras, and El Salvador meet. On this day his shrine is thronged with pilgrims from all Central America and from Mexico and New Mexico; he is the center of a pilgrimage fair like that of Copacabaña on Lake Titicaca, also a spot where borders meet.

Valley Town

Without a doubt Esquipulas is an ancient border god in a new guise, for all over the world the Church preserved pagan shrines, merely giving them new names. In ancient days this god, who may have been Quetzalcoatl, presided over a great international market where the traders from South and Central America met those from Mexico and perhaps from certain Caribbean islands. This habit of holding an international fair under the protection of a god is as old as trade itself, and as universal. Hermes-Mercury was the patron of fairs, traders, borders; like Quetzalcoatl, he was a winged god.

There is nothing farfetched in all this; the men of Teotitlán still make the pilgrimage to Esquipulas and sell their serapes in the plaza below his church. What is strange is Esquipulas, whom the valley people call "saint." He is not a saint at all, but the crucified Christ; and this Christ is very dark, almost black. He is the Indian Cristo.

In the Teotitlán church there are two images of Esquipulas, which are usually at a side altar. Today the larger Cristo stands before the high altar and the smaller one before the chancel rail. It is the same bronze-colored figure, wearing only a loincloth of the ancient type, of woven reed; and both are faithful copies of the miraculous image in Guatemala. There are many explanations of why this image is dark: it is stained with the copal incense of four centuries of worship; there have been chemical changes in the wood; the Indian who carved it hated the white Spaniards and so made his Cristo black. The Indians themselves think no explanation is needed.

All through Southern Mexico there are traces of a cult—merely a thin stream of memory or fanaticism—which centers on the Indian Christ, crucified for the Indians. More than once, among both Maya and Zapotecs, an Indian has offered himself for actual crucifixion, a rite carried through in deepest secrecy and deepest reverence. For these Indians say, "This Christ who died far across the seas, rejected by His own people, did not know of the Indians.

73

But if an Indian dies on the cross, of his own will, then we can be sure the sacrifice is for us." And in that spirit the sacrifice is made —rarely, but within the memory of living men. In the same spirit, many Oaxaca villages and two churches in the capital have a Good Friday rite in which a young man is tied to a cross and remains for two or three hours of pain, as a token of Indian crucifixion.

Esquipulas is thus the Christ closest to the Indians, who turn to him as the great healer of blindness and bodily ills; he is *muy milagroso*—very miraculous—because he is one of their race. The images in the Teotitlán church are hung with little offerings unlike anything you can see unless you go to the remotest mountain caves where the old gods are worshiped: strange little dried flowers, seeds, stones. The small image before the chancel rail is freshly decked for the day with a garland of pink roses, though the magic offerings remain on a cord around the neck. An old man who is nearly blind stumbles up to kiss the image, crooning, *"Esquipul, mi padrecito, las rosas de mi padrecito,"* touching the roses, then brushing their healing essence against his eyes.

Esquipulas, the beloved father, the dark Christ, is celebrated by those sons of the Bird of Heaven, the god of brightness, dancing in the atrium under the crag of Xaquia. For a moment Indian Time, vertical time, ties all together; for the dark god and the bright god are one. Quetzalcoatl's name means "winged serpent" and also "precious twin," for the Bird of the Sun is also god of the night. When Quetzalcoatl performed his final sacrifice, burning himself to ashes, his soul rose to heaven as Venus, star of morning and also the sunset star. It is a long, long story, hidden, mysterious. Perhaps the god who became Quetzalcoatl alighted first on this very crag of Xaquia; the fiery bird who in the valleys of Oaxaca is recognized in the splendid guacamayo, and in the rain forests of the Maya in the quetzal bird.

What do the elders of the village remember of this long story? One does not ask; they would not dream of telling you.

IV

ISTHMUS AND SIERRA

In the central square of Tehuantepec there is a hideous bronze bust which is perhaps the only public monument in the world to a woman of light character. The statue of Doña Juana Cata Romero, mistress and lifelong friend of Porfirio Díaz, expresses the ambiguity of the isthmus town. It has always been the crossroads between Mexico and Central and South America and a link between the oceans. An endless variety of peoples have left their traces in Tehuantepec: the tribes of prehistory, Aztecs, French, Negroes, American forty-niners, and modern drummers from Lebanon and Syria. In political crises Tehuantepec has always tried to straddle or, if a choice had to be made, has taken the side of property and power. Doña Juana is perhaps not too cruel a symbol of a town polyglot in spirit as well as blood.

The inscription on the bust praises Doña Juana for the works of charity that marked her old age, and the brassy portrait makes her look like a severely pious sodality sister. That is well enough for public purposes, but the tehuanas cherish her as their secret ideal, a woman who used her beauty to amass great riches which she administered shrewdly, a tehuana always fiercely loyal to her town.

There was a time when Porfirio Díaz, who developed into one of the world's most durable dictators, played on the side of the liberals. Born in the city of Oaxaca, of mixed Spanish and Mixtec blood, Díaz was confused in his social thinking, just as his future

75

rival, the pure Zapotec Benito Juárez, was clear and steadfast. The isthmus has always reflected dramatically the conflict between these two Oaxaca leaders, which sums up the history of the republic. Juchitán has forever fought on the liberal, democratic side; Tehuantepec has supported the political adventurer, the reactionary property lover. Even the physical appearance of the towns reveals this moral cleavage.

As a brilliant young officer it suited Díaz to support the liberals during the civil war that preceded the French invasion of Mexico and the tragic farce of Maximilian and Carlotta. In command of Tehuantepec, Díaz was captivated by Juana Cata, who came to the barracks to sell coconut candy and play billiards with the soldiers. The French traveler Brasseur de Bourbourg, who visited Tehuantepec at this period and saw Juana at the barracks, went into raptures at her brilliant beauty and her exotic clothes. "I never saw a more striking image of Isis or Cleopatra," he wrote.

Porfirio Díaz found that his enchantress had brains as well and used her as a spy to report the movements of the enemy. Later she ran off with one of the worst scoundrels of the day, and still later married, but the tie between her and Díaz lasted until they both died in 1915. Meanwhile, of course, Díaz became President, which gave Doña Juana immense power in Tehuantepec. She became fabulously rich, owning sugar and coconut plantations and much property, and built a pompous "chalet" which still stands in the center of town, directly beside the railroad. Here in the ballroom hung with crystal chandeliers she gave formal balls for the President whenever he visited Tehuantepec, and the elite of the town flocked to these sumptuous affairs. She balanced her worldly extravagance by rebuilding the old cathedral, convent, and cemetery and founding convent schools.

The railway that runs in front of her decaying house is a relic of the days when the isthmus interested foreign powers. This short, decrepit line which connects the Gulf with the Pacific is all that remains of international dreaming and scheming to make a great deal of the Isthmus of Tehuantepec. The early scheme was to dig a canal linking the oceans. The idea began with Hernán Cortés and is not entirely dead yet. Modern engineers have proved that there is not sufficient water in the isthmus to maintain a canal, but every now and then some American who is tired of political troubles in Panama revives the project.

A railroad, however, was feasible, and Europe and the United States had long regarded the isthmus with a mixture of calculation and romance. There were wild schemes in the United States for the colonization of this "natural paradise" (ignoring the uninhabitable swamps on the Gulf side), and before the Civil War a New Orleans company had a concession to build a railroad. However, American interest was diverted to digging the Panama Canal, and in the end it was the British, whom President Díaz always favored over the Americans, who built the Tehuantepec Railway. It was opened in 1907 and flourished, with twenty trains a day each way, until the Panama Canal began operations in 1914. After that the importance of the railway dwindled rapidly.

Its Pacific terminus, Salina Cruz, shows the marks of this debacle. It was laid out in broad streets strung with hotels and shops and warehouses but is almost a ghost port today, its paint long since scoured off by sandstorms. Texas oil, shipped by rail across the Isthmus, is transferred here to tankers which supply the coast to the north; otherwise very little moves in Salina Cruz today. Ixtepec, whose airport was built with American money for the protection of the Panama Canal, shows more activity, since it is the take-off for planes to Guatemala. But Ixtepec is an ugly town.

The most charming spot along the coast is the primitive little beach of La Ventosa, a fishermen's cove near Salina Cruz where the bathing is good unless one of the vicious northers is blowing. Here you can sit in a bamboo cabin which is little more than an open pavilion furnished with hammocks, a very rough table, and a few chairs. The children rush to the beach to bring oysters;

from her hammock an old woman directs somebody to open bottles of warm beer. It is all very peaceful, and on the beach the gauzy nets are spread as the dark-skinned fishermen take their afternoon ease. A marimba is playing in one of the huts.

"A dead child," they explain. "That's why the music is gay. For an older person's wake they play something more serious. But when a child dies we eat, drink, dance, because the *angelito* has gone straight to heaven."

There is something of this tender coziness in the cemetery of Juchitán, which is a village of miniature houses, all prettily painted and decked with flowers. Each dead soul, or each family, thus has a carefully tended home, and there is nothing somber about this village of the dead. But unlike most of Mexico, which makes a carnival of the Day of the Dead, the isthmus people celebrate it as a day of true lamentation, with much wailing at the graves. Nobody knows why this is so, but the isthmus is a world in itself.

Juchitán is a secluded world which has never become a backwash. It lies a mile or so off the Highway, a big town of twenty thousand people which produces so many intellectuals and artists that they must emigrate to Mexico City to make their careers. This is really singular. Here is an isolated town stretched along the arid sandy plains of the Pacific, a Zapotec town almost unmixed in blood, which means that it holds fast to many ancient traditions. And yet Juchitán has an enlightened perspective on public questions, its artists and poets are always in the vanguard, and its people reveal high personal standards and a hardy idealism. What is it that makes some people and some towns better than others? This is an important question to which it is not always easy to find an answer. But a foreigner observing the pure Zapotecs does find one quality very highly developed: self-respect.

For four centuries the Zapotecs have been treated by the Spanish, and by Mexicans with a mixture of European blood, as an inferior people. They never believed themselves inferior, even when they were branded and sold at auction as slaves, or when

78

modern tourists made it uncomfortable for their women to bathe nude in the river. On the contrary, they have a profound, disciplined pride in themselves and their race, and so you will find towns like Juchitán, or Ixtlán in the Sierra de Juárez, stamped with a preservative self-respect.

To achieve beauty in the isthmus requires a true instinct. These are not lush tropics, but almost desert sand flats, monotonous and blasted by atrocious summer heat and by the winter northers which fill the air with yellow dust and sand. Juchitán cannot be beautiful, but it has space and order. The streets are very broad, lined with tamarind trees, and except in the center, where there are Spanish-style houses with patios, the homes are set far back from the roads. Unlike the valley towns, where the houses have a blind side flush with the street, the Juchitán yards are unwalled, no doubt to give a better circulation of air. There is no such thing as a lawn in Oaxaca, and these spacious yards are mostly bare earth, but the houses have privacy and a suggestion of coolness because they are surrounded by trees and sometimes flowering shrubs like hibiscus and frangipani.

Flowers are abundant only because they are important to the *juchitecos*. During the winter the River of Dogs is dry stones, so water must be brought from a distance to keep vegetable and flower gardens alive. But it was in winter that I saw the most charming of all flower markets, in Juchitán. A line of women sat along a wall, with another line crouching in front of them. Their flat baskets held a riot of flowers, but zinnias were the motif that morning, and the women themselves were dressed in all the zinnia colors: magenta, crimson, pink, ocher, mauve. I am sure that they chose their blouses and skirts to do honor to the flowers.

The Juchitán market is run, like all those in the isthmus, by women and girls, and it is a model of order. Visit the market and the school, and you know the town. One very hot summer day, with a Chicago schoolteacher, I passed the huge school just as noon recess began, and at once we were inundated by children.

Zapotec

They swarmed around us, friendly as puppies, highly amused in true Zapotec fashion at our foreignness and not at all repressed in their giggles and silly questions. Where do children get such energy in a tropical climate? The Chicago pedagogue rushed to one of the schoolmasters who was watching the riot, begging for discipline. Discipline? He was incredulous. The children often quiet down in school because they are eager to learn or to draw, but no master attempts to make them act like grownups or sheep. And we two *gringitas*, he evidently thought, justified any uproar.

Juchitán, with its fidelity to tradition, makes the more famous Tehuantepec a disappointment. At the period when Doña Juana was giving her champagne suppers the little city had an air of meretricious gentility. Now it is a slatternly huddle of dun-colored houses slapped against the banks of the river. The once-elegant houses around the central square have degenerated into pool halls and beer parlors.

Because of its glamorous reputation and the fact that it is the first large town beyond Oaxaca, this is a letdown. For four hours one has been motoring down the Highway through an endless mass of mountains so jumbled together and so steep that the only hamlets are down in an occasional valley with a stream old enough to have built up a ribbon of soil. The road is almost empty of people and inexplicably full of livestock. In the dry winters the cows and burros, which must belong to some farm hidden in the mountains, come to crop the leaves of the young trees and shrubs along the Highway, and one pities them. In the summers, alas for the motorist, there is a verdant border of grass along the road, so the animals return, bringing their young—*burritos*, colts, calves, kids—which have no conception whatever of the machine age. The bull calves are the worst; truculent, defiant, unteachable, they stand stock-still in the middle of the road until it pleases them to amble away. All the animals are fat and sleek in the summer; the mountains are clothed to the top in brilliant dense green, very different from the tawny winter dress. But the newcomer to the isthmus is agog to see the fabulous city of Tehuantepec, and what he finds is very nearly a shantytown.

The hideous iron railroad bridge takes one into the tousled center. Farther on there are lovely groves of coconut palms, and here there is a new tourist hotel with affable waitresses in the native dress. But I once spent a midsummer night in a native hotel just off the main plaza and found it surprisingly agreeable. The inn was built around a large patio where guests parked their cars and the family swung in hammocks. Meals were served on a veranda overlooking the patio, and after dinner we lingered to drink colas from the electric cooler, which is now becoming standard in Mexico, as the Singer sewing machine has been for two generations. We were soon teaching the proprietress canasta. The tehuanas are full of curiosity about novelties in clothes or amusements, and unlike their more reserved sisters of valley and sierra, they have easy manners with strangers.

This is long habit. The women of Tehuantepec not only manage shops and market stalls, but they like to travel far and wide to sell isthmus products: pineapples, turtle eggs bought from the Huave of the lagoons, live iguanas—huge lizards whose meat is considered a great delicacy—sweetmeats, sugar cane, chickens. A group of tehuanas always take the bus to the Saturday market in Oaxaca; others travel back and forth on the trans-isthmus train or cover the whole network of nearby towns. They have the right temperament for this work, for there is something of the gypsy in the tehuana which goes a little deeper than the Romany suggestion of trailing skirts, gold earrings, and brilliant, calculating eyes.

In valley and sierra it is usually the men who make the market trips, while the women stay home, tied to a handicraft. But the isthmus men have little time to circulate. They leave home at dawn to labor in cornfields, orchards, and sugar plantations, or to range the mountains as professional hunters of wild boars, deer, curassow, armadillo, and the destructive jaguars for which they are paid a bounty. Others are fishermen who have an expanding market now that ice and rapid busses are available. For those who work the land the irrigation problem is an added burden to pile on the climate of alternating windstorms and spells of atrocious heat. The *istmeños* are extremely hardy, but they come home tired at night.

Perhaps this explains why some of the isthmus fiestas are merely an excuse for the men to get drunk. But they used to mean a great deal more. The opening of the Highway and the inroads of modernity have meant that in Tehuantepec at least the traditional fiesta is rapidly going to pieces. The town is divided into a dozen wards, *barrios,* each with its church and patron saint, and until a few years ago the fiesta celebrating the saint's day was a matter of ceremonious dignity. But that slipping and sliding from the old standards which is so apparent in Tehuantepec today is ruining its fiestas. Those standards were always easy, threaded with compromise, but the infection is now reaching vital sources of strength.

The ward of San Blas celebrates its festive days late in July, beginning prettily enough with a procession of women carrying masses of white spikenard to the little barrio church. By evening, when we went to the church, the redolence of the *nardo* was suffocating. Near the altar a rakish Santiago sat his splay-legged wooden horse. A few of the older women were praying, but the muddy streets were dark. Everybody was early abed or else celebrating the carnival at the other end of the barrio.

The hotel people had insisted on sending their son along with us, and this protection seemed odd in Oaxaca, where foreign women are safe at all hours. No, he said, we must not go to the carnival, it was simply not the thing to do. The next afternoon we were grateful for his stubbornness; we would have run into a horde of extremely drunk men feeling expansive.

Whether or not it is traditional, San Blas staged an equestrian feature the next afternoon. It was only a group of teen-age boys

mounted on mustangs, racing madly from one end of the barrio
to the other. They yelled and beat their nags, but all they accomplished was to stir up clouds of dust, for the usual rain had been
omitted that day. However, the street was lined with spectators,
sitting in the doorways, perching on walls. The little boys were
often stark-naked, in isthmus fashion, but the little girls were
fetching in miniature tehuana costumes. Like their mothers, they
wore their second-best clothes, omitting the pleated lace flounce
and head-huipil which require many hours of ironing. Second-
best in the isthmus is a bright, ground-length calico skirt and the
huipil which has become the rage: a red-and-yellow concoction
which an expert seamstress can make in two long days at a sewing
machine. The material is either red or yellow, and the square neck
is decorated in solid machine stitching in the contrasting color. It
is a charming and expensive garment.

Conscious of their finery and the fresh satin ribbons in their
braids, the little girls aped their mothers by gliding barefoot along
the broken sidewalks, toying with the string of black beads which
someday would be replaced by a chain of gold coins, and casting
sidelong glances from lustrous eyes.

As in New Orleans and Haiti, a mixture of French and Negro
blood results in exotic beauty, and now and then you find this
type in Tehuantepec. But as a rule the blend is far more complex,
and the pure Zapotec type of Juchitán is becoming rare. The
isthmus dress, so Cretan-classic, was designed for a slim, proud figure such as every Juchitán girl tries to preserve until she is safely
married. In Tehuantepec, where a fat placidity is the style, the
girls begin to get heavy and even dumpy in their early teens, and
their faces, too, seem broader and heavier-boned than those of their
rivals in Juchitán. There is great jealousy and bickering between
the towns about good looks, hair styles, and clothes. In any rivalry
of manners the tehuanas are clear losers; their market women are
often strident, bawdy, and deliberately rude. This is not Zapotec.

And when we reached the carnival area we found the sort of

Zapotec

Mexicans familiar in the slums of Mexico City or the honky-tonks of Tijuana on the California border, the tragic mixed-blood Indian who has mingled with too many cheap foreigners and has become a nondescript. To be sure, these raucous istmeños were blind-drunk, but not in Zapotec fashion. Anybody who loves fiestas is bound to see a good many intoxicated Zapotecs, but somehow they carry their liquor quietly, though they may relieve themselves against the nearest wall. For every drunken Zapotec there are two devoted friends who have stood their mezcal better and who look after him with great courtesy. It is bad manners to laugh at a drunk.

A side street in San Blas was solidly lined with stands selling odorous snacks, *totopos*—great crisp tortillas baked in a deep pit—but mostly beer and mezcal. The men, especially the older ones, wavered from one stall to the next, getting more sodden and vociferous with each stop. The younger men were dancing away the late afternoon in the usual bamboo pavilion hung with bunches of green coconuts, where the band alternated with a marimba orchestra. In the sweltering heat the dancers stood glued together, hardly moving and hardly able to move because most of San Blas was packed around the dance floor.

There was no real gaiety. The virile young men and the plump sensuous girls, their braids down their backs, moved slowly in a sweaty embrace, bathed in the odors of onions and beer and hot fat from the stalls. There was a debauched sense here of tropical carnality, a fetid ribaldry.

In the generation since Diego Rivera first painted the most exotic women of America their allure has faded, along with their town. But Juchitán has never compromised, and one can hope that its girls will long be as bewitching as they are today.

SIERRA DE JUÁREZ

One should not attempt long mountain trips in the summer, for the rain can transform a road into a bog or erase it altogether; it can sweep away bridges and create impassable torrents in barrancas bone-dry in winter. As for Yalalag, the mountain town I wanted to visit, it can be reached on horseback during the winter, but in the rainy season one would have to make a three-day journey afoot with no burro to carry packs, and find a guide who knew alternate routes if the usual paths were washed out. "Nobody goes to Yalalag in the summer," everybody said.

As it turned out, my stubborn attempt to get to Yalalag failed, but the failure meant that I saw Ixtlán de Juárez, far more than a consolation prize.

Still, I want to see Yalalag someday. This town, hidden deep in the mountains northeast of the capital, is a reservoir of the old ways, and its people are charming. I had a friend, Rosalia, who came down from Yalalag to sell the fine weavings of the town, and though we could communicate only when somebody was there who knew her town's special version of Zapotec, she had invited me to visit her home. We Americans often felt a childish impulse to pick Rosalia up and hug her, for she was small and dainty as a Chinese doll. The Yalalag women look like little girls ready for bed: they leave their hair hanging loose down the back and wear long white tunics as shapeless as old-fashioned nightgowns. But for fiestas they wind their hair around a heavy coronet of black wool, exactly duplicating the classic headdress of old Zapotec queens and goddesses.

This is just one of the things they have never forgotten since their region was Olmec Land. Also, there is the mystery of the three Yalalag crosses of silver which the padres found the women wearing. . . .

So three of us started off for Yalalag in the rainy season. There is a saying in the American colony in Oaxaca that if you ask information or advice you are bound to get at least five contradictory answers, and by then you concoct your own version. So it was; we had decided to take the bus to the mine of La Natividad in the Sierra de Juárez, and there we would be "sure" to find horses and a guide to take us across the short intervening space (on the map) to Yalalag. My companions, a veritable Osa Johnson of Latin American safaris and a young California naturalist, had prepared for all contingencies and climates.

They brought along everything but a camel to carry their gear. They had tents, jungle hammocks with complicated mosquito nets, three camp stoves, a mound of blankets, a tremendous first-and-last-aid kit, lanterns, pillows, enough food for a chuck wagon, a ten-gallon water bottle in a straw container, pots and pans, impressive changes of attire, including large sombreros, riding boots, and bed jackets. Dick, the naturalist, of course had special gear, prepared to collect all fauna except possibly a live jaguar. He had glass jars of all sizes and shapes, pressing equipment and a very long net for butterflies, a snake stick, bolo knife, and, as a final touch, a huge multiple-dwelling bird cage. The only thing lacking was a yellow rubber life raft, which, considering the weather we were to encounter, might have been useful.

The bus driver was appalled but equal to anything. He got extra ropes and managed to tie our preposterous baggage on the top of the bus, with the bird cage crowning our silliness. The passengers were fascinated by our luggage, but neither giggled nor asked questions. They were hardy mountain folk, with the best manners in all Oaxaca.

We started across the valley floor along the old Camino Real with its little hidden villages. Beyond Teotitlán del Valle we climbed into the sierras, and the mettle of bus and driver became the test of survival. We were following a slightly widened foot trail with grades never intended for motors, a one-way road with sudden sharp curves. When we met a car bound in the opposite direction, one of us had to back up around those short bends for perhaps quarter of a mile to a wide spot. Our driver was so calm and skillful that I developed a blind faith in him and in the engine of the rickety old bus, which must have been a powerful truck motor, or we never would have climbed the ladder-steep grades.

Isthmus and Sierra

Up and up through the riot of summer, rivers and waterfalls brawling where in winter there were only dry arroyos. All was green and lush with bloom, with masses of wild cosmos, morning-glories like great purple stars in the meadows, dahlias and bird-of-paradise, crimson *sangre de toro,* and higher up grand oak and pine forests, decked as for a fiesta in orange *Bromelia* and less familiar air plants.

All this dramatic, barren country belongs to the border sèrranos, the poor, blighted folk with scraggly beards and deep-sunk eyes under their peaked hats of black felt. Their corn patches are almost perpendicular, their houses graceless huts. They come down to the Oaxaca market with wood and charcoal and at Christmas bring mosses and orchids. I had visited several villages in this region one winter, depressed that there should be such poverty, such evident hunger for everything, beginning with food, in these glorious forested mountains.

We circled from one mountain system to another, the country almost deserted for long stretches, and then by afternoon we came, amazingly, into an old settled world, a bountiful land where the vistas were wide, the mountains mild and clothed in checkers of green and gold, the fields bordered with old trees. The towns were exquisite, lying in cups and spreading up the paternal sierra slopes, and the people in the bus began murmuring their names: Yavesía, Lachatao, Ixtlán, Guelatao, all the lovely old far-off towns, each a different color. Guelatao, where Benito Juárez was born, was all white, Ixtlán a soft gray-beige.

Here the Rio Grande flows, in summer deserving its name, a first-class, nobly curving river, creating a wider stream of dazzling green meadows. Here the people are sturdy, with glorious red cheeks. There is a cheerful tidiness in the villages, and geraniums spill from every window. This is a self-contained world, part of the ancient Olmec Land.

The Sierra de Juárez is probably older than the valley. There are many buried towns in the region, towns with huge masonry works that suggest an era of greatness before the birth of Christ. The sierra was once more thickly settled, by Zapotecs who may have been an independent stream of the race; there is a deep cleavage between sierra and valley forms of the language, just as there is a wide neutral zone of poor mountain lands separating them.

It was the sierra people who put up the stiffest resistance to the Spanish, fighting from ambush with long flint-edged lances or bows and arrows. Cortés had to send three expeditions against them, and still the guerrilla warfare went on. The Zapotecs used a special whistling code which was one of their best weapons in fighting the Spanish and which they have by no means forgotten, for often it saves a day's journey. They call from mountain to mountain, whistling simple messages and even identifying themselves and the person to whom the message is to be delivered.

We had to remember, going through the tempting towns of Guelatao and Ixtlán, that we were bound for Yalalag, just across a mountain or two. So we rumbled on to the hideous mining town of La Natividad, and immediately there were torrential rains, which served us right. Nobody there had ever heard of Yalalag, still less of horses to hire. Everything in this wretched town was alien; it seemed no part of Oaxaca. The mining installations and the sodden huts spilling down the sides of the ravaged mountain, the drunken, brutalized Mixtecs in the cantinas around us, the very savagery of the rain were alien.

The mine superintendent rescued us, offering us supper and shelter in the guesthouse. Piece by piece Dick and I moved our safari gear from the bus station, the rain cascading from our ponchos down into our shoes, and I chanted curses on each and every item, the nylon tents, the bundles of bread, the snake stick and the bird cage, Anne's various riding habits. No horses, no Yalalag. The rain poured down all night.

La Natividad was instructive. There are many mines in Oaxaca, a great number of them abandoned with their lodes almost intact because the Oaxaqueños so hate to work away from the sun. As one of the richest mines in Mexico, its ores bearing gold and silver together, La Natividad has been worked steadily since the Conquest. It lies near the Upper Mixteca, whose people have the bitter choice between starving and working as migrants. So it is Mixtecs who go two miles into the mountain to take out the gold and silver. No wonder they spend Sunday getting drunk.

During the night I remembered a story about the Sierra de Juárez. When the new governor was installed there was a conference of five hundred mayors from all over the state, and since most of them belonged to the party machine they had come to dip into the barrel for whatever they could get for their towns and themselves personally. In the midst of this grabbing a deputation arrived from a sierra village.

"We have very little money," they told the governor. "But we are content. We have a town barber who keeps our heads clean, we have a fine school, and our affairs in general go very well. But there is no proper road up the mountain to our village; we have only a path so narrow that it is hard going even for the burritos. We do not know how to make a fine road. All we can do is to take the stones from the side of the path with our hands and tramp them into the ground with our feet. Will you send us a man who knows how to make a fine road? We will all give our labor, and we will pay for this man. It may take us two or three years, but we want to pay for our own road."

The serranos did not get their road or anything else from the new regime, and yet when the general strike was called for the purpose of curbing the governor, the men of the Sierra de Juárez sat for thirty hours deliberating whether it was the just and dignified thing to join the state-wide revolt. They finally voted to strike but sent a message to the President of Mexico explaining that they were not rebelling against law and government but against a personal malfeasance.

This deeply ingrained respect for the law, learned through

many centuries of independent town government before the Conquest, is fundamental in the Zapotecs. In an isthmus town like Juchitán or a valley one like Teotitlán del Valle, which have managed to keep the party machine out, there is this same deliberation about the right and wrong of public questions. An illiterate village elder is a natural, long-winded orator and often has a shrewd, paternal sense of what harms or benefits the people.

This instinct for fair government was truest of all in Benito Juárez, who was trained as a jurist and then as President carried Mexico through its most critical period, by respect for the law and for the rights of others. He never for a moment wavered, but stood calm and stanch as the sierra that now bears his name.

After the degradation of La Natividad we returned to Guelatao and clarity. Don Benito's birthplace is a simple village with an alpine air because of the bright window boxes against the tidy white houses, and because the people are sturdy and thickset like the Swiss. Guelatao has not forgotten its great son; behind the plaster arches at the front of the little square there is a tall pedestal bearing a tiny bronze statue of Juárez in his presidential frock coat; and at one side is the Internado Indigena, one of the two boarding schools in the sierra for promising Indian boys. The other feature of the village is the "Enchanted Lake," which looks like any other cow pond and seems to have no story. But it has always been enchanted.

Here Benito spent his first dozen years, knowing no Spanish and longing for a school. Orphaned early, he lived with an uncle and tended his sheep, now and then mounting a rock and addressing his flock in ringing Zapotec. One day some muleteers passing through the village stole a sheep, and Benito spent the night reproaching himself for his carelessness. He could not face his uncle and before dawn was on the way to the city, where an older sister lived.

This is almost the stock beginning for a great man's story, or even a fairy tale, and in the lovely afternoon, mounted at last on veritable horses, we enjoyed Guelatao with its high clean air, its climbing geraniums on the cottages, the schoolboys whistling on their way to the Enchanted Lake. This was the proper setting for one of those tales that belong to all the people.

We rode back the short way to Ixtlán, head of the sierra district, calling out our *"Buenas tardes"* to the little groups of serranos we met across the mountain. One must be careful about these greetings. There were four of us, because the son of our hostess had come along. Suppose we met five people on the trail: each of us would greet each of them and immediately say good-by as we passed, so there would be *"Buenas tardes"* twenty times and *"Adiós"* twenty more, which made a little song in the sunny air.

There is a feeling of solidity and richness about Ixtlán, and this kept amazing us, because in the center of the state nobody hears about this town. We had more or less blundered into it, and it was such a model in every way that we began to wonder how many more charming old towns were hidden in the sierra. Quite content to leave Yalalag for another season, we went up and down the winding streets with a growing sense of approbation.

Ixtlán evokes an approval with a moral content because it is so plainly the home of Zapotecs with that powerful self-respect we mentioned earlier. Every child goes to the fine new school, every citizen speaks Spanish, and you feel that this acceptance of modern education and the national language was made with a fuller consciousness of how a proud old Indian race should live today than is possessed by valley Zapotecs. Choosing the road of enlightenment only makes Ixtlán more truly Indian. For the highest culture of America was bred in these very mountains and the coastal lands beyond them on the Gulf.

Much of that old inheritance is in the sierra people, the monolithic strength of race. In the physical sense, Ixtlán dates from the Spanish Colonial period, when wealth was pouring into the town from the Natividad mines. Its pleasant plazas are rimmed with dignified public buildings; most of the houses are large stone resi-

dences with patios where rich Spanish once lived. They are shabby
now but are kept in order and are bright with flowers. There have
been three successive churches in Ixtlán; the post-Conquest one
has been torn down, and we did not visit the newest one. But the
small cathedral built in the eighteenth century in high Chur-
rigueresque style is a jewel. It blazes with the pure gold of La
Natividad; it is as sumptuous in its inspired gimcrackery as the
famous churches of Puebla and Taxco.

All prowlers in Mexico know that there is some powerful
solvent in the air which makes it possible to mix any and all colors
and styles and even sorts of people and make them belong together. Thus Don Mario's shop, an abstract study in geometrical
neatness, lived very happily near the jewel-box cathedral. It was
such a wonderful shop that we kept inventing errands to take us
there. The counters, the floor, the walls were radiantly clean and
scrubbed. The bolts of cloth were put on the shelves with milli-
meter precision; huaraches and lanterns hung from the ceiling in
neat festoons; cheese, honey, frosted cookies were covered with
sparkling glass domes. Behind the counter Don Mario and his wife
presided, spotless, comely, comfortable, radiating that particular
quality we found everywhere in Ixtlán—a personal sense of right-
ness, of being exactly where they belonged—that is expressed in
a grave, beautiful courtesy.

Ixtlán is a sequestered town, unused to strangers. But it accepted
the inexplicable trio of two middle-aged women and a bumptious
youth who without preliminary would try to enlist everybody
into collecting lizards, birds, snakes, or what not. Quite calmly the
town accepted our sudden fevers—for horses to ride when walking
was more practical, for collecting old church paintings with
which the walls of many houses were hung. Snakes? Birds? Paintings from the old torn-down church? Simply out of courtesy
Ixtlán tried to satisfy our whims, and when most of the town was
abed, some young girl would come running to tell us that Don
Andrés had some pictures his grandfather had left him. Or Dick

would rush about the *zócalo* catching moths in his butterfly net, while on a bench outside the cabildo three old white-clad men sat in cozy silence, pretending not to notice this madness.

There was more than courtesy in our relation with Doña Esperanza, in whose house we were living. She showered love on us, as she did on everyone about her. Her soul was in a state of great activity because there were American missionaries in the town who had more or less converted her to the Protestant faith and had given her a Bible, which she was reading with a great sense of discovery. What she was discovering was that the Sermon on the Mount expressed a universal ideal by which Zapotecs and all gentle people had tried to live all along. But she was much too humble to realize how closely the Beatitudes described her own personal and racial aspirations.

Doña Esperanza is a widow with, as she expressed it, "everything to see to." She has teen-age children and a feeble-minded nephew and has recently adopted two tiny girls who were orphaned. Mornings she keeps a stall in the market, and the rest of the day she manages her big house, one of the old Colonial places gone shabby, her livestock, her neatly fenced cornfield. She is small and fragile-looking but has the spunky energy of a Nantucket woman. A born manager, she keeps everything around her humming, but she is too wise to try to manage spiritual questions briskly.

In the little room at the corner of the house where she and the younger children slept she went deeply into the religious question. She was unwilling to criticize the church in which she had been bred.

"There is good in all religions," she said. "But what is important? To do as the Bible says—feed the hungry, clothe the naked, give shelter to the stranger within thy gates."

These were not parrot words she had learned from the missionaries. For when we left she would not let us pay for our shelter. And there were the little orphans, sitting round-eyed and quiet beside her. The odd thing is that as a Zapotec Doña Esperanza would have received us as guests and would have taken in the homeless children simply as a matter of long tradition. Now the missionaries had told her that these acts had a religious dimension. No wonder she was confused.

We were comfortable under her roof. The house ran along two sides of the patio, which had now become a barnyard with turkeys and pigs left loose during the day (her household was walled and gated) and locked into one of the side rooms at night. Only a few of the original rooms were still used for living purposes; we were bivouacked, tropical hammocks and all, in the huge old *sala* furnished with rough tables and chairs and a wooden platform where the feeble-minded nephew unrolled his petate at night.

On the walls were the usual chromo calendars alternating with the amazingly lovely, though half-ruined old church paintings which the grandfathers of many townspeople had bought when the old church was pulled down. During our search for canvases small enough to buy and carry home we saw houses much prouder than Doña Esperanza's, houses that had gone through the war of independence and a succession of civil wars and the Revolution of 1910 and still had the air of Colonial luxury. There is a preservative quality in Ixtlán.

By the time we left, the busses had stopped running because roads and bridges had been washed out, so we rented Doña Esperanza's three nags, using the strongest one as a pack horse, to ride back to Oaxaca. We left at dawn, but she had already been long astir getting our horses fed and saddled and the food prepared for her son, who was to bring the horses back.

She embraced us with great tenderness. "If only I weren't a widow with everything to manage, I should love to come with you to Oaxaca. But you will come back to Ixtlán and this house that is yours. May all go well with you, my friends. Go with God."

V

BELOVED CITY

Certain cities have such a romantic appeal that they are regarded as common property. Just as we all boast about San Francisco, Charleston, or New Orleans with a citizen's pride, Mexicans claim Oaxaca as their own. They like to come and bring their families for the Easter or Christmas fiestas, and the next year they are back again. It is one of those places for which people feel a deep pang of homesickness.

Oaxaca has no night life and virtually no intellectual life; people come for something else, for nothing as definite as beauty and balmy air and rich sight-seeing. There are Americans living in the city whose sole occupation is to sit at a table in one of the portales and watch the people come and go through the central plaza; and they are never tired of watching. It is the Indians who give Oaxaca its charming modulations of mood, the gentle, fervent Zapotecs who somehow remind one of Tuscans.

Today Oaxaca is the Zapotecs' emporium and religious capital, but they did not found the city. When the Aztecs conquered all Middle America, just a generation before the Spanish Conquest, they set up a garrison at this strategic spot where the three central valleys merge. Thus Oaxaca began as a detested and alien settlement, and continued so under Hernán Cortés. When things settled down, rich Spanish families and hordes of Dominican brothers arrived, and it was they who gave the city its physical beauty. Earthquakes have done some damage, but Oaxaca remains a gem of

Spanish Colonial, and of its many churches at least a dozen are superb, and one, Santo Domingo, is often called the most beautiful church in North America. It is the final word in baroque, and some people find it overluxuriant.

The city was built in a lavish spirit as the seat of Cortés and the favorites of the Spanish King. The powerful Dominicans were able to build 160 proud churches during their first two decades in Oaxaca, using Zapotecs and Mixtecs, who had been masters of the arts connected with building before the Christian Era began. The Indian tradition was one of monumental architecture, of simple masses decorated with stone carvings and painted surfaces; and this tradition has combined with the Spanish to produce a style peculiar to Oaxaca.

Thus the larger buildings and the churches have a solidity and fine proportion that recall classic Indian times, and they are decorated, just enough, with carved façades and the wrought-iron work which is a local specialty. The houses, too, have fine stonework, and their shallow balconies just above the street level and their gates are often of exquisite iron tracery. Moreover, the houses are painted in pastel wash—pink, salmon, saffron, apple green, blue, lavender—so each street is a faded rainbow. The local stone of which the larger buildings are made is a pale sage green, and when this stone gets wet in the rainy season it is smooth and precious-looking like jade.

All this jewel richness is muted by age, so that Oaxaca conveys the general sense of a city the color of wine, cupped in mountains of a darker color. The Sierra Madre del Sur rings the horizon, and Oaxaca has its nearer, private mountains: the long majestic ridge of Monte Albán with its pyramids, and the double crest of San Felipe, an extraordinarily beautiful mount which in most lights is a throbbing purple. The city lies between them.

Best of all are the valleys seen from a height at sunset. On one side the city has a lofty brim, a natural belvedere which commands the whole central plexus of Oaxaca, which once meant the heart of Middle America, expressed in Monte Albán. Perhaps ancient Zapotecs lived here, for they often chose such a natural bastion for their towns; at any rate, their harvest goddess had her shrine here, and the pagan rite is still remembered in the July fiesta called Lunes del Cerro, Mountain Monday. In this most mountainous part of the Americas, the Zapotecs have singled out this sierra and call it simply El Cerro. At its outermost thrust stands a fine monument to Benito Juárez, and its peak has an obelisk honoring the flag of Mexico.

With all this, and the entrancing view, the Oaxaqueños are forever trudging up the steep streets on the rim of the city, past the villas of prosperous doctors and bankers, up the shaded walks to the level where the waterworks spout their fountains amid gardens of hibiscus and rose, and then up broad, crumbling steps to the escarpment. Before one rounds it to the Juárez monument and the grand view, there is a long pause to look down at the city, which is positively golden in the slanting light of sunset, all its colors molten and trembling. The twin towers of the churches rise like tall blooms above the one-storied houses; in the plazas the Indian laurels, a dense, dark green, keep the picture from dissolving. These Indian laurels are the most wonderful trees in Oaxaca; all the year they are in full, spicy leaf; they are round and heavy like the trees children draw. Patriarchs of the arboreal world, they preside majestically over churchyard and plaza.

Pomegranates, palms, orange and lime, Australian pine, banana and bamboo, the casahuate with its trumpet-shaped white flower, jasmine, magnolia; and here the bougainvillaea may grow into great trees. By March, when the jacaranda is in full bloom, the view from the Cerro is almost too beautiful to bear; this elm-graceful tree, with its fan of lilac-blue, flowers at a time when there is a dusky haze over the city, the dust of the dry season's end, so that the jacaranda blossoms seem to float on a cloud of rosy smoke.

On this side of the Cerro you can see the valleys opening southward to Zaachila and the Pacific, and southeast to Tehuantepec.

Then around the curve of the promontory you are above the valley leading northwest to Puebla, and directly opposite Monte Albán and its attendant monticles. In a few minutes the sun slips behind Albán and a ruby fire leaps along its entire length, outlining the Great Plaza and its pyramids.

Going down the broken steps under the pepper trees, you fall in with three youths singing their way home. One of them plucks a guitar, choosing songs about faithless loves and vain longings as the adolescent will when he is bursting with contentment. In the streets the dim electric bulbs shine inside the open doors, and there is a smell of burning charcoal and crushed chiles. Noiseless on their little bare feet, the women flit by on their way to the corner shop for sweet buns or ginger ale. Suppertime, and the first star is out.

Oaxaca has the largest Indian market on the continent, and it is the most important part of the city, more essential than the Government Palace, for the people could survive without a state administration, but their economic life hinges on the market. When it was closed during the general strike the city was, to all intents and purposes, dead.

The Mercado is vast, stretching under roofs for blocks, and spilling over the adjacent streets on Saturday, the big day when all activities are trebled by the arrival of buyers and sellers from the whole surrounding country. All Friday night you can hear the dainty rap of burro hoofs as the serranos come into town with their charcoal and the rough unpainted furniture they will sell in a certain side street; other burros are laden with huge net bags or barrels packed with the pottery of Ocotlán or Coyotepec. The families and their beasts put up at one of the *mesones* near the market, a sort of burro hotel with rough rooms around the courtyard where the people can unpack their goods, prepare a hot meal on the little charcoal stove they have brought along, and perhaps catch a few hours' sleep. But by dawn these mesones are noisy with the protests of animals about to be sold: pigs, sheep, turkeys and chickens and goats. Oxen are not sold in Oaxaca; there simply is not room, so the campesinos go to the Sunday market in Tlacolula down the valley for their oxen.

Meanwhile the busses, whose stations rim the market, have been clattering in, packed tight with people and goods from all the valleys. They bring vegetables, fruits, grains, and flowers, and each town has its own place along the sidewalks and in the roads. People from the southern towns and the isthmus fill up the streets nearest the bus stations; on the other side of the market are the serranos and the Near Eastern peddlers, who spread their bolts of cotton, their laces and ribbons and household gadgets on ground sheets.

In the market buildings themselves, through which it is possible to walk on weekdays without undue jostling, every square foot of space is crammed with goods and vendors, and people are supposed to get through the pack somehow, which they do with the utmost good nature. Basically there is no confusion in the market, since it follows, as all traditional marts do, a strict plan of organization. There is a section for flowers, another for fruits, a lane where nothing but rebozos are sold, an island where Oaxaca's fine cutlery gleams, a region of almost cathedral quiet where at least fifty varieties of chiles await the connoisseur, and near them, logically enough, are tomatoes, avocados, and onions.

In the same way, the stalls selling candles and cheap chromos of Guadalupe or Soledad are near the flowers, since these things belong on the home altar. And it is not an accident that the wizened little curanderas, who sell herbs, the pagan incense copal, love potions, and every sort of magic remedy, are stationed nearest the market church.

San Juan de Dios, embedded in the heart of the market, gets short shrift from the guidebooks because it is a humble and rather ugly church for a town like Oaxaca. It belongs strictly to the market and the Indians who come there, and St. John thus becomes to Oaxaca what Hermes-Mercury was to the ancient world,

99

the god of merchants, markets, and wayfarers. In the morning the Indians come into the church to pray for a prosperous day, and in the evening they return to thank the saint for whatever luck has been theirs. But then the church has its kneeling figures at any hour of the day, and usually it is campesinos, humble and devout, their knotted hands crossed over the breasts, their unfathomable dark eyes fixed on the altar. This is the church of the white-clad Indian, and those black-robed women of Spanish blood who are always in the prouder churches never step inside. San Juan de Dios is as primitive and innocently pagan as the herbwomen crouching in its shade.

There are sections of the market which are hard for the stranger to take, for hygiene, too, is primitive in Oaxaca. There are the mingled smells of eating stalls and latrines in the center, and nearby a horrid lane where women fry indescribable animal innards in deep fat. Worse, there are the meat stalls where strips of beef or mutton hang, completely black with flies. Here one encounters those wretched dogs which are skin, bones, and perpetual hunger, for in Oaxaca everybody loves puppies and nobody feeds dogs. If a household pet has a cold he may be given a necklace of limes, but he is expected to forage for himself. How cats and dogs manage to survive and breed is a mystery, like the general attitude toward them.

On the other hand, the Indians so love birds that the market women bring along their macaws and parrots for company, and they perch on the stalls, making sardonic comments. The youngest children of a stallkeeper have to spend a long day in the market, and they are remarkably good. The babies are either nursing or sound asleep, but the toddlers, for their own safety, are put into crates, where they yell bloody murder. It is rather a relief to find that the angelic Zapotec children resent frustration in the normal fashion. More fortunate are the families in the pottery and basketry section, where each stall is like an open-front shack. Here, during the afternoon lull, the small children are bathed in a great earthenware basin glazed in green, the most delectable sight in the market.

Domesticity of this kind belongs in the market; one sees courtships, gossip coteries, acts of neighborliness, political discussions, tribal and intertribal attitudes, the confiding of secrets, and many occasions for chuckling or laughter. This is home, this is the center. The market, with its strolling bands and *mariachis*, its masses of beautiful vegetables, fruits, flowers, arranged with tender artistry, its multiple smells, all pungent and most of them delightful, the gaily dressed people pushing and shoving and joking— what could be more jubilant than the market? This is abundance, heaped up and running over. Almost everything you see in this happy emporium is the gift of nature or has been made by hand: serapes, rebozos, huaraches, knives and machetes, baskets, pots, tin candlesticks, straw hats, dishes, toy animals, deerskin jackets, belts, saddles. All are honestly made and are as attractive as possible. Even the ropes that tie burdens on the burro have gay touches of red and green paint.

Give any people at least a thousand years of the classic market, in which they meet to exchange the products of their hands and their gardens and orchards and fields, and you will have civilized and happy folk. It is the best possible place for smoothing off the edges of the ego, for learning to get on with others. However, it is true that some races get more from this excellent school of human relations than others. The isolationist Mixe and the neurotic Mixtecs do come to the Saturday market, but it is the Zapotecs who run it and have most of the fun.

They have a vivid sense of the human comedy. Shrewd, intuitive judges of character, they miss no nuance of the differences between people and are tolerant of them. They live on close terms with their neighbors and will help each other out with the greatest good nature, but they avoid such pitfalls as suggesting how others should handle their problems or criticizing what they do. This is not circumspection so much as a regard for independence.

Zapotec

On weekdays the market people have more time to amuse themselves with byplay and running jokes and the endless fascination
of observing their fellows. Because the life around them is so rich,
they have the air of rich people who can afford to be gracious.
They will stick to their price for a handful of green beans because
their financial margin is a sliver. But then, when you have paid,
they will give you a few more with a warm smile and a "May you
go well." This is their pride and their grace.

All Oaxaqueños have a passion for sweets, snacks, and soft
drinks, which is indulged so incessantly that it gives the city a
juvenile air. Often you will walk down a street, and everybody
you pass, young or old, is munching something—peanuts, candy,
frosted cakes, sugar cane, toasted squash seeds, fruits candied or
fresh, water ices on sticks, *tacos*, the small tortillas wrapped around
a savory nugget and fried in deep fat, or pineapple slices dusted
with red sugar. The per capita consumption of soft drinks is beyond belief; the American cola types bottled locally, the native
refrescos, which include fruit ades of every description, infusions
of tamarind or Jamaica flowers, coconut or papaya juice, a thousand cooling concoctions in a climate that is never really hot. Just
as almost every corner of the city has its tiny shop for odds and
ends, there will be in front of it a soft-drink stand.

Even the poorest people can afford small treats, which in the
dull seasons between fiestas satisfy the need for something enjoy-
able. Another indulgence which the men allow themselves is the
weekly visit to the barbershop for a haircut and mustache trim
and male gossip. Men who possess store shoes sit on the cement
benches of the Zócalo like lords while the shoeshine boys officiate.
The more bourgeois citizens who sit at an arcade table over a game
of dominoes or a political deal also love to have a bootblack working on their shoes. There is plainly some sensual satisfaction in
having shoes shined that belongs to the male make-up.

Amusements fall into a racial pattern; in general, the Indians still prefer the traditional pleasures of the fiesta and whatever music they can listen to for nothing. The mestizos flock to the all-American game called "*beisbol*" and to the cinemas, modest little houses that show mostly Mexican films which are often interrupted by a dim-out of the city's feeble electric supply.

The machine age has hardly made a dent in Oaxaca as a whole, and in the city its partial conquest is still a matter of wonder to Indians from remote parts of the state. They are enraptured by the mere sight of a sleek automobile or a display of gadgets in the window of a hardware shop. They hold no brief for modernity or for tourists; they merely scrutinize unfamiliar people and machines with interest and care.

Rural people who have never used a fork or slept in a bed accept a blaring sound-truck advertising some commodity more calmly than they should; they gather near the open door of a shop dispensing radio or juke-box music. But two or three strolling musicians are surrounded by a dense ring of people who rush to listen, and the better the "live" music, the bigger the crowd. When Diego Innes conducts his Sunday-afternoon concerts in the Zócalo, somehow making the brass band sound like a symphony orchestra, the faces of his huge audience are wonderful to see.

Anybody wearing a wrist watch and a friendly expression is apt to be stopped and asked the time. This is merely the fascination of the small mechanical timepiece, for the Indians are not interested in the time of day to the minute. In this latitude the sun and the length of shadows outside the door tell the housewife when it is time to start her charcoal stove; everybody is up with the first light and goes to bed when the stars are out. What more does one need?

Moreover, the cathedral clock strikes every quarter hour, playing the usual little tune for anybody who wants to know the time. It is a rather special clock, connected with a clapper that strikes a bell in one of the towers. This bell is under the solemn sentence of the Inquisition of Spain to be hammered every fifteen minutes

103

as long as it shall survive the punishment. It is one of the bad bells of Mexico.

It used to hang in a church in Toledo, Spain. One night, when no human hand was near it, this bad bell began to ring. This was plainly the work of the devil, and the Inquisition made a formal trial of the bell, which at the trial was stubbornly silent. It was sentenced to be exiled to America, to be struck by hammers *in perpetuum,* and the Viceroy sent it to Oaxaca, perhaps to remind the people there that it does not pay to traffic with the devil. However, Satan is still at work and recently had the bell striking nineteen times for every hour around the clock.

A friend who lives in San Miguel Allende in the north reported the case of another bad bell. This miscreant, its rope suddenly frayed, fell on a boy and killed him. There was a formal court trial, and the bell was sentenced to life imprisonment. "It's in the town jail today," she said.

Church bells are of course blessed, and most of them behave. We happened on a charming ceremony down the southern valley, in Ocotlán, when the town was installing a chime of new bells. They had been cast in a foundry set up in the atrium of the church, everybody had contributed to pay for them, and a three-day fiesta celebrated their hanging. We arrived at the crucial moment when the bells had just been blessed in a solemn ceremony in the church and the people were pouring out into the atrium to listen to the sanctified bells speak for the first time. The roof was covered with excited lads, the towers were wreathed in masses of fresh flowers, and when the signal came and the ropes were pulled there was a mighty moment of brazen music, and everybody cheered.

A generation ago there was a good deal of social life among the Oaxaqueños of Spanish blood: opera and theater, gaily dressed *charros* riding in to town, balls and dinner parties with the guests in formal dress. This style persisted even after the Revolution, which liquidated what few haciendas there were near the city. For some reason this ostentation has vanished, and the non-Indians have a very dull life. Today Oaxaca is a city in which the Zapotecs represent what is vital and growing, and the state bureaucracy is more and more parasitic. Little as the "white" Oaxaqueños appreciate the Indians, they will side with them against the bureaucracy in a crisis such as the general strike. A great many of the intelligent and ambitious families have moved to Mexico City, along with the Zapotec intellectuals of Juchitán, and in the capital there is a Oaxaca colony of 35,000, almost as large as the city of Oaxaca itself.

Of the "*gente de razón*" who remain, only a few have degenerated into the sort of government servants in demand nowadays. Instead, they run the hotels, keep the larger shops—along with a fresh contingent of newcomers from Spain—manage the banks and the businesses, and go into the professions. The Institute of Arts and Sciences, which gave Juárez his education, trains only doctors and lawyers, and many of them remain in the city because they could not bear to emigrate. Despite the lack of intellectual and social excitement, the cultivated Oaxaqueño can make himself an agreeable life on a very small income.

Until a recent spurt in living costs, which may prove to be permanent, Oaxaca was famous in Mexico for its low prices. For the equivalent of a hundred American dollars a month a family can still live in a comfortable house with plumbing and patio and keep a servant or two. Lower-income families will live two or three in a house and still have plenty of room, and the many Zapotec families in the city live in the same Spanish-style home, its patio graced with a lime, a pomegranate, and an assortment of potted plants and shrubs, but several households live together.

Only those Spanish-blood citizens who work nearly as hard as the Indians—and the ambitious ones do—escape the almost lethargic dream bred by the perfect climate and the isolation of Oaxaca. A typical lawyer will get up about seven, putter about his garden, and breakfast at nine. He will open his office at ten-thirty or eleven, knock off at one for a gossip in the arcade over beer or a mezcal or two, and go home for the heavy meal of the day. From one-thirty until four all the shops are closed. This siesta period rarely means a nap, simply a peaceful interlude for digestion and mild domestic chores. The lawyer may then go back to his office, or he may sit in the arcade with friends, for in the early evening the Zócalo is animated. The excellent State Band tunes up at seven, and everybody takes a turn or two under the laurels. At nine or ten the lawyer and his family have a light supper and immediately go to bed.

Some of these professional people are so lulled by the large proportion of leisure in their days that it becomes almost impossible for them to make a definite move. An American woman who had lived long enough in Mexico to achieve property-owning status told me of her struggles to get the deed to her house signed. All that was needed was her signature, but her lawyer kept putting off this decisive moment.

Finally she arrived early, at ten, determined to finish this elementary bit of business. For an hour the lawyer fidgeted, answered the telephone, went out to look over his stenographer's shoulder at whatever she was typing, drew doodles, filed his nails, stared out of the window.

"I'd like to sign the deed," my friend reminded him.

He went back to the window and after long deliberation turned around. "Señora, why do you weary yourself today? Let's see, today is Tuesday." He confirmed the fact by going to the calendar and also asking his secretary. "Yes, today is Tuesday. Why not come back, let us say, on Thursday?"

"But all I have to do is sign the paper."

He picked up the deed, read it with knitted brows, put it down, and shrugged. "Señora, surely not today."

"But why not?"

He went back to the window and made a hopeless gesture.

Beloved City

"*Pues*, señora, today there is too much wind."

Men of this sort often end behind a desk in the Government Palace, where the only decision that needs to be made is whether the affair brought to their attention will yield a *propino*, or sweetener. If not, it is referred to three other people, and so on until, as a swollen dossier, it ends in the limbo of lost papers.

Meanwhile there are bankers, businessmen, doctors, teachers, devoted sons and daughters of Oaxaca, who spend most of their waking hours wide awake. They have an intense local patriotism; they realize that Oaxaca is an Indian state and that it is their business to understand and help the Indians, after four centuries of exploitation. A growing number of this intelligentsia which will determine Oaxaca's future are young Zapotecs who have managed to get university or business-school training. With their energy, sunny manners, and natural clarity of mind they are so outstanding that only the very stupid people of Spanish blood still try to keep up a pretense of race superiority.

Oaxaca has the most famous fiestas in Mexico, and the cycle at Christmas time draws all the tribes of the state to the city, to say nothing of tourists from both Americas. The holiday round begins on December 12, the Feast of Guadalupe, Mexico's patron saint, and ends with Epiphany on January 6, when the children set out their shoes on the balcony and receive their presents. During all this time the city is thronged with Indians in their regional dress, there is a continual fair of the choicest works of popular art, a never-ending carnival with Ferris wheel, merry-go-round, and such mechanical attractions, and there are moments of exquisite beauty.

The market heralds the approach of fiesta. Down the old Camino Real the little burros trot, bearing great sheaves of the *flor de Noche Buena*, as the poinsettia is called. Often the young mother and her baby are mounted amid the crimson bracts, while the father runs alongside, so there is a Christmas picture to start the holiday feeling. And then the little serrano women come down with their delicate burden of wild orchids and mosses and spread along the market street nearest the Zócalo. Now the picture becomes sylvan, exotic, for these air plants grow in the greatest profusion and variety in the mountains of Southern Mexico, and one does not see them anywhere else. Some of the *Bromelia* are the size and shape of isthmus pineapples, and their brilliant vermilion spikes are tipped with bright blue. There are tiny yellow-and-brown orchids, long sprays of the larger mauve ones, and they bloom from the carpet of mosses that covers the dusty street, the lush emerald velvet ground moss, stiff, curly lichens torn from trees, hillocks of Spanish moss. The shy little serranas crouch beside their treasures, and as the hot sun mounts they fill their mouths with water and carefully spray their delicate trove, in Chinese-laundry fashion.

In the same street are stands selling the materials for crèches, which every household creates. These *Nacimientos* are a folk art in themselves. Often a whole corner of the main room is built up into a hillside where flocks of sheep graze, and in a little grotto on the top is the manger with the Christ child, the Madonna and Joseph, and a host of animals, including oxen and burros, looking on. The Three Kings with their camels and entourage are often approaching the manger. Families are always enlarging these Nativity scenes, adding to the materials stored from year to year, as we store Christmas-tree decorations. The mosses from the mountains and small glittering stones and miniature trees are arranged into a landscape, and if the *Niño* is only a celluloid doll from the factory, these Nacimientos, glimpsed through open doors as you walk down the streets, are lovely and touching.

There is a feeling in Oaxaca that at Christmas time everybody should be dressed up, and this applies to the holy images in the churches. The Madonna and Child are freshly robed in whatever seems the height of fashion—nowadays the sleazy pink satins and machine laces the Lebanese and Syrians import. Between them,

Beloved City

the Indians and these merchants from the edge of the Holy Land create effects that are startling but never offensive. You are often startled in one of the humbler churches; you may find a Cristo with long bright red hair curled in tight ringlets, or a Santiago wearing brand-new silver spurs from a certain stall in the market.

Some of the churches have managed to preserve older finery, and in the church at Tlacolula, one of the finest in the state, there was a charming tableau behind the altar rail: Mary and Joseph in the guise of a Dresden shepherd and shepherdess. Joseph wore a yellow robe and green cape, and Mary a dainty seventeenth-century gown, and both wore brimmed hats of straw.

It may be significant that the two Virgins celebrated in December are not Madonnas with an infant but women beautiful as goddesses. Guadalupe, in her rose brocade gown and blue mantle, is celebrated in a feast of flowers, and the little boys dress up like courtiers with tiny serapes folded over their shoulders, and burnt-cork mustaches. Soledad, the most beautiful Virgin in Mexico, is honored in a festival of lights.

The Virgin of Solitude by the Cross, patron of the state, has such a profound hold on the people that they save and deny themselves all year so that they can come to the city to honor her fiesta. Her arrival in the city was miraculous and happened long ago, in 1543. A campesino was driving twelve burros to Oaxaca, and just outside the town he stopped for the night. In the morning he was amazed to find a thirteenth burro with his own animals. Almost at once this strange burro died. When the campesino opened the chest it carried, he found the image now known as La Soledad. The padres at once erected a church to stand on the spot which the miraculous burro had evidently chosen. Like Santo Domingo, the original church of Conquest days was replaced by the present baroque structure late in the seventeenth century.

The best way to grasp the significance of Soledad is to compare her church with Santo Domingo. (As sometimes happens,

109

the Cathedral of Oaxaca is simply the formal, official seat of the state hierarchy, and no special feeling attaches to it.) Santo Domingo is the most splendid church the Dominicans built anywhere in the world, and somehow it remains a tour de force, an expression of pride and perhaps of rivalry, for the other orders were coming into the state. Though much of the pure gold leaf that ornamented the high altar and the chapel of El Rosario was chipped off by French soldiers during Maximilian's empire, the church is an inspired extravaganza of richness. The nave is lined with superb images of church fathers, and the ceilings are covered with polychrome and gilt sculptures in high relief. Those in the chapel are in the form of a genealogical tree of the Dominican order. The whole church is magnificent—but nothing ever seems to happen in Santo Domingo.

The Church of Soledad is the true center to which the people throng in fiesta or in heavy trouble. It stands well above the street in the middle of three broad terraces which have been artificially filled out on the slope of a hillside. All these terraces are paved and cooled by trees and fountains. The atrium of the church is very large, and here, during the fiesta, hundreds of families sleep. The Plaza de la Danza, just above the church, is flanked by the old Augustinian nunnery, which is now the Normal School, and the Fine Arts School, both of which are training some of the most progressive young people in the state, so that the whole complex of buildings has a good meaning.

The church itself is very lovely, of tawny gold color, and the statues in the façade and the chapel porch have a winsome beauty that is almost Florentine, almost Verrocchio. The whole interior is a glowing frame for Soledad, who stands in a glass-and-gold enclosure in her Elizabethan gown and ruff, with a priceless diadem on her head. Her face is high-bred, of austere, almost remote, beauty, and it is remarkable how this proud, brooding face can change by accidents of lighting or the mood in the church into one expressing pure compassion. Perhaps Soledad has a deep hold

on the Indians because she reflects something in them: the power
to suffer greatly and endure.

But she is splendid too, the Queen of Heaven. The fishermen
have given her priceless pearls, which she wears with a robe of
black velvet solidly embroidered in gold and studded with precious
stones. She possesses the jewels and the wardrobe of a queen,
laces and costly brocades and robes of the finest convent needlework. In older days she had her maids of honor, certain well-born
Spanish ladies who attended her to her room behind the altar and
disrobed her at night, exactly as if she were a queen. In a less
ostentatious way she is still cared for by women of the church.

Without being frivolous, one feels that the Oaxaqueños, who
so much revere beauty and fine clothes, take great pride in Soledad's worldly wealth and her regal air. The isthmus women, particularly, convey this impression, for in their harmless Venus cult
Soledad embodies all that they most admire. At her fiesta one year
there were regional dances in the plaza above the church, and
when an exquisite creature from Juchitán stepped from the line
of sandunga dancers and delivered an oration to the beloved
Soledad, there was more than a hint of pagan emotion in her words
and in her voice. And at that moment, when Monte Albán on
one side and the harvest goddess's Cerro on the other were luminous with sunset and between them Soledad's church was rimmed
in lights, the old days sprang into life.

Soledad's three-day fiesta begins on December 18, close to the
winter solstice, so that purely on theoretical grounds one might
assume that it revives those ageless rites to the sun which remain
in the memories of all the peoples of earth. Plainly it is a festival
of brightness in which the whole city seems incandescent.

At the most solemn ceremony on the morning of the saint's day
the church is ablaze with lights. From a thousand prisms the
crystal chandeliers pour tiny rainbows down upon Soledad, and
the diamonds at her throat and wrists spurt crimson, emerald,
purple fires. The lovely baroque angels hovering over the nave

lean down with fiery lanterns in their hands. Soledad stands as if in a lake of white lilies, each an altar candle cupped in gold. Beyond the rail a dense throng kneels with lighted candles in their hands. All is a quiver of light, every face is aglow with wonder. From the choir the voices of the incomparable choirboys of Morelia come like a wind that is full of golden flames.

At night there are fireworks in the atrium, culminating just before midnight in one of those set pieces Oaxaca loves. This is a *castillo*, a little castle, with Spanish soldiers on the battlements who begin to spin round and round, shooting off their toy cannons, as the pinwheels in tier above tier ignite and shower cataracts of red, green, white, mounting higher and higher in a tower of loveliest light until finally the crown at the top of the castle assaults the dark sky itself with rockets of bursting stars and suns, ending in a salvo as from great guns, a royal salute to Oaxaca's Queen of Heaven.

These are wonderful moments of the long festival which never has a letdown. The bourgeois families are very gay with dances and children's parties and *posadas:* they sit at the portal tables, parents and children together, eating oysters from Salina Cruz, listening to the band and the marimba and the many strolling players who appear at holiday time. The bootblacks all have new clothes and indulge themselves in pralines and pink-frosted cakes and the delicious tamales special to Oaxaca, filled with raisins and spices and wrapped in oiled banana leaves.

The real pageant is the Indians in their beautiful clothes, strolling through the fair at the foot of Soledad's church, playing bingo games in the carnival section, giving their children rides on the merry-go-round. The isthmus women are no longer the sensation, for at this fiesta you see the people who stay hidden in the mountains or the tropics all the rest of the year, the Mixe women in their green homespuns and their multiple strands of glass beads, Chinantecs, Mazatecs, and other highland women in their long embroidered huipiles, Mixtec girls in full red skirts, and Huave from the lagoons with folded white towels on their heads.

On December 23 there is a little fiesta peculiar to Oaxaca called Radish Night. Long ago somebody discovered the humorous possibilities in a variety of radish that grows in the shape of people or animals. Thus a competition began for the funniest or most original creatures people could make out of radishes. Every year stalls are put up around the Zócalo displaying these whimseys, many of them merely bawdy, but some with faces carved into skillful caricatures, or figures of men riding elephants or burros, gnomes and elves and comic hags.

Along with these jokes the stalls offer charming little wares seen only on this night: swans and peacocks made of tiny ever-lasting flowers, miniature animals of seeds or straw or feathers, airy fluted wheels of cellophane, anything that is capricious and gay. On this night everybody eats a *buñuelo*, a great flaky wafer dusted with honey and paprika and sold on an earthenware plate. When you have eaten the pastry you make a wish and then break the plate.

After this evening of puckish humor comes Christmas Eve and its poetry. The *calendas*, a procession with *tableaux vivants,* is a rite that belongs to Oaxaca and that one sees, more and more rarely, on the eve of an important saint's day, but Querétaro in the north also has calendas on Christmas Eve. It is difficult to explain to people who have never been in Oaxaca and felt the innocence of its people how very moving the calendas are. Each section of the procession is prepared by one of the humbler churches of the city, which is to say that it is an effort of the Indian heart to express the tender beauty of the Nativity.

It is a cold, still night, and the full moon has swept the sky clean of all but the bravest stars. On all four sides the Zócalo has been filling with people, and everybody, even the tourists, is very quiet. The strolling players have melted away into the darkness, for from a street below the square the first lanterns bloom. The paper lanterns, carried by men and women of the Church of Carmen, are pale pink and yellow, shaped like tulips. Behind them comes an artless band playing one of those nondescript tunes one can never identify, but the men walking beside it are shooting off rockets, so the tune does not matter. Then comes a float bearing the Christmas picture.

This is the Nativity as people who are children at heart see it —no humble manger, but a picture of glory, the tender Madonna with the Babe, attended by angels and shepherds. Sometimes the scene is set in a blazing star, sometimes on a tropical seashore with palm trees and a glimpse of gleaming sand and ocean, or it is a living copy of an old church painting, or a scene within a great golden chalice.

The tableaux are played mostly by children, who look literally angelic in their white robes and golden fillets and gauzy wings. The Madonna and the little angels wear earrings and necklaces, and often the children near the Niño (who is not a live baby, but a doll or an image borrowed from the church) hold sparklers to illuminate his little face. All the actors, from the little boy who plays Joseph to the smallest cherub, remain absolutely motionless during their slow progress through the streets.

One after the other the calendas appear, coming from the four quarters of the city with their flowerlike lanterns, their rockets and bands and exquisite pictures of the Noche Buena. When the last of the long procession has left the plaza the townspeople go home to light the candles before their own Nacimientos, and their children sing a Christmas lullaby to put the Niño to sleep.

The Indians have accepted the Christmas story, as they have a few other things brought from the Old World, because it expresses something that all people feel. Who does not rejoice at the birth of a child? But they will not accept what is alien to them. These Oaxaca natives gathered in the city for the fiesta are a constant amazement to visitors who know Indians from other parts of America. They are not the remnants of a great classic civilization; they *are* classic. They are warm, living people who have little or no objective knowledge of how great their inheritance is, but instinctively reflect it in everything they do.

The great days have vanished, but they live in the people. Thus their story, which began so long ago and so mysteriously, is not a closed book, but a part of today.

PART TWO

VI

MONTE ALBÁN

Of the thouands of Americans who come to Oaxaca primarily to see Monte Albán, no two have the same blend of reactions. There are exhilarations of many sorts on the mountain: the heady altitude and naked sun, the wondrous views, the grandiose dimensions—for the ancient city and its suburbs covered twenty-five square miles—and all the elements that fire the imagination and tax credulity: the Great Plaza with its pyramids and observatory, the tomb paintings, the stones carved with glyphs in an unknown tongue, the grotesque Dancers, and the ball court, perhaps the earliest in America.

It is all too much for some visitors, whose bewilderment results in a sensation of boredom. Others climb Monte Albán dutifully, as in Egypt they would journey to the Sphinx and the Pyramids, and come back with little more than the tourist's self-approbation. It is even possible for people to be so mesmerized by the jewels of Tomb Seven, which are safe in the museum downtown, that they neglect the sacred mountain itself.

But there are many other people who, at their first sight of the Great Plaza, are filled with an inexplicable excitement, which mounts as they rush from one pyramid to the next, climbing the giant staircases at the four points of the compass as if more glory than a fresh view were to be gained at the summit. Perhaps there is; this is an individual matter. It is as if this ceremonial city, laid out twenty-five centuries ago in a spirit of exaltation, were still capable of exerting its spell.

Beyond these physical and emotional impacts, the bare fact that Monte Albán was built in this place, by 600 B.C. or earlier, is a challenge to the imagination. In 1839 John Lloyd Stephens, hacking his way through the jungles of Honduras, came upon the great Maya city of Copán. We have had more than a century to absorb the shock of realizing how old, after all, the New World is. Monte Albán, whose excavation is recent and still incomplete, comes as rather an anticlimax; we are used, by now, to ancient pyramids and exquisite stone carvings. But in reality, because the Zapotec region has been revealed in a period of great advance in archaeology, with new scientific methods of dating and studying sites, Monte Albán has become the most baffling mystery experts on the ancient American world have encountered. In itself a massive question mark, it demands that we push dates back and back and keep enlarging our ideas of the world that made Albán possible in 600 B.C.

Unless future excavations in Middle America change the picture—and in Mexico alone there are still twenty-five hundred ancient sites to be explored—Monte Albán will stand as the *earliest full revelation of a great Indian civilization on our continent,* a culture which was already, centuries before Christ, fully formed, many-sided, and noble. It was the herald of the amazing high culture developing among the peoples of Middle America, the first of the brilliant galaxy of sacred cities: Uaxactún, Palenque, Teotihuacán, La Venta, Cholula, Xochicalco, El Tajín.

Six centuries before Christ, before the Persian Wars and the Golden Age of Athens, centuries before the first dated Maya stone, the Indians of Oaxaca had already worked out the calendar which was eventually adopted all over Middle America. They built the earliest observatory so far found in the New World, and the only one of its kind. They were superb engineers, stone carvers, and potters, and they had a written language. These same Indians built another sacred city at Tilantongo in the Mixteca about the same time, and many more ancient cities of Oaxaca lie buried under vegetation.

Americanists are still in doubt as to what people built the earliest ceremonial city, though all agree that Monte Albán was Zapotec from the beginning of the Christian Era until its occupation by the Mixtecs a century before the Conquest. There is good reason to think that the Zapotecs were on the mountain in the centuries before Christ as well. Art treasures from all over the Zapotec region of Oaxaca, dating from the earliest periods, show an amazing continuity of development, as do the pieces from Monte Albán itself.

In physique and habits the Zapotecs have evolved without sharp change, so that without straining the imagination we can fill the Great Plaza with people from the crowded streets below the mountain. Over and over in the Saturday market in Oaxaca or the Sunday market in Tlacolula you will find the living replicas of faces on Monte Albán urns; and the potters of Coyotepec still cherish their agate polishers as did the men who developed the famous Polished Black of the mountain.

The people of Xoxo on the flanks of the mountain, and its traditional guardians, have even preserved the Zapotec name for Monte Albán, which was believed lost. But the late Wilfrido Cruz found oldsters still using the name Danibáan, Sacred Mountain, which the Spanish friars, considering the shrine an abomination, had twisted into White Mountain. In Old Zapotec, Cruz explains, *báana* meant holy, and the ancient name for Mitla was Liobáan, Holy Mansion. In the same way, the Zapotec word for mountain, *dani*, was combined with *báana* to make Danibáan, the name which expresses the function of the high city.

For Danibáan was created in a spirit of religious exaltation, and its beauty has the enduring quality of its purpose. It was a place of pilgrimage for many peoples, perhaps the first Mecca of our continent.

Zapotec

Nature made it the core of Oaxaca, an isolated mountain mark-
ing the junction of its three central valleys. The long crest lies a
thousand feet above the merging greens of the plains, enclosed
in the wide sweep of the Sierra Madre del Sur. In the old days
much of the valley floor was covered by a lake, and if anything
could be more entrancing from the heights than today's city of
Oaxaca in its tapestry of fields and groves, it would be a lake
reflecting the red and white temples of Albán.

Starting with this dramatic site, the builders sculptured the
entire mountain and its outlying spurs as a home for the gods.
They leveled off the highest crest and laid it out in a central plaza
a thousand feet long and 650 feet wide, with massive pyramids
bearing temples at north and south, and along the sides huge
masonry platforms supporting the palaces of kings and priests.
The nearby hills were crowned with smaller structures, temples,
and tombs.

Using only stone tools to subdue granitic rock and stubborn
quartzite, the builders then proceeded to transform the mountain
to its very base, hewing terraces and courts and roads out of its
rocky flanks. Finally they achieved a huge sacred area covering
miles, rising level on level from the adobe huts and milpas of the
humble citizens to the higher abutments where kings and priests
were buried, and finally to the crowning plaza. Monte Albán is a
natural fortress not intended for military use; it had no water
reservoirs, and no weapons of any kind have been found in the
graves. It existed in what the Spanish friars called the "Zapotec
peace," which they were told had existed for a thousand years
before the Conquest. Perhaps the peace had endured another
thousand years before this long truce.

Monte Albán was built for a single purpose: to exalt man into
communion with divinity. The Great Plaza still expresses this idea,
though its temples with their brave red stucco have vanished, and
the stones which paved the entire plaza lie buried under a carpet
of scorched grass and wild verbena. At the north a great pyramid

staircase 135 feet wide leads up and up to emptiness, and only the masonry columns which supported the temple roof are there, whittled down by time. But nothing can change the dimensions of the plaza, achieved by a superb artistic intuition.

The exaltation which one feels today on Monte Albán is the wonder of the sky. One climbs a thousand feet from the valley floor to stand in a roofless temple a thousand feet long—simply to become conscious of the sky. The stones of Monte Albán were laboriously piled, and its proportions calculated, to give the mind as vast an illusion of infinity as it can entertain. When we stand on an open plain and look up through emptiness, the will soon relinquishes this endless journey; it demands a goal. But in the Great Plaza the tall ramparts of the four sides serve to concentrate the senses, just enough. The walls are just on the periphery of vision, so that wherever you happen to stand they never interrupt the pure awareness of the sky pouring down its golden light.

Our spatial sense cannot have changed much in all these centuries, for the proportions of the plaza still act upon body and mind so that one is released from the human scale and lifted into a grander perspective. Here, the builders intended, men were to conceive not infinity, which no one can grasp, but the reality, the almost tangibility, of godhead.

The men of Monte Albán worshiped the physical forces of heaven—sun, rain, thunder and lightning, winds, clouds and mists, and, more faithful than any of these, the stars which gave mankind its true north and its cardinal points. It is significant that the Great Plaza contains as central structures an altar of sacrifice, a lofty sundial, and the observatory, which is the most extraordinary building in Middle America. For here, as Dr. Alfonso Caso, excavator and interpreter of Monte Albán, declares in one of the few sweeping statements he has allowed himself, there was worked out "the most genuine and perfect achievement of American indigenous cultures." He is referring to the Zapotec calendar, the *pije*, which became the Maya *tzolkin* and the Aztec *tonalpohualli*.

Zapotec

This "magic calendar" became the basis of Middle American religion, an intricate chapter in itself. Here we are standing under the high sun and looking at an odd little ruin where the priest-astronomers measured time. It bears no slightest resemblance to Mount Palomar and never possessed more instruments of precision than the human eye. But here was perfected a system of measuring time that was much closer to absolute star time than the European system.

The old rubble has been cleared away from the observatory, but not from our notions of early history. It is when we come to the Middle American calendar that we are most misled by the fact that the history of this region was written hind foremost. First, the Spanish discovered the Aztecs and their calendar and concluded that they had invented the whole Indian Time system. In reality, they were the latest of all the Mexican peoples to hear about it and never learned a great deal.

Second, the Spanish discovered the Maya, and the friars wrote down certain symbols which took on meaning only in the last century, when scholars scattered all over Europe and America managed by many years of hard work to decipher and understand the Maya calendar. As we all know, the Maya were obsessed by measuring and recording time because they thought their lives literally depended on it. We will not know for many years to come how much of the final elaboration of the calendar is to be credited to the Maya alone. Until the riddle of the Zapotec glyphs is cracked, we cannot know. But it appears probable that the calendar did not originate in the Maya area.

Third, we come to the Zapotec calendar, still going back in time, for it is the oldest so far found. One becomes shockproof about Mexican antiquity and ready to believe even in the remote possibility that still older time systems may be turned up by the archaeologist's spade. But the Zapotec system is ancient indeed, using partly understood Old Zapotec terms for the names of days and months. And these symbols, laboriously analyzed by savants like Eduard Seler, revealed a mother system of chronology which made it possible to explain the calendar symbols of other Middle American peoples.

Fifty years ago, in a fat volume of essays on the subject by five German scholars, published by the Smithsonian Institution, Seler concluded that "the Zapotec country was more than a region of interchange; that it was the land in which the Mexican calendar, a most important factor in our knowledge of the Mexican races, had its origin. Indeed, among no other races did the calendar and the determining of fate connected with it exert so powerful an influence over all the relations of life as among the Zapotecs."

Since then Monte Albán has been excavated and dated, and the very observatory revealed as the birthplace, or at least the nursery, of the "magic calendar." The Zapotecs were well grounded in astronomy before the Great Plaza was laid out, for its temple pyramids are on a north-south axis, and the observatory, shaped exactly like an arrowhead, points due southwest at the winter solstice.

Today one can reach the unroofed space at the top of the building where the astronomers worked, by climbing an outside staircase—or by squirming eel-like up very narrow passages within the building itself. Either way, you arrive at the top with the same instruments the ancients carried: a pair of eyes. They used buildings and steles as lines of sight, and the angle at which the observatory was set, bisecting the ninety degrees from south to west, gave them a further refinement. Slits in the masonry wall offered a line of sight along the azimuth of the meridian. That was all, aside from the clear atmosphere and a patience enduring over very long periods of observation.

Like all early peoples, the Zapotecs were familiar with the solar year and its fraction over 365 days. They knew the movements of the moon and planets, and of the constellations in their annual circuit of the North Star, expressing this yearly round in a cross of the four compass points. Here a remarkable mysticism entered, for in this cross they tied time and space together. The universe and eternity were thus merged in one symbol.

The Zapotec solar year was divided into quarters, each tied to a cardinal point, and began on March 16 under the year-sign of the greatest god, the lord of rain, Cocijo, who lived in all the points of the compass. The Zapotecs based their number system on 20, obviously derived from the fingers and toes, and they had 18 solar months of 20 days each, leaving five "indifferent" or uncounted days at the end of the year.

Why could they not be satisfied with this system? One is tempted to say simply that they carried to an extreme length the human passion to find out everything and then to harmonize everything they found. They must have felt that certain disparities in the heavens could be reconciled by finding a key to the mystery, and the key was mathematical. The sun made its round over Monte Albán in 365 days plus. The Venus cycle was 584 days; Mercury's revolution, 115. Here were three very different time cycles with no apparent arithmetical connection, but the Zapotecs could not be happy until they had solved the puzzle. Never mind how many centuries of observation it must have taken, *in this same latitude*, to establish their computations. They finally found an esoteric formula for setting the heavens in order, which has had more than one savant muttering "Chaldean" in his beard.

They combined their basic number 20 with 13 (and no wonder this is considered a magic number). The formula $20 \times 13 = 260$ is the pije. The 260 days of the pije, running in an interlocking system with the solar year, make in the course of 73 pijes the "calendar round" of exactly 52 years, the period required for the solar year and the magic year to coincide in their date symbols and start the round again. This calendar round of 52 years became the basic unit by which all Middle Americans measured their history. At the end of the cycle all life was believed suspended until certain ultra-solemn rituals ushered in the new era.

But the magic of the pije went further. Venus made exactly 65

MARJORIE CORDLEY ROUILLION

1. Oxcart on the old Camino Real, Valley of Oaxaca

2. Girls returning from church festival, Isthmus of Tehuantepec

ARMIN HAAB

3. Stormy sunset, Tehuantepec

4. Azompa man unpacks his ollas at the Etla market

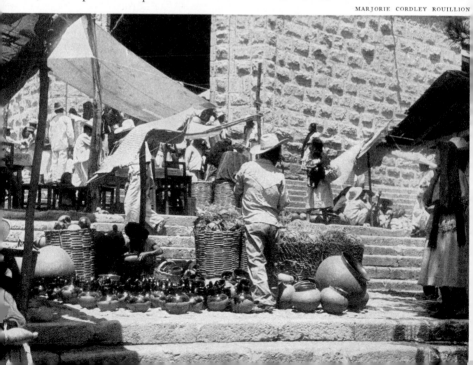

5. Mazatec women in the Plaza de la Danza

SAMUEL G. ATKINS

6. Fording summer-flooded river near Oaxaca.
   The third burro is buried under cornstalks

7. Mitla women chat beside organ cactus fence

MARJORIE CORDLEY ROUILLION

8. The Ocotlán market is huge, orderly, charming

9. Plume Dancers pose in Don Leopoldo's dooryard

ARMIN HAAB

10. Isthmus women wear second-best for a small fiesta

11. The Great Plaza of Monte Albán, observatory in foreground

12. Four of the mysterious "Dancers" of Monte Albán

GEORGE HOYNINGEN-HUENE—COURTESY OF J. J. AUGUSTINE

13. Preclassic Zapotec wearing bird headdress

B.

A.

14. Clay figures of Classic period:
   A. Warrior
   B. Priest with Bird of Heaven headdress
   C. Jaguar God
   D. "Old God" of fire and sun

C.

D.

15. Figure of corn god above entrance of Tomb 104, Monte Albán

16. Intricate stone mosaics adorn walls of high priest's palace, Mitla

17. Grand staircase of a Classic temple pyramid

18. Old Dominican church, Teotitlán del Valle

19. Façade of
Santo Domingo,
called the most
magnificent church
in North America

SAMUEL G. ATKINS

20. Walls and ceilings
of Santo Domingo
are covered with high
reliefs in polychrome
and pure gold

ALFONSO RIVAS

21. Serape weavers and their wives, Teotitlán del Valle

22. Shaded corner of a village market

SAMUEL G. ATKINS

23. Woman potter incises freehand design

24. *Adiós, niño y burrito!*

SAMUEL G. ATKINS

revolutions in the course of 146 pijes, and Mercury made 104 rounds in the course of 46 pijes. So much for celestial harmony. To the common people and to the kings and priests guiding the nation, the magic calendar of 260 days meant an intricate system of divination. Thus the fate of individuals and peoples was bound up with this little observatory on Monte Albán.

We have not yet finished with this fascinating building, for it also served as a sort of Zapotec archives. Carved upright slabs are used as facing for the outer walls of the observatory, and some of the glyphs they bear have been decoded, for they represent Oaxaca towns which still exist. The symbols of the towns are over a human head placed upside down, to signify that these cities were conquered by the Zapotecs. One stone has the glyph for *tepec*, place, with three chiles on top, spelling out Chiltepec. That is still its name, the newer version of its old Zapotec title. Other towns recognized are Tolstepec, Rabbit Town; Caltepec, Mount of Houses; and Ixtepec, Flint-Knife Town.

No key has yet been found to the written language of the Zapotecs. Dr. Caso can decipher a few place names and day signs, the symbols for sun, heaven, and such important elements, and numbers under 20. Bars are used for five and dots for units; 13, for instance, is two bars with three dots over them. This bar-and-dot system was adopted by the Maya and other early peoples.

One very important Zapotec word has recently been discovered by Howard Leigh of Mitla. It is the name for the tiger god, *Béeze*, which had been lost in obscurity, like the Zapotec name for Monte Albán. All the earliest peoples of the region centering in Oaxaca worshiped the jaguar, and images of this god occur frequently in the early period of Monte Albán. Perhaps the *tigre* was the totem of certain ancient tribes; perhaps he was chosen as the most formidable of the real animals they knew. The Mexican jaguar, which still ranges the wilder parts of the republic, is a terrifying beast which only the toughest hunters care to tackle. He is also beautiful, and ideal as an art form.

Zapotec

Throughout Middle America the jaguar represented the earth, and especially the darkness and mystery within the earth. His jaws were a cave from which the creators of mankind sprang and into which the dead returned on their journey to the underworld. The earth jaguar was worshiped for centuries, especially in the Tehuantepec region, and not even the later cult of Quetzalcoatl, the Plumed Serpent of wind and sky, quite dislodged him. But the Zapotecs had meanwhile merged Béeze with their own great sky god, Cocijo.

Tantalizing unread glyphs are cut on the Dancers stones, the most puzzling and hilarious objects on Monte Albán. The *danzantes*, so called because of their lively postures, are carvings in low relief on slabs which once decorated a building on the west side of the Great Plaza. Evidently they stood in a long double row facing each other. They are all life-size figures of naked men, almost the only ones of ancient Mexico drawn with genitalia. These grotesque variations on the human theme belong to the early period, and nobody knows what to make of them.

Some have the chubby contours and drooping mouth of the jaguar cub, which was an early "Olmec" obsession; some are decidedly Negroid, others are old bearded men with Semitic features. They wear large round earplugs of the sort prevailing in this region, but their headdresses suggest Assyria, Egypt, and even Greece.

Carved with the vivid, easy lines and the suggestion of caricature which mark the early style, these antic creatures have a strong appeal. Their supple bodies are contorted in positions which do not suggest dance gestures so much as a protest at their pains or their hard lot. For every one of them is a freak, or deformed, or diseased. Some are dwarfs, some hunchbacks; others have clubfeet or flat heads or abnormal jaws. There is a hermaphrodite, there are several figures with the empty expressions of idiots, and one man is scratching his armpit and making a grimace, as if he were suffering from a skin disease.

Did they belong to the cult of the abnormal and the grotesque which had a powerful hold in many areas of the ancient world? Were they clowns used to relieve the solemnity of ritual dances? Were they the private freak collection of some king, or simply sufferers coming to Monte Albán to be cured? Or did they express the cosmopolitan nature of the city, even in this earliest period? The glyphs which accompany many of the figures might suggest the answer; meanwhile they are admirable works of art, these lugubrious and lively Dancers.

The American passion for ball games got an early start, and all through Middle America a ball court was part of the ceremonial city. On Monte Albán the court flanks the northeast corner of the plaza and has been restored enough to suggest how it looked centuries ago when the uncomfortable stone "bleachers" were packed with spectators betting their fortunes and sometimes selling themselves and their families into slavery to pay an unlucky wager.

Like everything on the mountain, the game was in honor of the gods, and the flight of the ball may have symbolized the journey of the sun through the sky. As a contest it was exciting and dangerous, and the players were almost literally idolized. Even their helmets, belts, and loincloths were objects of reverence.

The ball was heavy, about the size of a basketball, and made of solid rubber. This proves that the game started in the rubber country in the Vera Cruz-Tabasco region, an important part of the Olmec area. It was developed by the Zapotecs and Old Maya and much later was absorbed by those human sponges, the Aztecs, who called it *tlachtli*.

As the Zapotecs and Maya played it, the game resembled our modern soccer, but it was decidedly more hazardous. The court was shaped like the Roman numeral I, a narrow central alley with slanting walls, and at the ends transverse corridors which provided the handicap for the teams. The ball was propelled solely by the hips and knees, never kicked or thrown. The game was to bunt the ball into one of the dead ends of the court and then keep the opposing team from returning it.

When the Maya of Yucatan and the Aztecs took up the game they played it more like basketball. They set two stone rings hardly larger than the ball in opposite sides of the central alley, and whichever team managed to knock the ball through the ring won the game. This type of ball court is preserved at Chichén Itzá. At Monte Albán the slanting walls and the rules about touching the ball only with hips and knees imposed conditions which only expert players, willing to lose their lives in the game, could face.

Until 1931 the rich field of Monte Albán lay fallow under its verdure, visited by prowlers in search of valuables, by a few Zapotecs leaving offerings at the ancient shrines, and by scientists of many nations who cried aloud for the excavation of this site, which promised to be the most important one of the continent. In that year Dr. Caso began the systematic work of clearing and studying the ruins, and after seasons of intense effort ending in 1937 he had only begun to discover the treasures and the problems which the mountain holds.

It was fortunate that the work was delayed until the modern era, when excavation is an exact and delicate science. Monte Albán's sister city of Teotihuacán, excavated earlier, suffered the vandalism of a period when a self-appointed "archaeologist" might use dynamite to speed his work or expose priceless murals to destruction by the elements. Dr. Caso and his distinguished colleagues, Jorge R. Acosta and Daniel F. Rubín de la Borbolla, found evidence of much amateur digging and blasting, and opened many a tomb only to find it had been despoiled; but considering the age of Monte Albán and the troubles it saw even before the Conquest, it is amazing how much they were able to salvage.

For one thing, the peoples of Middle America had the fortunate habit of preserving the original ground plan when rebuilding was done, erecting the new structure around or on top of the old and often using its dressed stones. At Monte Albán the excavators could sometimes peel off a sample sounding which revealed successive constructions, one within the other, like the concentric layers of an onion. Four different eras of construction were revealed in the great pyramid staircase at the north, and one structure had been rebuilt *in situ* seven times.

In the core of the pyramid which supported the King's Palace (now ruined) on the west side of the plaza one can see the original wall, made of huge stones fitted together without mortar and capped with even heavier stones weighing tons. The sundial outside this pyramid was erected in the same arduous fashion by an army of slaves. It is an enormous monolith set in place without block and tackle, then unknown in the New World. Probably the builders used the system, common to certain Pacific islands, of dragging the giant stone to the site and up the slanting side of an earth ramp, and then tugging until it plopped over the steep side and down into a prepared pit.

In protected crannies of the structures one can still find small patches of the extremely hard and smooth stucco which once plastered the exterior walls, and even bits of the red paint that covered them. But nothing remains of the temples and palaces which topped the pyramids and which were undoubtedly decorated with external murals in the prevailing fashion.

The great centers of Middle America usually fall into five periods like Monte Albán, though none of them lasted nearly as long. These stages of development have been correlated by the labors of scholars, many of them ceramics experts who can examine an urn from Costa Rica and tell by its clay, firing, design, and decoration whether it is contemporary with, say, Cholula I or Teotihuacán II. The man opening up a new site expedites their detective work by using the science of stratigraphy.

Zapotec

Dr. Caso would sink a vertical pit in a refuse dump until it struck living rock or empty subsoil, noting at each successive level the pottery fragments which revealed the type of ceramics made at that level. A change in pottery styles always ties in with shifts in architecture and other cultural factors. What the ceramic sleuths call Polished Gray might show the wrinkled face of the Old God of fire and sun but never the plumed head of Quetzalcoatl, who belongs with much later ceramic types; and this is just as true of a piece from Tabasco as it is of a Monte Albán urn.

In this way the Americanists, by continually swapping reports of their finds or studying pieces already in museums, have been able to establish from three to six levels of culture for each excavated city and to correlate them with each other. But it was impossible to give them definite dates. With due scientific caution they tried to keep their estimates within the Christian Era.

Quite recently, nuclear physics simplified the dating problem, incidentally calling for drastic revisions in the accepted chronologies. Dr. Willard F. Libby of the University of Chicago developed a method of listening to objects, especially ancient ones, with a Geiger counter and letting them report their own age. Much simplified, the process is this: All living things, plant or animal, contain radioactive carbon (Carbon 14), which keeps disintegrating, making sixteen ticks per minute per gram of carbon, a tiny sound caught by the Geiger counter. When plants or animals die, they cease taking in fresh radiocarbon, and the tick slows down at a constant rate. Half of the radioactive atoms will have exploded over a period of fifty-six hundred years, slowing down the count to eight per minute.

It is now a matter of routine for archaeologists to consult a radiation laboratory—Dr. Libby's or a few others capable of performing this very delicate test on samples of charcoal, lake mud, wooden furniture, animal bones, textiles, shells, anything that once received charges of radiocarbon. The laboratories cannot keep up

132

with the requests for dating, for often interpretations and whole theories depend on knowing the sequence of events.

The exact dates Dr. Libby gave samples from the first period of Monte Albán and Monte Negro at Tilantongo were 649 B.C., with a plus or minus correction of 170 years. Thus these samples may date 819 B.C. or 479 B.C. But Dr. Libby and the archaeologists who are keeping him busy realize that Carbon 14 dating is freakish. For unknown reasons, four out of five datings have proved correct by other tests, but the fifth one varies, nobody knows by how many years. Until a great many more tests are made from all over Mexico, the age of the Oaxaca sites is uncertain. They may well be older than their Carbon 14 dates, because there are definite correlations between Monte Albán I and the less advanced sites of Zacatenco and Tlatilco on the central plateau, and these towns have been dated both by Carbon 14 tests and geologists at about 1500 B.C.

The trend among archaeologists is to push back the dates of early cultures into an antiquity undreamed of a few years ago. Another move has been to put the cultural epochs of Middle America into three grand periods: Preclassic from 1500 B.C. to the Christian Era; Classic from A.D. 1 to 900; and Postclassic from A.D. 900 to the Conquest.

Because of its antiquity and its central position, Monte Albán exerted a tremendous influence on the developing cultures of Middle America. From the first its culture was sturdy and independent, borrowing little from its neighbors. Though the Zapotec and the Maya were close in their religious concepts, each went his own way in art expression. Here the Old Maya were the masters; no Zapotec piece yet discovered has the plastic beauty of Copán's young corn god, or the two heads found in Palenque in 1952. But the Zapotec style, again in the early periods, has produced objects of truly classic beauty.

It is difficult for the hurried traveler to get any idea of Zapotec art. Carvings and ceramics found in the last fifty years or so are scattered in the museums all over Europe and the United States, and Europe has some of the best. The Monte Albán yield is divided between Mexico City's National Museum and the State Museum in Oaxaca, but many pieces are still under study in what Dr. Caso calls his "workshop" in the suburbs of the capital; in reality, this workshop is an entrancing treasure house.

However, the new Zapotec Museum in Mitla, based on the Frissell collection, and Howard Leigh's private, small, but choice collection across the patio show in rich detail what Zapotec art is and how it developed. These pieces have been gathered from all over the state, and yet they correspond in style and often in quality with the masterpieces of Monte Albán. And they support Leigh's conviction that from first to last Oaxaca art was Zapotec and not imported, as some theories insist, "from somewhere else." The Mitla collections show clearly how the unmistakable Zapotec style developed without a break from one era to the next.

"In the first place," Leigh said, "almost everything Zapotec was a pot. There are of course solid figures, but by and large, Zapotec ceramics were made to hold something, perhaps offerings of food and drink for the dead man's journey to the underworld. And the next thing that marks a Zapotec piece of any period is the fact that the back is left plain, or even unfinished. These urns or figurines or what not were meant to stand on a shelf or in a niche, so all the decoration was at the front."

The earliest Zapotec figures are usually nude, except for ornaments and headdress. Gradually the style changes; a ribbon is slung loosely around the neck and other ribbons are sometimes drawn through the ear lobes; a loincloth is tied around the waist to fall in a triangle at the front, or a curious short kilt is pleated under the belt. By the third epoch the figures are fully clothed.

The men themselves are Zapotec. While the famous "Olmec face" with its flat nose, coarse mouth turned down at the corners, and Mongoloid eyes appears on some of the Dancers stones, it is rare in Oaxaca ceramics. The racial type is plain throughout in the narrow face, high-bridged and shapely nose, and delicately modeled lips that mark the Zapotec.

Because the "Olmec face" often appears in Middle American art, changed just enough to suggest the jaguar, one should mention here the slow transformation of the jaguar into the Zapotec rain god, Cocijo, an extremely important process that alone ties the first four Monte Albán periods together as Zapotec. The change had already begun when the city was built, and the oldest urns show Cocijo as a potent sky dragon wearing the jaguar mask of earth, thus uniting the two paramount Indian conceptions into one symbol. Through scores of pieces one can then see Cocijo evolve as a god altogether of the sky.

Having tied Monte Albán together as the evolution of a single culture, we can now sketch the accepted epochs, with tentative dates:

MONTE ALBÁN I (1500 B.C.–272?)

The ground plan of the ceremonial city was laid down, astronomy was studied intensively, and the magic calendar perfected. Great events and their dates were recorded in glyphs carved on stone and probably on wood and other media which have perished. The earliest Zapotecs were not only superb architects, but masters of low-relief carving and the difficult art of carving jade, which they prized above all stones.

They buried their dead in flat-roofed tombs of dressed stone, along with offerings of pottery and jade. Some of the most splendid pieces are very large, almost life-sized standing figures of men or of animals, especially jaguars; or urns shaped as heads or bearing heads at the front. These portraits could hardly be more simple or more noble in conception. Often they suggest the archaic, the long squared contours of the face running without a break up to the austerely plain *tocado.* or headdress. But they are modeled by a sophisticated hand.

Zapotec

This highly evolved simplicity of line marks the ceramics, produced in a great variety of sizes and designs. The typical wares are
Polished Gray (a dark slate color), but beige and Polished Red
also appear. The polished pieces were finished by rubbing with
agate. The decoration is restrained: geometric designs scratched
in the wet clay, a piecrust rim, or the same fluting around the
break of a curve. Images of men, of Cocijo, or of small animals
often have a delightful, half-humorous quality.

MONTE ALBÁN II (272 B.C.–A.D. 1)

This short, brilliant period produced some of the most beautiful
pieces of all, and its influence carried on into the next, Classic, era.
Cocijo continues to evolve as the sky god wearing the jaguar
mask, Polished Gray turns to Polished Black, and the scratched
designs are now apt to be filled in with red paint. Perhaps this
innovation suggests experiments in polychrome pottery, which
result in glorious urns and plates. Along with them are mono-
chrome pieces which are very large. The gifted potters of this era
excelled in portraiture and in catching the charm of animals. They
modeled jaguars, dogs, rabbits, turtles, birds, monkeys, and all
the creatures about them to perfection; and as a further tax on
their ingenuity they would sometimes decorate a small pot with,
say, a monkey head, which became a perfect lizard when the pot
was reversed.

Tombs were now built with a vaulted roof and niches holding
some of the most splendid works of ancient Mexico. One master-
piece is a mask of jadeite representing a creature half bat, half
jaguar, but most of the treasures are of terra cotta. There are
heads and standing figures of patricians whose expressions range
from sober to genial; their lips are parted in the invariable Zapotec
style, which lends animation to the most dignified face. Their
tocados are tall and severe, of striking designs.

The ultimate triumph of this style is a portrait head (now in
the National Museum) of a lusty man who carries his evident

authority with jovial ease. He wears the usual round earplugs and an unusual circular collar of Pilgrim Father cut. His dramatic tocado is a stylized bird whose beak curves over the man's forehead and whose wings are stretched behind the head in a great oblong.

MONTE ALBÁN III (A.D. 1–900)

This was the golden age, the long flowering of Zapotec culture. It was a time of the utmost splendor in arts and ceremonials, of wealth and grandeur, when the city on the sides of the mountain had many thousand inhabitants. It is marked in the ninth century by the final arrival of metals, in the working of which the Zapotecs quickly took first place in Middle America. Little copper bells and gold beads and ornaments appear.

As works of art the small urns of the early part of this era are the most exquisite of all. The typical Zapotec urn developed during Epoch III into a figure of Cocijo, or a priest wearing his mask, and the figures become more and more elaborate in dress and ornaments, supporting a tremendous tocado with elements of the jaguar, serpent, or bird, and a great fan of quetzal plumes. But in the early pieces there is a much simpler portrait, often of a young man who has the sensitive, brooding face of a poet. These urns have the power of a great plastic conception; they seem nearest, in sheer loveliness, to the best of classic Maya art. To modern eyes the Zapotec face is more beautiful than the Maya with its heavy nose and lips. It is happier, more ardent. Over and over in Oaxaca you can see this very face today, fine-boned, aristocratic, eager, among women as well as men. For there is an epicene quality in the classic Zapotec which is most apparent in these portrait heads, which as art are perfection.

The tombs of this period are the most elaborate in ancient America. A temple was often built over them, and the tomb itself was like a temple, with a richly carved façade and an antechamber leading to the burial room. The niches on three sides of the burial chamber held fine carved jades and the great funerary urns on which the Zapotec artists lavished more and more of their energies. There are medical curiosities like the trepanned skull in Tomb 80 and another skull with efficient dental fillings. There are stylized serpent heads and spirals which announce the arrival of Quetzalcoatl in the Zapotec pantheon, along with the fantastic god of spring, Xipe Totec. But the greatest find of the period was frescoes.

Tomb 104 has an elaborate façade, with an urn over the lintel bearing the seated figure of the corn god, Pitao Cozobi, whose image is painted also on the walls of the burial chamber, along with Xipe Totec and a jaguar wearing quetzal plumes. These paintings are on a coat of stucco, the figures first sketched in red, then filled in with red, blue, yellow, black, and gray, and finally outlined in black. The painting was hurried and not comparable to the fine frescoes in Tomb 105, unfortunately less well preserved. There is a replica of Tomb 104 in the Museum of Natural History in New York, for it is in every way remarkable.

A large temple was built over Tomb 105, which stands proudly by itself on a hillock. The tomb itself is cruciform, partly cut from the living rock and roofed with giant slabs laid flat. An antechamber sealed with great stones led to the burial chamber where, curiously enough, nothing was found but a lone skeleton, without the usual rich offerings.

But the murals are a priceless document, especially since the Zapotecs seem to have painted no codices. They show nine pairs of gods, each lord with his goddess, and no doubt they are deities of the underworld. These figures carry symbolic objects, and from their mouths comes the word symbol, decorated with jewels, which means that they are singing. Their name glyphs are beside them, and most of them have been deciphered. In style these frescoes resemble those of Teotihuacán, then in close alliance with Monte Albán, and it is apparent that the younger city got its number system and written language from the Zapotecs.

Monte Albán

MONTE ALBÁN IV (A.D. 900–1420)

Like all classic periods, the great age of Zapotec culture was followed by one of decadence, of overblown arts, endlessly repeating the funerary urns and overdressing Cocijo. This was true on the mountain, where Zapotec artists were simply imitating themselves, but the creative vigor of the race had shifted to Mitla and the building of its perfect temples. It was a period of expansion to the isthmus and of trouble with other tribes, especially the Mixtecs. Monte Albán declined as metropolis and religious center; Zaachila became the home of the kings and Mitla the seat of the high priests.

MONTE ALBÁN V (A.D. 1420–1521)

The new masters, the Mixtecs, occupied the mountain and created a period stamped with their peculiar genius in ceramics and the working of metals. Their black and polychrome pottery is the most beautiful ever made in Mexico and their jewelry work incomparable. The Spanish Conquest shattered this brilliant renaissance of the mountain.

In Mitla there is already a legend about Dr. Caso. One night in the Great Plaza of Monte Albán he saw a spring of crystal water suddenly gush from the base of a monument. Bobbing on it was a red gourd, and in the gourd was a golden fish. The fish advised him to investigate Tomb Seven.

This would have been New Year's Eve, the time of portents, as 1932 came in. It was Dr. Caso's first winter of work, and he was still down in the low numbers of the 169 tombs he eventually opened. He already had his eye on the mound marked Seven on his map, because it evidently held the substructure of a temple such as the Zapotecs built over important burials. With Juan Valenzuela and Martín Bazín as associates, he began the year by opening Tomb Seven.

The workmen cleared off the surface soil, dug down through

the ruins of small rooms floored with thick red stucco, then dug a vertical pit, only to encounter a second stucco floor. Things looked more and more promising. They found a conch-shell trumpet, two collars of fine jade, and a pair of jade earrings, evidently final offerings above a tomb that lay still deeper.

Late in the afternoon of January 9 they lifted one of the slabs roofing the tomb. Caso turned his flashlight down into the opening and saw a skull and what looked like a vase of gleaming black pottery. Valenzuela wormed his way down the narrow opening and a moment later shouted like a man gone mad. Caso at once wriggled down the shaft—to find himself ankle-deep in jewels— gold, silver, turquoise, pearls, jade.

Thus began the richest archaeological find in American history, rich in art treasures, in potential knowledge, and in intrinsic value, for the exquisitely worked jewelry alone weighed almost nine pounds.

They found the skeletons of nine men, probably priests, ranging in age from a boy of sixteen to a man in his sixties who had evidently died of a brain tumor. He was the important personage, the most bejeweled; on one arm he wore six bracelets of gold and four of silver. The whole small chamber was crammed with treasure, over five hundred complete pieces of jewelry and other art objects, all of incomparable workmanship. Some of the turquoise mosaics which had been made on a matrix of wood or skin had disintegrated and were scattered all over the floor, along with little gold bells and pearls, one the size of a pigeon's egg. The floor itself had been inlaid with flint-polished turquoise.

For the next week nobody thought of sleep. Caso at once gathered some of the chief treasures and took them down to Oaxaca for safekeeping, and then with his wife and assistants crouched in the tomb day after day, carefully photographing, gathering, and listing the trove.

The high priest wore a diadem and plume of thin beaten gold which may have come from Peru, but the rest of the objects were plainly Mixtec and had been interred not long before the Conquest. Perhaps the burial had been hurried, for a Zapotec tomb of Period III was found under this one, indicating that the Mixtecs had pressed an old excavation into service.

One of the strangest objects was a human skull inlaid with turquoise, and the greatest marvel was a rock-crystal cup. Even with modern tools rock crystal is almost impossible to work, and this exquisite vase must have taken nearly a lifetime of labor, with sand or perhaps powdered sapphire as abrasive, since diamonds were unknown.

The jewels are much copied today by local goldsmiths, one of whom has mastered the lost-wax process used by the Mixtec craftsmen. There are solid-gold necklaces of round beads, of tortoises, of plaques strung so as to form a collar; there are pendants of a series of square gold plates ending in a mask of the death god; masks of Xipe Totec, belt buckles and fan handles and wonderful rings with eagle heads, earplugs of obsidian polished down to transparency. There are strings of pearls, turquoise, jade —and, for the first time in Mexico, jet and amber.

A jewel representing two solar disks has one lappet of gold and the other of silver, joined without visible soldering by some process modern goldsmiths are unable to divine. But to Caso the most priceless find was thirty-five flat, thin jaguar bones with delicate carvings which rank with the best ivories of India or China. He recognized the figures as Mixtec glyphs like those used in their painted codices, but nobody could read them. Recently an old Mixtec map turned up at the University of Texas, providing a sort of Rosetta stone for the language, and now Caso is translating the text on the carved bones, along with the eight Mixtec codices which escaped the wholesale destruction of Indian records after the Conquest.

As yet the presence of jet and amber in Mexico is a mystery, and no turquoise or jade deposits have been found. Turquoise may have filtered down from New Mexico and certain Zapotecs are said to know of a jade deposit. When the Aztecs conquered Southern Mexico before the Conquest, they exacted a yearly tribute of turquoise and jade from Oaxaca and the neighboring region of Guerrero, which Caso thinks must mean that both these stones were native.

The treasure of Tomb Seven went up to Mexico City under heavy guard, but finally, after Oaxaca sued the federal government for repossession of the jewels, they came back to the city of Oaxaca, where they are displayed in a special strong room of the museum.

Tomb Seven was a spectacular find which turned the attention of the outside world on Oaxaca. Those who know the region best are sure that more excitement is in store, but to them new caches of jewels would not be nearly so welcome as new light on many vexing problems. Monte Albán is still, after two decades of study, a profound mystery. In the real sense every metropolis of ancient America is still a buried city.

The great question has not been answered: What hands fashioned these everlasting stones; what minds conceived gods so noble that for them a whole mountain must be sculptured as an altar?

VII

THE SHADOW OF GIANTS

In trying to get behind Monte Albán we are entering a realm
which is clouded almost as much by the dust of battle raised by
conflicting theories as by the fogs of the unknown. But we must
explore this terra incognita, with the help of a few experienced
guides, if we are to understand what we can actually see today in
museums and on excavated sites, and if we are to follow the new
discoveries and theories which are constantly being made.

We live in an age when the whole story of the human race is
slowly being pieced together. Archaeology is becoming a One
World science; the man digging in Afghanistan may turn up something which illuminates the finds of the delver in the Ohio Valley;
and both these men, no matter what they find, are helping us to
understand the world in which Monte Albán was built. And by
the time American prehistory is clearer, our notions of the whole
ancient world will take a more definite shape.

Middle America, in the centuries before the Christian Era, is
a complex of small puzzles and great mysteries. The men of early
Monte Albán already had wide horizons. They were in touch
with other cities in Oaxaca, with the pre-Maya in Guatemala,
with nations living along the Gulf of Mexico, and with the peoples
of the central plateau. We see great ceremonial cities rise over an
expanding area, cities wondrous in their stepped pyramids, their
carved jades and steles, their colossal stone heads, and even more
amazing in the mental powers they reveal. There are three re-

markable things about these cities: they all belong to the same unique, highly evolved culture; this culture is quite unlike that of other regions in the Americas; and it appears fully formed, without prelude. No transitional epochs lie under the stones of Uaxactún or Monte Albán or La Venta; these magic cities might as well have dropped from the sky. As Dr. Caso remarked when we were discussing this enigma, "The Middle American culture is incredible, inexplicable—but there it is. We must accept it without being able, at the moment, to understand it."

The high culture did not arrive in a world empty of people, but among Indians who had been living for a long time on a very simple level. There is little dispute about how the New World was populated, for those theorists who insist that there was a second cradle of the race in the Americas have almost nothing to back them up. There are sporadic traces of extremely ancient man in the Americas, but by and large our Indians were Mongoloids who crossed over Bering Strait from Northeast Asia during lulls in the Ice Age and shortly after the last glacial retreat. By ten thousand years ago, when that important cosmic clock of Dr. Libby proves that the ice gave up its siege of America, these Mongoloids had settled from the Pacific Northwest to the southern tip of South America.

Only recently have actual traces of the primitive roving hunter who crossed over from the Siberian region been unearthed in Mexico. Now several finds have been made in the area near Mexico City, the most dramatic one the fossilized skeleton of a Mongoloid hunter, together with the bones of a mammoth which had stood fourteen feet shoulder-high. This Tepexpam Man has been dated by radiocarbon at about 9000 B.C. He belonged to the primitive, roving level of man before agriculture was developed.

Then there is a gap in time—and also in digging—until we reach what we can call the eternal Mexican Indian. He has made a tremendous advance over Tepexpam Man; he is raising corn. Where he got his corn nobody can say. Clearly he did not bring it from

Siberia; almost certainly it came up from Middle America, but there for the moment the trail is lost. However, this Preclassic Indian himself is distinct; many of his towns have been dug up near the site where his ancestor killed the mammoth. A newly revealed town, Tlatilco, dated by Dr. Libby at 1450 B.C., is especially rich in detail. The fact that the Indians were by then living in towns is important; corn made settled community life possible.

Tlatilco people were not markedly different from Indians living in sheltered corners of Mexico today. They hunted a little and fished a little but depended mostly on corn, beans, and squash for food. They made simple pottery and wove various fibers into nets, baskets, and clothes. They were not greatly preoccupied with religion, but their female figurines of baked clay may represent an earth goddess of fertility. Some of their domestic gear, especially the metate for grinding corn, has not changed in thirty centuries.

Dr. Manuel Gamio, who was a pioneer in discovering these Preclassic towns, once drove his cook out to a site he was excavating. She was unclear in her mind about archaeology, but when she came upon a metate several thousands years old she went into raptures.

"Oh, señora!" she appealed to Mrs. Gamio. "Please buy this metate for me. I've looked all over the markets in Mexico City, and this is better than any metate I've seen."

Nothing could illuminate more clearly the basic trait of the Indian: continuity. When Indians have evolved a tool or a way of life that fits them and their soil, they are loath to change it. Dr. Gamio's cook demonstrates the deep gulf between basic, eternal Indian culture and the new stream of influences which created Middle American civilization.

Where these new influences originated is a matter of dispute among Americanists. Some of them think that the major center of development was in the Olmec region along the southern part of the Gulf of Mexico and that other areas borrowed from this center. In this theory, which is held by scholars on both sides of the Rio Grande, the Maya and Zapotecs were the earliest branches of the young Olmec tree, and their ancestors had lived side by side in remote times in the Pánuco basin near the modern city of Tampico.

However, there is a group of Americanists who suspect a quite different origin for the new influences which so transformed the Archaic Indians of Mesoamerica. We shall follow some of their speculations later. Meanwhile, simply for convenience, we shall call the unknown mother culture of Middle America "Complex X." This term covers a whole set of important elements such as ceremonial cities with stepped pyramids, a mastery of astronomy, and a written language; it means exactly what "Olmec" does when used to describe the whole evolving culture. But "Complex X" has the advantage of not identifying the mother culture with the Gulf and its peoples. For it may prove that this culture was incubated in the highlands of Mexico, where conditions of life were far more favorable than in the steaming jungles along the Gulf.

Getting back to Tlatilco, we find a vivid picture of Olmec influences from the rubber country of the Gulf arriving among Indians living on the simple traditional level. The earth jaguar arrived in the town, the ball game with its sacred helmet and belt, exquisite figurines of clay or polished serpentine, funerary urns bearing figures of men or animals, and the curious doll-like figures, sometimes double-headed, which belong to one of the Gulf cults.

This little town is a cloudy mirror which reflects the dim shape of a cultural movement much larger than Middle America. The excavators found objects that related now to the Gulf, now to Oaxaca or Central America. But the most persistent correlations were with the mysterious Chavín culture of Peru. It is facts like this which make the careful scientist withhold final opinions about where and when and how the new culture originated.

During the Preclassic period from 1500 B.C. to the Christian Era the broad lines of regional cultures were laid down: Central Mexico, Oaxaca, Northern Gulf Coast, Olmec, and Highland and Lowland Maya. These cultures all continued through the Classic era, though shifts in population or in influences modulated each local picture. Of them all, the Monte Albán culture showed the highest continuity and the longest history. Thus we have six regions in Middle America which, within the span of roughly twenty-five centuries, developed their independent civilizations, while at the same time they were closely linked by a common religion and by the interchange of trade and ideas.

Coming now to the Olmec sites proper on the Gulf, Tres Zapotes was built late in the Preclassic era, followed by La Venta and the less important Cerro de las Mesas. These jungle-buried cities were excavated in the early 1940s by the Smithsonian Institution under the direction of Matthew W. Stirling, whose discoveries created a sensation.

The name "Olmec" is confusing. It comes from *olli*, rubber, and was applied to peoples who once lived along the Gulf, including Mixtecs, Mazatecs, and Popolocas. We shall call these ancient Rubber People by their Spanish name, "Olmecas." As for "Olmec," the term was used loosely for puzzling art objects found years ago in the Gulf region and then, in spite of Dr. Stirling's own best efforts, to his discoveries there. Nowadays it is used by Americanists who believe the Olmec was the highest of the ancient cultures, to cover the whole civilization which flowered in Middle America.

The Gulf peoples made colossal stone heads, simply fifteen-ton heads that never possessed bodies or even necks. They represent round-faced young men wearing a casque like a football helmet. Another rubber-country obsession was a rage for the infantile, the jaguar cub, the human baby with a turned-down mouth like an infant jaguar, or dwarfs who look like children and young jaguars combined. There is a strong suggestion that children or dwarfs, or both, were sacrificed in certain emergencies by Gulf peoples and Zapotecs, though human sacrifice was rare and strictly controlled.

Here we will mention only those strange discoveries which have started so much speculation and serious study of Olmec origins.

Zapotec

There were hundreds of beautifully worked jades, a few of them the "jewel jade" supposed to come only from Burma. The spectrograph shows that ordinary examples of this precious stone have a different structure from oriental jade, and it is believed that they are native to Mexico. But as Miguel Covarrubias pointed out,[1] there are curious parallels between the Olmec and the Chinese treatment of jade:

"The ancient Chinese and Mexicans saw magic and divine attributes in jade and regarded it as the most precious of materials. Both carved it exquisitely, wore it as an amulet, made offerings of it, and buried it with their dead. While the Mexicans often placed jade beads in the mouths of corpses, the Chinese of 2400 years ago placed a cicada of jade in the mouths of theirs. . . . It is hard to explain why both Chinese and Mexicans painted their funeral jades with a coat of bright red cinnabar. Furthermore, the style of ornamentation of some of these jades is often strikingly similar, variations of the squared spiral motif."

However, most of the unexplained finds in Middle America are not Chinese in style. Dr. Stirling dug up objects which revived the old excitement about the legends of "bearded white strangers" who had visited both Americas in ancient times and who would one day return, the folk legends which made the Spanish Conquest easy, since the fabled white visitors had been sages and friends to the Indians.

At La Venta, which was built early in the Christian Era, he found a fourteen-foot stele showing a handsome old man in profile, a grandee with a flowing beard, a tremendous hooked nose, and an elaborate headdress, snarling at a plump little figure who is as native to the region as the Semitic type is alien. The plump little man has no face; it was deliberately smashed, as were many of the La Venta monuments, by a later people who, one must assume, were on the winning side of the argument, along with the bearded old man.

[1] *Mexico South*, 1947.

148

The Shadow of Giants

At Tres Zapotes, and later at Cerro de las Mesas, Dr. Stirling made other freak finds: small clay heads of apparently the same man, with an aquiline nose, Vandyke beard, rather slanting eyes, and exaggerated creases in cheeks and forehead. As somebody remarked, he is the spitting image of Mephistopheles in a Metropolitan production of *Faust*. Nobody attempts to explain him.

Even more dramatic are several carved stones showing an actual battle between round-faced men, typical Rubber People armed with clubs and long spears, and evident intruders who are bearded and dressed in a vaguely oriental style. The contrast between these two racial types and the fury of their battle tell one chapter of an unknown story.

The massive fact of Monte Albán, with its Dancers, its observatory, its pyramids honoring sky gods, is inexplicable in the sort of society Tlatilco represents. Complex X includes elements which seem non-Indian in the traditional sense and which could not have been brought to the Americas from Northeast Asia, where nothing of the sort existed. But these elements do seem to relate to the oldest parts of the Old World: to the Middle East, Egypt, India, China, Southeast Asia, and Indonesia.

There is a perfect welter of parallels between the Complex X areas of the Americas and this part of the East, and at first they seem to make no pattern, nor do they make sense. On Monte Albán one is tempted to think of Sumerian-Babylonian ziggurats and mastery of astronomy, including an exact observation of the movements of Mercury. Some of the Dancers are apparently wearing headdresses from this region; and in Tlatilco, the Chavín sites of Peru, and the Maya country cylinders have been found which, when rolled over a surface, print a row of figures, like the Babylonian roll seals.

But other areas are also suggested in Complex X. Panpipes were found in Peru and at Tres Zapotes which resemble the Greek syrinx; pipes discovered in Brazil are similar in pitch and scaling to those of the Solomon Islands. The ancient Mexican game of *patolli* is like India's pachisi, especially the version played in Burma. Pachisi was popular all across the area from Syria to the Philippines, and it had an esoteric significance which ties in with the pervasive cardinal points of the magic calendar. The "flying pole" or *volador* game performed by the Totonacs of Papantla has its parallel in India, and again this ritual ties in with the cardinal points.

At Chichén Itzá in Yucatan there are friezes with complicated lotus designs which are amazingly like motifs originating in Amaravati in Southern India. But El Tajín in northern Vera Cruz has other motifs of interlacing spiral bands which might have been inspired from bronzes of the Late Chou Dynasty in China. Certain Maya temples recall Cambodia. So it goes; various intricate metalworking and weaving techniques are common to the more southerly parts of Asia and the Americas; numerous details of architectural design and decoration; oddities like the parasol as a symbol of rank (and the same two designs of parasol); religious conceptions and rites without end.

Finally in 1950 the Museum of Natural History in New York City arranged an exhibition of pre-Columbian objects from both sides of the Pacific, and many of them were so similar that their labels might have been switched. What were the anthropologists who set these exhibits side by side trying to prove? That the world is full of odd coincidences? That human beings are so alike that even in complete isolation from each other several different races will arrive at the same techniques, art forms, tools and weapons, and elaborate styles of architecture?

Not at all. The exhibition was arranged by Robert Heine-Geldern, an authority on Asiatic cultures, and Dr. Gordon F. Ekholm, associate curator of the Museum's Department of Anthropology. Dr. Ekholm is a student of ancient American cultures who has done enough digging in Mexico to suspect that its enigmas fall into a certain pattern. He and Heine-Geldern belong to the increasing group of diffusionists who believe that there were contacts between Asia and the Americas over routes undreamed of a few years ago. Since the diffusionists are to be our guides in exploring what lies behind Monte Albán, it is only fair to say that they are violently opposed by equally eminent men who belong to the older, non-diffusion school.

Theirs is the standard, accepted theory, which runs something like this: The Indians of the two Americas were Mongoloids who crossed Bering Strait and evolved their various cultures with no subsequent contact with the Old World until Columbus. The high civilizations from mid-Mexico south must be explained as the result of long residence in extremely favorable areas where corn, to mention one factor, was developed early enough to give quite ancient peoples a staple diet, abundant leisure, and the civilizing influences of community life.

Any resemblances between the Old and New Worlds, this theory insists, are purely coincidental results of the fact that human beings are very much alike. This safe-and-sound theory has become fixed in the popular mind as the only explanation that is not the work of cranks. This is unfortunate, because its main import—that American Indians, without the slightest help from the Old World, created a marvelous civilization—is somehow lost by busy people who appreciate having a problem of which they know little reduced to simple terms.

Let us say at once that the diffusionists who have felt forced to restate this theory are not racial snobs. They agree with all but the closed-box aspect, the insistence that from the Ice Age to Columbus no influences touched the Americas except those brought by fresh waves of immigrants crossing Bering Strait. They believe that the high cultures of the Americas developed among Indians so highly developed and fortunately placed that these cultures should rate as an independent creation. But they also feel that the old closed-box theory, formulated before the high civilizations of Middle America were understood and even before most of them were discovered, is now too rigid and too incomplete to cover today's enlarged picture of ancient America.

For mixed in with the basic culture of the Middle Americans, the diffusionists would say, are certain elements, some trivial, some important, which appear to have arrived by routes other than Bering Strait. These elements seem to relate to a certain area of the globe, especially Southeast Asia, and we find them beginning early and lasting well into the twelfth century of our era. For some traits there is a dim trail from Southeast Asia across the Pacific via the Polynesian Islands to both Americas. Though contacts across the Pacific were maintained (with long interruptions) for a specific purpose, there was no wholesale importation of South Asiatic culture into Mexico, for instance, or Peru. Instead, we have a spotty and confused picture. That is fine. That is exactly what we ought to expect if our theory is right.

The Indian prince Ixtlixochitl, prompted by the first Spanish friars, wrote a history of Mexico which modern scholars often consult. Writing of the great pyramids of Cholula, he said that they were built by a race of giants called the Quinametin whose chief, Xelhua, was born of the Milky Way. These giants owned the world in the second age and were followed by the Rubber People of the Gulf, lords of the third age.

In the Society, Samoan, and Hawaiian Islands there are traditions of early inhabitants, Manahune, whom the Polynesians arriving from Indonesia in the fifth century A.D. had to conquer. Though the Manahune were "dwarfs," they had erected pyramids and tall steles and had devised marvelous irrigation systems. Those in Hawaii could erect a temple overnight, passing the stones from hand to hand in a long line of workers from quarry to site.

It may turn out that these giants and dwarfs were of ordinary size and actors in the same stupendous drama. The Quinametin, as the brilliant historian Jiménez Moreno sees them, were intellectual giants and the builders of colossal monuments. The Manahune, the

Polynesian authority Sir Peter Buck explains, were called dwarfs by the newcomers in an attempt to belittle their powers and their stiff resistance to the invaders.

Folk legends of this particular sort often turn out to be history. If Heinrich Schliemann had not taken Homer's epic as a document, he would never have found the site of Troy. In the same way, the Bible story of the Flood came very much alive to Leonard Woolley when he dug below the foundations of Ur of the Chaldees and found eight feet of river mud deposited by the very deluge described in Genesis.

These are dramatic but relatively simple instances of old legends coming true after the passage of many centuries. However, to explain what the tourist sees today on Monte Albán, scientists in many related fields must range over a huge and unexpected section of the globe, over a long time span, and take into account clues from the Indus Valley to the shores of the Mississippi. Something far bigger than a battle or a flood is involved; something that already has the shape of an epic involving many lands and many ages, and thus is too vast to be contained, except piecemeal, in folk traditions.

It happens that in every country of Complex X there are legends of bearded, long-robed "white strangers" arriving to teach the people the arts and sciences; and these tales may eventually stand up as descriptions of actual visiting sages. But for present purposes it is best to forget them, and certainly to forget the modern romances which purport to explain in one volume a mystery which two or three generations of hard-working scientists have scarcely begun to describe, much less solve.

Ever since John Stephens electrified the Victorian world with his description of the wondrous Maya cities, cranks and pseudo scientists have been busy with their moonshine: the sunken continent of Atlantis and Mu, its Pacific counterpart; lost colonies of ancient white men in the jungles of Brazil; wholesale migrations of Phoenicians, Egyptians, or Chinese to America over mythical land routes. Even before those Semitic-looking grandees turned up on the steles of the Gulf and their writhing compatriots among the Dancers, there were circumstantial accounts of the Lost Tribes of Israel emigrating to the Americas, and for a long time Quetzalcoatl was believed to be none other than the apostle St. Thomas.

All this romancing started in the era of P. T. Barnum, who made a fortune out of the harmless human relish for the barely credible. It was also the period of white supremacy, when the whitest skins went along with the best people and had to be imputed to the classic folk of Greece and Rome, who were about the color of southern Mexicans. This aspect of the fun was so pernicious that the closed-box theory, which firmly insulated the Indians from Old World contacts, was at least a healthy reaction.

Books are still rolling off the presses to solve, once and for all, the Great American Mystery. They furnish names and dates, they pin-point all the scattered and ambiguous evidences of diffusion as coming from one particular spot at one particular time. A recent book has the fleet of Alexander the Great (whose movements after the world conqueror's sudden death are conveniently vague) crossing the Pacific to establish all the civilizations of the New World. A still more recent volume has the founder of the most ancient civilization known, Sargon I of Sumer, arriving in Peru about five thousand years ago and his grandson then bobbing up in Mexico as Quetzalcoatl.

There is one interesting thing wrong with all these thrillers—they are not daring enough to make sense. Their authors cannot bring themselves to conceive more than a single, dazzling crossing of Pacific or Atlantic. As a result, they must make us believe that one person, or one group, having braved the unknown terrors of the deep, still had the strength to transform the lives and thoughts of many nations of American Indians. And Indians have the self-preservative virtue of being the hardest people on earth to influence.

Still, we prefer our sagas to conform to pattern. The Alger hero has now evolved into Superman, but our favorite story is still of an individual overcoming impossible odds to perform the incredible. Thus we cherish the story of Columbus in 1492 as Chapter One in the American epic, ignoring the prelude of Icelanders making rather frequent trips to Vinland centuries before Columbus. The moment a tremendous feat is repeated it loses its shock value.

It is going to be hard to popularize the earliest voyages to America because they must have been plural, and it is extremely doubtful if we will ever know what people made them. The diffusionists are not prepared as yet to furnish us many details. If we accept their hypothesis, we must entertain the possibility that an unknown people or peoples blazed a trail across the Pacific which was later followed by missionaries, artists, and the intellectual elite, and that this seven-thousand-mile voyage was made in both directions by fairly large groups of people over a period of more than a thousand years. This is staggering; it is too big to be credible, and it is too complicated to make a good story.

Moreover, it all happened much too long ago. Revelation of the whole Middle American complex has made us uncomfortable. The general public of European descent is asked to believe that Indians knew the orbit of Venus and belonged to an inter-American league of splendid cities at a time when our own ancestors were roaming the forests of Europe. Now we must add to this the notion that perhaps three thousand years ago Asiatic astronomers crossed the Pacific over routes that had already been proved safe enough for such important persons to travel, and were beginning observations of Venus in the new latitude. Our atomic age, with its by-product of precise dating, has presented us with the challenge of the observatory on Monte Albán in 600 B.C. It is a test of our democracy about time.

History has been written in such a way that a certain snobbery about time is apt to develop. We think of time as a one-way stream which is "getting somewhere," and so modernity must be better than antiquity. We want to think that modern people are better in every way than their forebears, that evolution is constantly improving the human race. It is a terrible blow to discover a fine civilization at our very doors, not only created by Indians, but created so very early. Has the human race not made as much progress as we had thought? Is it even slipping a little?

The human race, as the facts of history prove, does not move onward and upward in a sort of pilgrim's progress. It moves like waves in crests and troughs, up and down in the vast ocean of time. In the Mediterranean the crest of Minoan culture was followed by the trough of barbarian Dorian, mounting to another crest in the Age of Pericles. The Dark Ages followed Rome and led to the Renaissance. Dates have little to do with the values or accomplishments of the human race.

The culture revealed by Monte Albán was one of those seventh waves in which human powers mount to a high point. Not only must we accept it as the first proud American tradition, but we must enlarge our ideas of the world in which this Oaxaca city was possible. We must jolt our imaginations and see ancient peoples as great adventurers and travelers. They were just as curious about unknown parts of the world as we, having exhausted the secrets of earth, are now curious about the moon. And since astronomy was an exact science in Babylonia long ago, man could navigate by the stars as soon as he had the proper craft and had screwed up his courage.

We may take the courage for granted, and large seagoing craft evidently developed much earlier than we had thought. Since ships were built of wood, which is perishable, we can never reconstruct the ancient history of sailing by looking for specimens. There are records of other sorts. An old Chimu vase found in Peru has a good picture of a Polynesian double canoe of the sort which could and did carry sixty families and provisions for a long voyage across the Pacific; and there are memories of the double canoe all along the Pacific coast of the Americas. Nobody knows when the huge Chinese junks and other oriental ships built of sturdy teak began to defy the typhoons of the China Sea.

Heine-Geldern, in an article[2] written in collaboration with Dr. Ekholm, gives us interesting information about early sailing ships. Even in Ptolemy's time, in the second century A.D., vessels navigated from India to the Malay Peninsula and Indonesia, not hugging the coast, but sailing across the Bay of Bengal. When Fa-Hien, a Chinese Buddhist, returned home from India about A.D. 400 he sailed in a ship carrying more than two hundred sailors and merchants, which went directly across the ocean from Ceylon to Java. There he embarked in a similar ship which went straight up the China Sea to North China. As our Yankee captains well knew, any ship that could navigate the Indian and China seas and pass Java Head safely would have no trouble crossing the Pacific.

Navigation requires courage and skill in any age. The skippers who drove the first American ships into the Pacific just after the Revolution had tiny vessels of less than a hundred tons, stripling crews, no mariner's charts or instruments more elaborate than a sextant and a compass, yet they rounded Cape Horn, went up to the fur grounds of the Northwest, crossed over to China, and returned home around Africa safely, circumnavigating the entire globe.

It seems unlikely that the Phoenicians ever reached the Americas over either ocean. But by 1000 B.C. they knew enough about navigation to have made such a voyage. They were supplying the fairs of Tyre with amber from the Baltic and tin from Cornwall; they were venturing far down the African coast for gold and ivory.

We have purposely put Phoenicians, Yankees, Polynesians, and Chinese Buddhists in the same boat, so to speak, to indicate that crossing the Pacific is not a matter of dates or even variety of craft; it is a long, hard job, considerably lightened by the islands which dot much of the surface and by ocean currents moving in both directions.

[2]*Tlatoani*, December 1952.

Zapotec

This brings us to *Kon-Tiki* and the man whom everybody from Sir Peter Buck down is tempted to call Wrong-Way Heyerdahl. He has Polynesia peopled from the wrong direction, and much too late, and in a craft such as the Peruvians evidently did use in their trade with Middle America but which was hardly designed for transpacific work. Buck's classic *Vikings of the Sunrise*[3] is still the best description of how the Polynesians spread *eastward* across the Pacific in their big double canoes. Since Buck mentions earlier settlers, the Manahune, as having preceded the Polynesians to the very islands which form convenient links across the Pacific, his delightful book has a revived value today in helping to explain the earliest American mystery.

However, Thor Heyerdahl has done a real service in reminding the general public that oceans can be used for migrations and that Atlantis and Mu were never necessary to explain the peopling of the New World. The ancients were great navigators as well as patient pedestrians, and whenever one recalls that long trek from Mongolia across the ice of the glaciers and down the coast from Alaska to Tierra del Fuego, it is a relief to think that some of the ancients were fortunate enough to have made the trip by sea.

The diffusionists who think that we may one day be able to tie all the ancient civilizations together, including those of the Americas, as spreading from one center, are getting a good deal of encouragement of late years. A tremendous amount of digging has been going on in the Near East, where the ancient cultures of Egypt and Babylonia flourished; and, as usual, dates are being pushed back so that we can get a glimpse of what was there before the pyramids and ziggurats. A Stone Age man of 75,000 years ago has recently been found in Iran, and this man began, somewhere between 16,000 and 8000 B.C., to raise grain.

About 4000 B.C. an interesting process began: the slow forging of a chain of influences beginning in the Near East, running

[3]New York, 1938.

through India and Southeast Asia and down into Indonesia. The last links in this chain may eventually have reached the Americas. Its early stages have been traced recently by Walter A. Fairservis, Jr., a brilliant young archaeologist of the Museum of Natural History. He found abundant evidence that cultural traits of the Near East flowed down the Arabian coast, which was passable then, and up into Central Asia. From then on, Mr. Fairservis said in a letter to the author, these influences may have spread over a tremendous area:

"If these cultural traits were diffusing along the southern route from the Near East at an early period, as they undoubtedly did, then eventually much of India might be affected at an early period. Over the next three thousand years the diffusion of certain of these traits into Indonesia and Oceania, and eventually perhaps the Americas, could well take place. Movements of people did occur of course, and undeniably some of these movements affected the character of the inhabitants all along the vast chain. . . .

"If origins of the 'high cultures' of the Americas are Asiatic, those beginnings may be accountable not to mass migration and displacement of peoples but rather to minor and erratic contacts with people who on the Oceanic side of the sea and land bridge to Asia received cultural traits originating in the Near East and which, slowly diffusing and changing, reached to the Pacific islands. The number of these people who reached the Americas with the knowledge of these traits would probably have been very small indeed. However, even such a small number with knowledge could change an entire way of life."

The middle part of this diffusion has long been familiar, but Mr. Fairservis, by finding proof that it began in the Near East, and speculating on the possibility of an American terminal, has suggested a bold pattern which in a general way satisfies every question that has been raised as to the origin of the ancient American high cultures. The great enigma of these cultures is the fact that they show links now with one country, now with another; that these curious parallels occur at different periods; and that they are never too pat, but seem to have passed through several screening processes. Only a broad hypothesis can furnish the key.

Here we must warn the reader that the hypothesis which follows is entirely the fabrication of the author, who has no scientific reputation to lose. The scientists themselves will probably never be able to reconstruct very clearly how Complex X was transferred to the Americas. While diffusionists suspect that various voyages were made from Southeast Asia through Polynesia to both Americas, beginning early in the Christian Era, they are unprepared as yet to speculate about such voyages in the centuries before Monte Albán.

However, the mother culture of Middle America contained curious and apparently South Asiatic elements early enough to have transmitted them to the ancestors of the Maya and the Zapotecs. This takes us far back in time, and yet there must be an answer, or a speculative theory, to explain Complex X. The combined work of Americanists and experts on ancient Asiatic and Pacific cultures may eventually come up with a hypothesis quite different from the one which follows, which is offered merely as an amateur's guessing game.

The people who interest us were living in Java and Sumatra several centuries before Christ, the descendants of D.P.s from India, China, and all Southeast Asia. These proto-Malayans were largely Mongoloid with a strain of Caucasian blood, and authorities agree that some of them spread into the Pacific as proto-Polynesians (or Manahune). Much later the Polynesians proper followed them, emigrating from the East Indies also, and they still speak a dialect of the Malayan language.

The proto-Malayans were a blend of many races and influences, the ideal people to use in our guessing game. Because of pressures from the mainland of Asia, they began spreading out into the Pacific, thereby becoming our Manahune, whose historical existence is no myth. Their probable route of expansion was through

The Shadow of Giants

New Guinea, Fiji, Samoa, and the Society Islands, all volcanic islands which could have supported them as the barren atolls could not. This is the path taken by the food plants of Polynesia, all of which came from the Indo-Malayan region (except for Heyerdahl's famous sweet potato, which is no problem here).

Let us assume that at some point in this slow progress of the Manahune eastward certain daring decisions were made back in Asia, just where and by whom we shall probably never know. By reading from result to cause, a happy process denied the rigid scientist who describes but does not explain, we deduce the nature of these decisions.

The outstanding quality of the Middle American culture is that it was a tremendous religious movement. Every ancient site was a ceremonial city dedicated to the gods; all those beautiful objects we see in the museums were the visible forms of worship. From Monte Albán and other centers in Middle America an intellectual elite, priests and astronomers, carried the secrets of the magic calendar and the divination of fate far and wide. Like Islam and the Christian world and the kingdoms of Buddha, the Middle American culture possessed a great dynamic power, the drive for spiritual conquest of the entire world.

Where should this drive originate except in a region deeply mesmerized by a cult based on astronomy? Because of the early migrations from the Babylonian world where these sky cults were born, these concepts had been introduced into Southeast Asia. Therefore, we deduce that sometime in the years before Monte Albán was built certain zealots in South Asia resolved to sail eastward and make a conquest of souls.

At this point a fascinating question comes up: Did they know where they were going? Had the Manahune and their food plants spread far enough across the Pacific so that word had come back of their discovery of the New World? Would missionaries have started on a long and difficult voyage without a definite goal and the certainty of finding human material to work on? They might

well have started out, knowing little of what lay eastward and re-
quiring no other guarantees of success but the predictions of their
astrologers. Thus we arrive at a romantic version of the discovery
of America: The world's supreme astronomers saw this event
foretold in the stars, and they had the authority to command that
the feat be accomplished.

The Manahune, as we shall see, left a definite trail across the
Pacific, through Melanesia to Samoa and Tahiti, and probably on
to the Marquesas. Sir Peter Buck did not visit this group, but early
records indicate that a highly evolved people whose description
corresponds to that of Manahune elsewhere lived in the Marquesas
for a long time. This island group would have been the last stopping place for argonauts bound to the New World, unless they
happened to hit the Galápagos. Probably both island groups were
maintained as way stations.

From the Marquesas to Peru there is a stretch of four thousand
miles, which with a favoring wind could be sailed by a double
canoe in three or four weeks. The Galápagos are less blessed by
nature, but Heyerdahl, who is still turning up interesting finds
which he interprets to fit his own theory, has found Indian arti-
facts and mainland plants there, which indicate that it might have
been used as the last stage of the American journey. If voyagers
left the Galápagos, the equatorial countercurrent would have
helped them across the three thousand miles to the Gulf of
Panama. There are indications that the earliest landings were in
Middle America and spread later down to Peru.

We now imagine the Asiatic sages making their way up to the
Isthmus of Tehuantepec. At this point we hesitate. Did the sages
begin their mission in the high central valleys of Oaxaca? Or did
they cross the isthmus, take other ships, and land at the mouth of
the Panuco River below Tampico?

The first fragment of anything resembling Mexico's ancient history concerns the landing of strangers at Pánuco. Fray Bernardino

The Shadow of Giants

de Sahagún wrote down what the Indians could tell him of their earliest story, and some of these accounts have been reinforced by archaeological finds. The "Olmec" school of Americanists—many of whom are non-diffusionists—like the legend of the Pánuco landing, not because it suggests the arrival of evangels from Asia, but because it mentions the Pánuco region, which some of them think was the early nursery of pre-Maya and pre-Zapotec peoples, and indeed of the whole mother culture. According to this view, the Maya were incubated in the Pánuco region (where the Huastecs, a Mayance people who early went to seed, still live); and the Maya then moved down the Gulf coast to Guatemala.

However, Dr. Ekholm has excavated the Pánuco site thoroughly without finding a trace of anything that could be called Maya or Olmec. This puts a dampener on the idea that pre-Olmecs, or a visiting band of Asiatics, developed Complex X in the Pánuco region. We mention the legend in connection with our first hypothetical landing, although we have a strong suspicion that it may apply to a landing centuries later, and one perhaps connected with that battle depicted on the Gulf stones. The legend is interesting for other reasons.

It is a tale of men arriving at Pánuco by sea and founding the town of Tamoanchan, where they lived for a long time. With them came sages and soothsayers, men able to write, but they did not remain long. They re-embarked and sailed east, promising to return just before the end of the world. After they left, four old men, Oxomoco and Cipactonál and two others whose names have been lost, undertook to regulate the calendar. The tradition connects these ancient newcomers with the building of the pyramids "by giants."

This is a remarkable story. "Sages and soothsayers, men able to write," and the regulation of the calendar by four elders condense the chief wonders of Monte Albán and the history of the Maya. No amount of digging has revealed among the Archaic Indians any knowledge of writing or of a calendar. These things were perhaps brought to Mexico by sages and soothsayers, the original evangels of Asiatic thought, who established a foothold on the Pánuco and then hurried on eastward to complete their mission. Four is the significant number for religion and government, and thus the "four elders" may have meant a school of astronomers, who naturally had to regulate the calendar to fit the new latitude.

However Complex X arrived, it was expressed in Oaxaca by the cities of Monte Albán and Monte Negro. They kept in touch with the pre-Maya at their site of San José in Honduras and with other cities. We have a vague picture of the new culture developing on both coasts of the Isthmus of Tehuantepec and on the highlands between, and finally flowing up into the central plateau to create the great pyramids of Teotihuacán and Xochicalco and Cholula.

The chronology of this remarkable expansion must wait for precise dating of the known sites and for more excavation. But its nature is fairly clear. The first conquest of Mexico apparently had as its chief aim the winning of souls. It was not a colonizing effort; it seems unlikely that great numbers of South Asiatics moved to Middle America at any period. It was, as the old tradition said, an invasion of sages and soothsayers.

They made little attempt to change the living habits of the Indians—which in any case would have been next to impossible— but they seem to have had great success in winning over the local caciques at least, so that they had a large army of slaves to build their ceremonial cities. The little ruling clique in each center set up a theocracy based on the magic calendar, which was evidently accepted without rebellion, since it was impersonal, infallible in the astronomical sense, and fascinating to every individual from king to slave, because his personal horoscope was cast from it.

Evidently the sages and soothsayers made a peaceful conquest. We do not yet know the date of those Gulf stones which show the battle between Rubber People and bearded invaders. They may refer to a later invasion and not to that shadowy picture of the landing at Pánuco. For the missionaries whose chief concern was the calendar were evidently followed by zealots of competing faiths, who have done a good deal to confuse the picture the modern archaeologist finds. These later missionaries were unable to make a mass conversion, for Mexico was still obeying the magic calendar at the time of the Conquest.

However, one great religion, the Hindu-Buddhist, made some headway among the Maya during the period from the first century A.D. until well into the twelfth. Heine-Geldern and Ekholm have made a careful study of this missionary movement among the Maya, which they see as the extension of the great Hindu-Buddhist sweep through Southern Asia and Indonesia. The specific art styles of certain Maya works stem, they think, from the center of Amaravati in Southern India. One of the Amaravati styles was a lotus-blossom motif with the leaves and roots of the plant stylized in rather a curious way. There is the mask of a jawless monster in the center, and the pattern is closed at each end by a fish or fish-like creature. This singular treatment of the lotus is found on several Maya friezes.

Since Southeast Asia and Indonesia—and the Mayance too—often used wood for buildings and sculptures in the early period, and the wood has perished, it has taken delicate detective work for Ekholm and Heine-Geldern to follow the lotus, the Maya cross, which is like the Indian tree of heaven, and a host of other elements through the mazes of the great Hindu-Buddhist missionary movement. But they succeed in proving that this movement did include Mexico over a long period, and conclude that "the traces of Hindu-Buddhist influence correspond precisely to those introduced in Southeast Asia by Buddhist and Brahman monks."

This fascinating study of one set of influences shows the quandary in which the modern scientist finds himself when he tries to explain ancient Mexico. He is dealing with just a few of the twenty-five hundred ancient sites of the country, for exploration has scarcely begun. Most of the written records of the Indians themselves were destroyed by the Spanish friars, and others are in

unknown tongues. The student of ancient Mexico suddenly finds
that he must know a great deal about the ancient history of Southeast Asia and Polynesia. The task, in short, is staggering, and it is a
tribute to the courage and hard work of our modern scholars that
even the vaguest and most tentative theories of the origins of early
American cultures can be formulated.

To the archaeological sleuth, pottery is as much of a godsend as
Dr. Libby's Geiger counter. Polynesia might give us a vivid picture of transpacific comings and goings. But there is no pottery on
the islands, for the simple reason that clay occurs only in old land
masses, and the islands are the work of volcanoes or creatures de-
positing coral. Without this firm index of changing ceramic styles
which tie up so closely with dates and reveal trade contacts or
actual origins, the links between Polynesia and the great continents
on either side are spotty and confused.

Again we have a mass of legends, which will one day be sifted
for bits of true history. We have unfinished stories. For instance,
Fairservis found in Pakistan what seemed to be a rudimentary
alphabet with signs remarkably like those of an alphabet previ-
ously found in the Indus Valley, which has never been deciphered.
Meanwhile, on Easter Island, the easternmost of the Polynesians
and in many ways the most mysterious, wooden tablets were
found with characters said to resemble those found on seals at
Mohenjo-Daro in the Indus Valley and dated 2000 B.C. Is there a
connection?

It is well known that Polynesians and Peruvians used the *quipu*,
a complicated system of knotting a cord as an *aide-mémoire*. But
one could fill an entire chapter with such parallels. What almost
proves the diffusion theory is that a similar tool or trait is seldom
found uniformly throughout Southeast Asia, the Americas, and
Polynesia, but more often in limited areas of two of these great
regions. For instance, tattooing, the flattening of the forehead,
filing and blackening the teeth, and certain forms of nose orna-

ment were common to both Americas, the Pacific islands, and Indonesia. But the fashion of making a shallow depression in a tooth and filling it with a precious or semi-precious stone was popular only with Zapotecs and Maya, a few South Americans, and early peoples in the Philippines, Borneo, and Sumatra. The Fiji Islanders and the Popolocas of Vera Cruz still follow an ancient trick of shaking a narcotic into the water to stun fish so they can be easily caught. But certain textile techniques such as batik seem to have reached the New World directly from Java and Sumatra and were lost in the Pacific islands for lack of good weaving fibers.

The Manahune have left their traces: great steles, temples, and pyramids, the Easter Island colossal figures, and on Kauai in the Hawaiians an irrigation system revealing great skill. When the Polynesians invaded Hawaii, the Manahune fled and perhaps went to the American mainland. Several of the Northwest Indian tribes have an assortment of Oceanic traits and speak Penutian, related to an ancient form of the Indo-European tongue which the Manahune may have brought with them from Indonesia.

Some of the Polynesian genealogies go back much farther than the known history of the islands. In the Marquesas one family tree went back to 2000 B.C., and the royal genealogy of Rarotonga records the migration of Manahune from Samoa to the Tongas in 450 B.C. The clearest picture of the Manahune comes from the peripheral islands, the Tongas and Marquesas and Easter, where the old strain had not been submerged by the Polynesian influx.

The Tongas were first visited by Captain James Cook, whose artists and amateur anthropologists have given us a glimpse of a proud, beautiful people living in an island paradise. Like their brothers, the Quinametin of Mexico, they carved steles, built elaborate tombs for their kings, and in penitential rites would cut off a finger joint. Very like them were the Marquesans, described by the first Yankee skippers and a few early scientists. Men and women were tall and regal, the men often wearing Vandyke beards and mustaches. Like the Tongans, they wore tall headdresses of precious feathers, breast ornaments, and heavy earplugs. These islanders would have been quite at home in ancient Mexico.

If our story proves true, these were the people who chose, or were commanded, to remain on the islands, cultivating their bread-fruit and taro, providing havens and rest stations for the passage of the great ones who even in that far-off day were dedicated to the task of binding the whole world together in worship of the sky gods.

VIII

CLASSIC AMERICA

The tremendous impetus of the new culture which transformed Middle America was not spent for two thousand years, and during all that time Monte Albán stood like the rock on which it is built, as the heart of a dynamic civilization. The great center of Teotihuacán lived only half that long, and the wondrous Maya cities endured only a few centuries. In Oaxaca we can see the earliest chapter of Complex X—though the first pages have been lost—and follow the whole story through its climax in a true golden age to the years of slow decline and the final tragedy of the Aztec and Spanish invasions.

Classic America was a unity, dominated by a religious impulse which was expressed in great pyramid cities, all built in the same evolving styles. It was one vast theocracy in which a ruling clique of priests and sages in each center kept in close touch with the rest of their brotherhood. The merchants, too, kept this vast invisible empire woven together with their comings and goings.

This unity was a marvelous thing because it existed only in the sphere of religion and the arts connected with it. There was no imperialism, no politics in the usual sense, no regimentation, and evidently very little bloodshed. The Maya and the Mixtecs fought and feuded between themselves, but there are no records in the Oaxaca region of any large-scale warfare until the time when the Classic age sank into decadence with the decline of the old gods. From beginning to end the Classic culture was extraordinary; it

Zapotec

achieved and kept unity, not despite the number of peoples who had a hand in it, but one might almost say *because* of the number of peoples who were allowed to make their contributions. The religion itself evolved; the arts connected with it kept growing and changing, until finally the golden age was achieved as the integrated work of all the nations of Middle America.

What the Classic age really meant was the period—roughly the first nine centuries of the Christian Era—when several great independent civilizations flowered. Each one—Maya, Zapotec, Mixteca-Puebla, Teotihuacán—was a fully developed, distinct culture which stood on its own feet, but never stood alone. The richness and beauty of each was the work of all in the long centuries of cross-fertilization.

One way of suggesting the extraordinary nature of Classic America is to compare it with Europe. The Continent is a unity on the map, it shares the Christian religion, and its arts have evolved as a synthesis of national creative forces. Now, if one could imagine a Europe never torn by wars, national rivalries, and chronic fears, one would get closer to realizing what Classic America was like. It was by no means ideal, judged by modern standards—but there must be something wrong with modern standards if they are still defended in a world destroying itself with wars and iron curtains.

The culture was evidently generated in a collision of opposites—the passive Indian and the dynamic South Asiatic—and it was nurtured in diversity. One nursery was the ancient "Olmec Land," a rather small area which included what is now northern Oaxaca and adjoining parts of Vera Cruz and Puebla. Every nation which shared in the early development of Complex X is connected with Olmec Land—Maya, Zapotec, Mixtec, Mazatec, Totonac, Chinantec, Mixe-Popoloca, to name the most important. It was a veritable fair of cultures, a melting pot that boiled as vehemently as the early crucible of the Near East.

Few Zapotecs live in Olmec Land today, but in remote times

170

SOUTHERN MEXICO and GUATEMALA during the CLASSIC ERA

CARIBBEAN SEA

GULF OF MEXICO

PACIFIC OCEAN

Pánuco

El Tajín

Tula

Teotihuacán
Tenochtitlán

Cholula

Cerro de
las Mesas

Xochicalco

Tres Zapotes

Monte Negro

Monte Albán

Mittla

Giengola

La Venta

Balenque

Piedras Negras

Tikal

Kaminal-Juyú

Chichén Itzá

Uxmal

Copán

palacios

they evidently were there, in close association with the other Oaxaca tribes and with the pre-Maya. Except for the Maya, all these peoples belong to the same language group, the Olmec-Otomangue. Since the Zapotec tongue was the first to branch off from the common stem, on language grounds the Zapotecs are proved to be the first of the independent races to emerge from the nursery of Olmec Land. When they moved down into the rich central valleys of Oaxaca, they left behind them certain mountain-loving Zapotecs and their kinsmen in language, the Chatinos and the Chinantecs, who are there today.

Nature made Olmec Land the funnel through which the arts and ideas generated in the southern lands poured northward into the central plateau, to transform the lives of simple Indians like those of Tlatilco. During the Classic era much of the cultural impetus flowed southward from the great city of Teotihuacán, which was in close association with Monte Albán and with Maya cities. Thus Classic America had three great centers.

Who the masters of Teotihuacán were is uncertain, but they worked in complete harmony with the Zapotecs, so that the city of the central plateau and the city on the heights of Albán marched in step. The Zapotecs were not in the same close relation with the Maya, nor with the people of the Olmec sites on the Gulf, though they traded and exchanged cultural ideas with these brothers of the common faith.

Despite all the libraries that have been written about the Maya, their prehistory is still shadowy. Some of the pre-Maya were in British Honduras quite early, since their city of San José there belongs to the first epoch of Monte Albán. The glorious old Maya cities of Copán, Uaxactún, Palenque, and the rest were carefully dated on their own stones, and all fall within the Christian Era. By the time they were built the Maya had absorbed the magic calendar and emerged as supreme astronomers, builders, and artists. All this earlier incubation may have taken place along the coastal edge of Olmec Land.

Thus, in a rough way, we have the Maya gradually establishing themselves in Guatemala (which then included Chiapas), and the Zapotecs settling down in the Oaxaca valleys. These two older races are now settled down; but the rest of the clan are numerous and, like younger brothers in general, they are in constant motion. To simplify an extremely complicated picture, it was these younger races who built the Gulf cities from La Venta to El Tajín and the venerable centers of Teotihuacán and Cholula.

In all this they were helped, and no doubt enlivened, by the delightful Totonacs, who may have been distant relatives but who arrived from the Pacific side of the isthmus quite early. In our concentration on the Gulf region we must not forget that the Pacific coast, especially along Guatemala and Chiapas, was another nursery of cultures, and that these cultures poured up through the secondary funnel of Tehuantepec and across the isthmus to arrive finally in Olmec Land. In their migration the Totonacs allied themselves with the Zoque (the eastern tribe now reduced to two villages in Oaxaca) and perhaps lingered in Monte Albán to stimulate the second epoch there, the shortest and in many ways the best of the five periods.

The Totonacs were gusty, happy people who made the famous "laughing heads" of terra cotta and elaborately carved stone yokes which ballplayers wore around their hips for protection against the heavy ball. The designs on some of them, squared spirals in interlaced bands, are almost duplicates of patterns decorating Late Chou objects in China. If the diffusion theory is right, the Totonacs may have been a later migration from a part of South Asia that was under strong Chinese influence. These migrations, we speculated, would have terminated in the Panama region and then trickled northward; and certainly parts of Central America, especially Costa Rica, made art objects very much in the Totonac style. The Totonac migration ended in the Papantla region of Vera Cruz, where members of this race live today and perform their breath-taking "flying-pole" game. In this region the Totonacs and the Olmec peoples built the marvelous pyramid of El Tajín, which is as South Asiatic as possible.

While the Totonacs did not belong to the family of nations in Olmec Land, they are among the very greatest of the Middle Americans, and evidence of their artistic genius and their jovial humor has been found over a wide area. Their unmistakable art forms have not occurred in Zapotec country, but one is tempted to think that in an oblique way they stimulated the artists of Monte Albán II. There is the same buoyancy, the same beautiful control of a daring conception.

Now we come to the third great stream that resulted in the culture of Teotihuacán, which began about the first century A.D. Jiménez Moreno is sure that the Totonacs were at Teotihuacán very early, either as masters or slaves. However, in a general way the development of the central plateau for the first millennium of the Christian Era was the work of the younger brothers: Mixtecs, Mazatecs, Popolocas, all of them nurtured in Olmec Land but wandering far afield before they returned home to the Oaxaca-Puebla border country. Of these closely allied tribes, the Mixtecs were the artists and the roving tutors of Central Mexico.

Father Sahagún said that the legendary Olmecas, the Rubber People, were Mixtecs; and certainly of all the Olmecas they are the most protean, restless, gifted, the catalytic agents in the cultural ferment. Their ancient home was in Olmec Land at Mixtán, but very early they spread all along the Gulf coast, which must have brought them in contact with the Maya. Some of the Mixtecs settled across the border in Guatemala, others were in Totonac country north of Vera Cruz, and still others spread across the Oaxaca-Puebla border country which was the western part of Olmec Land.

The Mixtecs were everywhere—except in the Mixteca. Evidently they did not spread down the western valley of Oaxaca to the Tilantongo region until many centuries after the ceremonial city of Monte Negro was built there. Their own written history in the Mixteca begins in A.D. 720, when they were still fighting for its possession.

It seems certain that it was the early Zapotecs who built Monte Negro on the ten-thousand-foot mountain of Tilantongo in 600 B.C. The excavation of the ancient Mixteca has scarcely begun, though the region is one of tantalizing promise. Mexican experts have hesitated to place the ancient Zapotecs in the western valley, but early in 1954 a large buried city was found in the southwest corner of the Mixteca overlooking the Pacific, with steles bearing Zapotec glyphs.

Dr. Caso dug into Monte Negro and found it built by the same people who were masters of Monte Albán. The ceramics of the two cities are closely akin, and this alone excludes the Mixtecs from the picture, for never in history have Zapotecs and Mixtecs worked in the same way. This is especially true of the ceramic crafts, in which the Mixtecs were later to excel in their own unmistakable style.

As if to emphasize the primacy of Monte Albán, the builders of Tilantongo did not expend themselves in an architectural marvel. Monte Negro was perhaps intended as a spiritual outpost to hold the great western valley; it has the appearance of having been built and occupied by secondary artists. Its tomb offerings, and the tombs themselves, are in Monte Albán styles, but of less artistic merit. Often the gray clay heads and urns are unpolished, and there are few of the inimitable animal figures found at the deepest levels of Monte Albán. The Zapotec magic calendar and bar-and-dot number system were used. Another proof that the Mixtecs were not at Monte Negro is the fact that a bar was used there for the number five, while the Mixtecs expressed numbers up to twenty by dots alone.

The Mixtecs absorbed the teachings of other races so completely that not until their independent arts were perfected can we trace them clearly. Even in medieval times they were so closely merged with Mazatecs and Popolocas and minor peoples that "Mixtec" is usually followed by a hyphen. It was these alliances, laid down very early with their relatives or neighbors of Olmec Land, which gave this instable race its powers.

But their arts need no hyphen. They may have been great architects in the early days, but so far the magnificent temples shown in their codices have not been excavated. They were good at small sculpture and intricate wood carving. Their genius was in painting, and while the great bulk of their work was destroyed by time and the Spanish friars, what remains is supreme in Mexico. They painted codices and ceremonial pottery with complete mastery, and when in the ninth century metals were finally introduced into Mexico they also excelled as jewelers.

Their manuscripts were usually painted on long sheets of deerskin coated with white lime. On this base they drew the figures of monarchs and temples, filling them in with brilliant colors and finally outlining the whole with black. These sheets were folded back and forth like a screen, a device also used in Sumatra. In making ceramics they used a very fine clay which they worked into elegant and varied forms and decorated them with scenes or mythological symbols done in polychrome and polished to a brilliant luster. Much later they taught these arts to the Aztecs, who were assigned all the credit for them by Prescott.

Beautiful as the Mixtec codices are in themselves, they turn out to have another value: they comprise the only written history of Indians in either of the Americas. The Incas did not paint manuscripts, and the Maya recorded only astronomical data. Codices long attributed to the Zapotecs are now believed to have come from other hands. But the Mixtecs wrote actual history, recording the names and dates of the Tilantongo dynasties together with a few details of their reigns.

By sheer accident Dr. Caso discovered that an old Spanish map in the library of the University of Texas related to the Tilantongo region. It showed the churches built by the Spanish missionaries and was clearly painted by a Mixtec artist, who was inspired by patriotism or rebellion to add to this churchly chart an abridged history of pre-Conquest days. Along the sides he painted in codex style the monarchs of old Tilantongo. With this map as a key Dr. Caso is now reading the eight Mixtec codices which escaped the friars' flames, and those delicately carved jaguar bones he found in Tomb Seven.

The Texas map is dramatic because it shows that the Mixtecs who fought their way down the western valley to Tilantongo in the eighth century were saturated with Quetzalcoatl worship. The central king on the map is Ocañaña, or Twenty Tigers, an in-carnation of the great god. It was the fashion in ancient Mexico to honor outstanding leaders as incarnations of the Plumed Serpent, and most illustrious of all was the semi-divine Quetzalcoatl of his-tory, whose real name was Topiltzin Ce Acatl. His father was a Toltec and his mother a Mazatec-Mixtec princess who conceived her son after swallowing a piece of jade. Ocañaña repeats part of this story; his mother was called Quetzal Bird of the Jewel. He was the fifth and last king of the first Tilantongo dynasty, and his ancestors trace back to 692, the earliest true historical date in America. At twenty he was slain in a dynastic war; like Quetzal-coatl, he was burned to ashes, and his soul became the planet Venus.

The picture writing of the map tells part of Ocañaña's story, which is filled out in four codices. It shows the vanished temple at Tilantongo, decorated with "Greek frets" like those at Mitla, and above the temple are Ocañaña's parents seated on mats and facing each other, as royal couples are always represented. The symbols of their names are behind them. The king's name-glyph is the sky represented by three stars and vapor coming down from it, spelling "Vapor That Falls from the Sky." The queen's name is a quetzal bird and a jewel (a jewel almost always means jade, the sacred stone). Above them (the codices read up, not down) is the martyred king-god himself, Ocañaña or Twenty Tigers, wearing a tiger-skin cloak and surrounded by twenty dots. His birth date is given as 972, which agrees with the codices and makes him come a little later than the historical-mythical Quetzalcoatl, whose reign ended in 947.

There is a line of people offering homage to Ocañaña in the traditional ceremony of seven nobles offering a quail for sacrifice, a box with three jade beads, a fringed royal mantle, and a bunch of quetzal feathers. After this brief moment of glory a new dynasty appears, a line of twelve kings. As an interesting side light, Dr. Caso proves that the Mixtec rulers, like the Egyptians, Incas, and many other peoples, practiced incest in order to keep the royal line intact. Kings sometimes married their full sisters or their nieces. But this practice was not permitted among commoners.

The royal line, of course, traced its ancestry straight back to the gods, and the Mixtecs who conquered western Oaxaca ruled by divine right. What people the invaders found in the western valley we do not know; perhaps some of them were the descendants of the Zapotecs who built Monte Negro. At any rate, they could claim that, unlike their conquerors, they had been in the Mixteca "forever." They called themselves *tay nuhu*, men of the earth, and said that they were born of the trees and rocks and rivers of their beautiful land. In this they were like the Zapotecs, who had literally been on the soil so long that they had no migration legends and told the friars that they had sprung from rocks and trees.

The tay nuhu said that their founder, Yacoñooy, sprang from a pine tree growing on a mountain near Tilantongo. At once he desired to found a sanctuary, and he was prepared to fight a single-handed battle for possession of the land. He looked in all directions and found the land utterly empty. Who, then, was the cacique of this unpeopled realm? There was only the sun; this land belonged to the sun. All day Yacoñooy shot arrows at the fiery lord of the Mixteca. Toward evening his enemy sank to earth, staining the clouds rosy with his blood. Thus Yacoñooy became lord of the Mixteca and father of its people.

Only when you travel down the Mixteca, which still looks so empty of people and whose very earths are stained red with ancient battle, does this legend come alive with tragic truth. The great lord has shed his blood to burn and shrivel up the land, and yet the Mixtecs cannot leave it, as if they were under a spell. And the "Mixtec Song" with its haunting cry, "O Land of the Sun," is one of sheer nostalgia, the longing of an exiled Mixtec for his beautiful, baleful home.

The Mixtecs were late-comers to central Oaxaca, and their most important work was performed far afield with their allies, the Mazatecs, Popolocas, and others. Even in the centuries before Christ these Olmecas were the civilizing agents of the central plateau, where they lived for perhaps fifteen centuries, always in intimate contact with the rest of Middle America. Like all the others, they were astronomers and the builders of pyramid cities, and the marvelous centers of Teotihuacán and Xochicalco and Cholula rose on the central mesa like replicas of the great volcanoes. Perhaps some of these Olmecas carried the Classic cultures up the Mississippi and Ohio valleys, for these remote regions were drawn into the spiritual empire dominated by Monte Albán.

The crucial role of this Oaxaca city was due to many factors besides the primary one of its being the geographical center of Mesoamerica. The Zapotec temperament explains much: the gift for harmonious relations with all sorts of people, for acting as persuaders and moderators. To say that the Zapotecs are born middlemen is to diminish them; they are people of real strength and amazing stability who dominate by virtue of these qualities but use the Chinese art of accommodation, which is a very different thing from compromise.

If the Maya or the Mixtecs had established themselves in the center of the culture at Monte Albán, it would probably have evaporated in a few centuries. These wonderfully gifted people did not have the centralizing and preservative powers of the Zapotecs. Maya and Mixtecs were really self-destructive; the Maya became so obsessed with measuring time, which was not the real point of the magic calendar, that time devoured them; and the Mixtecs were of such precious, volatile stuff that without the fixative of calmer bloods furnished by intermarriage or alliances they effervesced, leaving only the bitter residue of today.

The "thousand years of Zapotec peace," a phrase symbolizing a period perhaps twice that long, is a tribute to the unifying gift of the Zapotecs and also to their tenacity in holding onto conceptions which exerted great power on the imaginations of diverse peoples. The Zapotec religion was based on the boldest possible intuition: the unity of time and space in the symbol of Cocijo, and this idea, which at first seems so alien to us, must be natural to the Indian mentality. For two thousand years Middle America lived by a symbol expressed in a cross—the-four-quarters-of-the-year-four-quarters-of-the-world—and relinquished it only to accept the Christian cross.

This time-space abstraction was warmed into life by Cocijo, who not only ruled the four quarters of the year and the world but bound heaven and earth together in his own person. He was a great conciliatory symbol the Zapotecs had worked out to resolve the eternal war in Mexico between the earth jaguar and the Bird of Heaven. Even before Monte Albán was built the blending of these concepts had begun, to end finally in a perfectly unified god, Quetzalcoatl, the Plumed Serpent. During all the centuries of Monte Albán, Cocijo was evolving as the Zapotec version of Quetzalcoatl, and when Mitla was built toward the close of the golden age its exquisite mosaics celebrated the end of the rift between the Gulf peoples and their jaguars and the highland peoples and their birds. The celestial dragon, the Sky Serpent, had triumphed.

Cocijo, as god of a region which depends on rains for survival, had the added force of a deity closely tied to agriculture, and no doubt the simple people of Middle America worshiped him primarily as the rain god. The Old Maya had precisely the same lord of rain, the fourfold Chac ruling the calendar and the cardinal points like Cocijo, and it is interesting that after all the cults that the Maya adopted, the people today have gone back to their old nature gods.

The Teotihuacáns made the rain god the supreme lord, as at Monte Albán, and dedicated the great Temple of the Sun to Ocelocoatl, the Tiger Serpent, who was an aspect of Cocijo. In Oaxaca, too, this central deity had many aspects: the lord of rain and lightning wearing the earth jaguar on his headdress; the jaguar wearing a crest of quetzal plumes; or "Heart of the Land," the jaguar as the symbol of the inner forces of the earth linked to those of heaven.

It is hard to tell whether the commoners of any remote age were happy or unhappy, or just what their daily lives were like, because all over the world chronicles center on kings and the fortunate great. The Zapotec stone records are still undeciphered, nor were the reports of the Spanish in Oaxaca nearly so full as those about the Maya and Aztecs. We get hints of life in the golden age from the excavations, but it is the Zapotecs living today who are the best witnesses to their own past. In temperament and basic habits the Indians of Mexico change very slowly, and the Zapotecs and Maya, as the earliest defined races, have changed remarkably little.

The Classic era had a system of slavery and a theocracy in which even kings obeyed the priests. You could make this sound like a grim lot for the commoners or decide that things were for Juan and Maria pretty much what they are today: an adobe-brick house, a metate and a few earthenware pots, labor from dawn to dark in the cornfields, and every now and then glorious fiestas. The people are contented now, though the fiestas are not as splendid as they were on Monte Albán; and they were no doubt contented in the days of the Zapotec peace. Slavery and theocracy are not necessarily ugly unless sadism prevails.

It is impossible to impute sadism to a Zapotec of any period. They are reasonable people, temperate and happy people, and evidently have been so all along. In the urn collections there is a gallery of Zapotec faces, but you will never see a cruel or mean expression; gentleness and sometimes radiance are in these portraits. Nobody looks like Cotton Mather.

An estimated 100,000 people lived on Monte Albán in its great days, the priests and other elite around the Great Plaza, and the commoners on the slopes, where bits of their adobe-brick houses can be seen from today's road. The sacred city was a hive of activity, slaves carrying up water from the retreating lakes, quarrying stones, working in the terraced fields in the west flank; masons and artists dressing walls with stucco, painting them red, and covering them with murals; the musicians, dancers, and ball players perfecting themselves for a coming festival; the women grinding corn on metates and tending their fowls, the only domestic animals.

The amount of clothing people wore was in direct proportion to their rank. The commoners went naked above the waist, with a length of cloth to throw around the shoulders in cold weather. The men wore a loincloth, and the women a straight wraparound falda as now.

Priests, kings, and great lords were magnificent. They wore a straight sleeveless tunic which fell below the knees, and over it a mantle. Both were of cotton or maguey fiber, for wool came in only with the Spanish. With a maguey spine for needle the women embroidered garments for both sexes in solid geometrical designs; they wove lengths of cotton in stripes of contrasting colors, or bordered a red-dyed garment with blue and yellow. The brilliant feathers of tropical birds were woven into the finest mantles and even into slippers. Ordinary sandals were of deer hide or plaited fiber.

This was only the foundation for the richness of jewels and headdress. Lords and ladies wore bracelets, necklaces, and ear-plugs of jade, obsidian, or turquoise (no metals were used until the ninth century). Men often pierced the septum of the nose for the insertion of an ornament and wore a breastplate inlaid with mother-of-pearl and other lustrous materials. Both men and women of the upper class had a headdress, tocado, which announced their station and increased their height. The nearest thing to the classic women's tocado is still worn by the lovely highland women of Yalalag: a twisted turban of heavy strands of black wool into which the hair is wound. That is the Zapotec style; the Mixtec queens arranged their hair in a bun at the back and over it wore a turban ending in two pronounced horns in front.

The tomb murals and urns and the terra-cotta figures found on Monte Albán reveal the ritual significance of the tocado. Whether the figure represents a god, or a priest wearing the mask of a god, or a king or warrior or musician, the classic headdress has a sacred meaning. Among both Zapotecs and Mixtecs the tocado often symbolized the person's name—Four Tiger or Six Monkey, or whatever day-name his birthday bore on the sacred calendar. The animal or bird was combined with decorative elements and the whole crowned with quetzal feathers or heavy black plumes. As time went on these tocados were so overloaded with symbols as to be oppressive; they were intended not only as decoration but as a complete description of the personage wearing them.

The women of Olmec Land still wear the classic costume, especially for fiestas. The Chinantec, Mazatec, Cuicatec, and high-land Zapotec wear homespun faldas and long tunics coming almost to the ankle. Each tribe has its variations; the Zapotec women of Yalalag weave a creamy-white tunic which may be embroidered with colored flowers down the side seams or more simply dec-orated with a strand of bright silk floss hanging in two spaced tassels on the chest, both types with intricate inwoven detail at the shoulders. Their cousins, the Chinantecs, prefer tunics almost solidly embroidered in geometric designs, and the Mazatec women have evolved the decoration of horizontal silk bands. All these highland costumes are marvels of design, and the splendid women of Olmec Land wear them like queens.

Almost anywhere in Oaxaca you can find the women still using the ancient weaving tools and techniques: the clay spinning whorl and the saddleback loom, tie-dyeing and abstract motifs which are very old. In fact, to get an idea of how craftsmen worked and lived in the golden age you have only to drive in any direction from the city and take the first dirt road. You may find a village making baskets, or huaraches, or deerskin garments, or pottery, or weavings. But you will never find half the village making one thing and the other half devoted to a different craft. Nor will you find anything resembling a factory, or a shop selling the local products, or a guild system such as prevailed in medieval Europe. You will find each family closed in its own ample, well-swept dooryard, busily making the town specialty, which a group of villagers will take to the weekly markets in the region and sell direct to the customer. But the choicest products are saved to sell at a great religious fair, when all the families of the village, dressed in their finest, move en masse to the center holding the triple festival of trade, merrymaking, and worship.

This is the pattern of the fair all over the world, through all the ages, and it is a marvelous thing to find it thriving still in Middle America, as it does in the Andes region. Whether by diffusion or by its nature as the ideal way for strangers to meet under the happiest and holiest auspices, the fair has a universal and eternal pattern. Through all its evolutions and guises it has remained a threefold institution, a device for international wholesale trade in which the goods are carried a long distance to arrive at a certain center at a certain date. To safeguard merchant and goods and ensure honest dealing the fair must be held on holy ground; and since people have made a long journey it is natural for them to relax and enjoy a festival. The fair incubated our commercial law; banks and stock exchanges; standard weights, measures, and currency; and many of the arts of amusement such as the circus and the variety show. Thus it is hardly a factor to be overlooked as a prime civilizing force.

For some reason those students of Classic America who are mystified by the wide extent of its culture and the close ties among the distant peoples belonging to it have entirely overlooked the pilgrimage fair. The diggers in the modest site of Tlatilco in Central Mexico will find objects that relate to the Ohio Valley or even Peru; and Cocijo urns made by Zapotec artists are scattered far and wide. Undoubtedly many objects and influences were carried by traders who were also pilgrims. Just as Don Leopoldo Torres will trudge today over the old Andes Road to the fair of Esquipulas in Guatemala, carrying a pile of serapes to sell below the church, his ancestors of the Classic age went to the same spot, over the same road, and probably at the same season.

A network of trade roads, which were also pilgrimage roads, covered a large part of both Americas, and without a doubt fairs or standing markets were connected with them all. In regions where trade is heavy you will always find a year-round fair. Tyre, for instance, was the emporium through which the rich goods of the Orient poured into the Mediterranean. Kinsai in China, about which Marco Polo wrote rhapsodies, was a vast city which cleared the trade of a large section of the country; and medieval Champagne kept four towns busy with Europe's commerce.

Oddly enough, Marco Polo's description of the Kinsai fair and its intricate setup applies perfectly to the Champagne fair of the same period and also to the medieval Indian fair. All these marts were marvels of order and good organization, and all followed the Chow-li Laws of Markets and Fairs laid down in China twelve centuries before Christ. The best description of a Mexican emporium comes from Bernal Díaz del Castillo, and what he saw was an Aztec mart at Tenochtitlán (now Mexico City), which was simply copied from the market-and-fair system of the older Indian peoples.

All Middle Americans followed the magic calendar and had a monthly fair, held every twenty days in their chief cities. But there were others connected with the trade roads, and some of these may have been standing fairs like Tyre or Kinsai, or important shrines whose annual fair drew great throngs of merchants and worshipers.

One of the great routes started in the Valley of Mexico and followed roughly the line of today's Inter-American Highway to Cholula, near the modern city of Puebla. Then it cut farther east than the Highway, through Tepeaca, Tehuacan, and Teotitlán del Camino, all three lively trade centers. From this point it went straight across Olmec Land to Tuxtepec, and there divided into Gulf and Pacific routes.

The terminal of the Gulf road was on the eastern edge of Olmec Land, at the Lagoon of Terminos in Tabasco, near the ancient city of La Venta. There was definitely a big fair here, and probably a year-round one, in a traders' town called Xicallanca, which was the meeting ground for the Maya of the Gulf and merchants from the central mesa.

The Pacific route had no terminal, unless it was Peru. It went down through Tehuantepec, where there were undoubtedly standing or seasonal fairs, and followed the Pacific down into Central America. Since the coast was sometimes flooded in the rainy season, and since the Zapotecs did not conquer the Pacific coast tribes until later, they built an alternate route through the mountains of Chiapas and into Guatemala. This is still, overgrown as it is, one of the great pilgrimage roads of the world. It leads to the town now called Esquipulas, which must have had a marvelous fair in classic days, when trade was lively between Southern Mexico and Central and South America.

Classic America

The road continued as far as a land route can go, and stopped, as all highways must, at the impassable jungles of Darien. The ancient traders then sailed part of the way down the South American coast, perhaps in balsa rafts like the *Kon-Tiki*. In 1526 Bartolomé Ruiz saw a large sailing raft bound north along the coast of Ecuador, and he listed (and undoubtedly seized) its trade goods: black pottery, ornaments of gold and silver, mirrors, dyestuffs, and fine weavings with the figures of birds and fish.

Some students think there was direct trade between Oaxaca and Peru, not a mere trickling of goods up through Central America. While Peruvian trade pieces have been found at Teotihuacán and in the Mayance, they are scattered all over Oaxaca, indicating a heavy volume of commerce. The Zapotecs seem to have influenced their southern neighbors, for the wall decorations of Chan Chan are rather like the Mitla mosaics, and such things as ceramic patterns, purple-dyeing from the murex, and the turban-like coiffure of Oaxaca women were reflected in Peru.

South America definitely influenced Oaxaca by introducing the arts of metalworking. Here we arrive at a first-class mystery. There is no trace in Middle America, so rich in precious ores, of the use of metals before about A.D. 900. This is one of the chief arguments against the diffusion theory, since the Old World worked metals very early. One explanation might be that the New World had a religious taboo against metals which was finally dropped. Certainly gold proved to be the root of the evils visited against ancient America by the Aztecs and Spanish.

There is another explanation which at first sounds rather ridiculous: Middle Americans knew about metals but had no interest in developing them. Even when they became consummate artists in metallurgy they had no use for metals except as jewelry, and jade was still preferred because of its magic attributes. One must never underestimate the profound indifference of the Indian to anything that has not been "forever" in his tradition. The basic population, of Bering Strait provenance, arrived and lived quite

Zapotec

happily for centuries without metals. Our hypothetical South
Asiatics, sages and soothsayers, may have had an intellectual
knowledge of metals, but they would be as ignorant as the in-
digenes about how to extract, smelter, and work them. They
were not practical men, and even if they had been, they would
have had difficulty in persuading the Indians to delve in mines—as
the Spanish discovered later.

This metals quirk may turn out to be something like the indifference of Middle America to the wheel. The principle of the
wheel was long thought to be completely unknown in the Americas, and this was one of the favorite arguments against diffusion. But the Middle Americans knew all about the wheel.
They had no draft animals, so wheels were of no use—except to
amuse children. In the Valley of Oaxaca and several Gulf sites
potters made toy animals meant to be pulled around by children,
and these toys ran on four clay wheels. In the Asia-America
exhibit of the Museum of Natural History, Dr. Ekholm was able
to match up these charming little animals with wheeled toys from
China and India.

When Oaxaca finally dropped its religious taboo, or its indifference to metals, its artists performed wonders with gold, silver,
and copper. The whole development was extremely rapid. Suddenly Peru and Ecuador, and soon after them Oaxaca, knew all
about metallurgy; alloys of copper with tin, zinc, silver, iron;
gold-coating by the mercury process; and the lost-wax method
of casting, the most intricate process known. How did all this
mastery of a whole chain of operations come about?

Here the diffusion theory is indispensable. By the Classic era
the Polynesians proper, the late-comers from Java and Sumatra,
were settled all across the Pacific. They were evidently in contact
with South America, since its sweet potato was carried back to the
islands. In return, it seems highly likely that the Polynesians
taught the South Americans metallurgy and also textile techniques
such as batik, both of which they had learned in Indonesia. There

was a veritable renaissance in Peru, especially at Nazca, of the weaving and decorating of cloth.

These textile arts may have flourished, too, in Oaxaca, but the old weavings have vanished. The metals endure, and Zapotec goldsmiths quickly rivaled their brothers in South America and made solid-gold ornaments of such beauty that they were in demand all over Mexico. They also worked with copper in various alloys, which they used for little bells and rings, and axes cold-hammered to make a cutting edge. Money came into use all over Middle America, the Zapotec "ax-money" of thin copper shaped like a giant thin nailhead. Dr. Caso thinks that they used the mercury process for gold-coating copper or silver, deriving the mercury from the cinnabar they used so widely. They even coated clay beads with gold and managed to fool Juan de Grijalva's men with them in 1518. But the Spanish had an infallible instinct for gold and silver, and the amount of Oaxaca art treasures they melted down for the metals does not bear thinking about.

The Maya were never great metalworkers and got gold objects from Costa Rica and copper from Oaxaca. Colombia, Honduras, Ecuador, and Panama had their goldsmiths, but the rich mines of Oaxaca and the skill of the Zapotecs and later the Mixtecs produced the most superb goldwork of the Americas.

At about the time metals arrived in Mexico a mighty shift was taking place in the ancient world. In the south the Maya civilization was disintegrating; in the north turbulence was building up into a storm which would soon sweep the older peoples from the central mesa to their original home in Olmec Land. The barbarian warrior would replace the stately figure of the priest as the prototype of Mexico.

Monte Albán held firm. There was time yet for the reversal of currents from the northward flow which had brought the arts of peace to the central plateau; the tide of war and conquest was not yet flowing southward to Oaxaca. This was the golden moment, the fullness of maturity, and Monte Albán reached its greatest splendor. The Great Plaza and all the mounts flanking it were crowned with white and red temples decorated with murals; kings were buried in tombs as rich as palaces and, like the Egyptians, laid away in treasure rooms of precious offerings. The reign of Cocijo was supreme; his face was repeated on thousand after thousand rich urns, and it no longer had the ardor of a young poet half lost in dream. Cocijo had matured with his people; his face under the towering tocado with its multiple symbols was potent, grave, sometimes withdrawn and enigmatic.

Down the valley at Mitla they were building new temples, and Cocijo in his familiar guise would not be there. Instead, there would be the geometrical abstraction of all he had meant to the Zapotecs, the stone mosaics perfect as ice crystals and almost as cold.

At Monte Albán it was still the golden age, but the Maya were tearing themselves to pieces. They had abandoned their glorious cities and moved into Yucatan, where they built Old Chichén, only to abandon it and fall into a dismal succession of feuds and civil wars. Monte Albán, perhaps because of the impossibility of finding a stable center in Yucatan, kept its closest relations with the Maya city of Kaminal-Juyú, near the modern Guatemala City. During the golden age this was the southern center of the axis running from Teotihuacán to Monte Albán and Guatemala.

It is tragic that the Old Maya and the Teotihuacáns had such short spans. After their migration the Maya lost their supreme touch, leaving to the jungle Copán with its colossal steles, Tikal's intricate carvings in zapote wood, the figurines of Lubaantum, and perhaps saddest of all that most poetic of cities, Palenque.

Teotihuacán was destroyed by the Toltecs about 900, and though they created a brilliant renaissance there, the loss was a bitter one. The early city was a smaller Monte Albán, laid out in plazas with temple pyramids, its walls covered with stucco painted red and adorned with murals. In its stone carvings, its molded figurines and pottery, as in all else, the younger sister followed Monte Albán styles closely.

The greatest spectacle of Classic America must have been the Great Plaza of Monte Albán during festivals connected with the calendar. At the completion of the calendar round every fifty-two years, when the solar year and the magic pije made their union, these ceremonials would have been solemn and brilliant in the extreme. Once in the lifetime of a citizen of Middle America he would experience the moment when all life on earth was suspended and only the will of the supreme gods could bring about a general resurrection.

Those who know something of Oaxaca can imagine, without too much strain, what these festivals were like. Today, when the Plaza de la Danza outside the Church of Soledad is filled with people from all over the state dressed in their gorgeous regional costumes, you look up at Monte Albán and think that these beautiful people really belong there. Certainly they are an incredible apparition in the war-grubbing modern world. They belong in the Great Plaza on the mountain, in a festival drawing thousands of pilgrims from the two Americas who have come to the Sacred Mountain, Danibáan, to pray for a renewal of life on the earth.

One imagines that during the whole night before March 16 the plaza is massed with people in an agony of suspense. Will the sun rise? They do not know. All life has ceased; every pilgrim suffers his personal death, and in token of his sacrifice he draws blood from the veins behind his ears and under his tongue and catches the blood upon a little bundle of grass to offer the gods. On the central altar there are live offerings: turkeys, jaguars, perhaps human sacrifices. In the little observatory the astronomer-priests watch the sky. Will the miracle occur?

At dawn the eastern sierras grow rosy, gold and rose mount the sky, and the great sun leaps the mountain barrier, completing his fifty-two journeys at the precise instant when the sacred year has accomplished seventy-three. Life flows back into the people, who can exult in the kindness of the sky gods who are bringing their children a new cycle of happy and fruitful life.

The music begins, the exquisite reedy voice of the chirimía and the pulse of the tortoise-shell drum beaten with deer antlers—and this music you can hear today. The dancers appear, and it is not hard to imagine how they looked, for surely they are bearing on their heads the blazing disk of the sun, the brilliant guacamayos of Teotitlán del Valle.

Music and dancing; the pandemonium of the ball game, its stadium thronged with shouting spectators; the pilgrim from the pyramid city of Cahokia, Illinois, exchanging wagers with a trader from Xicallanca on the Gulf or a batik dyer from Peru; the great fair with its goods brought from every quarter of Classic America; the masses of flowers and caged birds and festive sweets and pungent chile-flavored chicken or beans wrapped in bland tortillas—no, it is not all lost. Pile the Saturday market in Oaxaca on its Christmas fiesta, move all this delightful noise and friendliness up to the Great Plaza, and you've made a start. For the rest, we must try to imagine what the world was like under the two thousand years of Zapotec peace, when people were so glad to be alive that the one miracle for which they met to pray was not immortality, but simply another half century of being privileged to live under the sun as brothers.

IX

THE SKY DRAGON

The town of Mitla lies prettily at the eastern end of the Valley of Oaxaca, which rises in a series of terraces broken by small hills and cut by streams. Above it is the natural bastion of El Fortín, on whose height very ancient buildings once stood. Thus it is a region of broad horizontal planes, and with great subtlety the Zapotec builders repeated these planes in four groups of temples lying at slightly varying levels on the natural terraces ending the valley.

The Mitla temples are as famous as any buildings in Mexico and have no counterpart anywhere in the world. They were built about a thousand years ago in a region already venerable, and possibly their unique style had been established long before they were built. Since all the buildings on Monte Albán except the observatory and parts of tombs were destroyed, we can only guess what they were like. But in a few places in the valley there are fragments of the extraordinary grecque designs like those at Mitla but much older. And the Mixtec map at the University of Texas has a small drawing of the ancient temple of Tilantongo which looks very much like those at Mitla.

If the squared spiral motifs which decorate the Mitla buildings go back to the very early days, the wonder grows. They have an elegance, an ultra-refinement, which belongs only to a people long sophisticated. Mitla, in fact, looks modern, which is another way of saying that it suggests the classic Greek style which we are still copying. This half-familiar architecture, with its chaste perfection of line, and the meticulous stone mosaics sometimes leave people cold. Mitla does not have the stunning impact of Monte Albán. One should see Mitla many times, in different lights, to appreciate what a pure and lovely scene the ruins offer.

Danibáan, the Sacred Mountain, was built for exalting the gods, but Liobáan, the Zapotec word for "sacred home," was built for the repose of souls. Therefore, its temples and palaces are not raised on pyramids but stand on the ground, as entrances to the underworld where dead souls go to join the ancestors. Subterranean chambers opened, it was thought, upon this vast ancestral cave where after a long journey the dead soul found his home.

Liobáan (spelled also Yoo-paa and several other ways) was not only the Zapotec burial place but also the seat of the high priest. Since this exalted man was the seer who went into sacred trances and pronounced oracles concerning the nation as a whole, it was appropriate that he should live in what was symbolically a cave, and his most solemn rites were performed in an underground room.

This, then, explains why Mitla is so unlike ceremonial cities like Monte Albán or Teotihuacán, which were designed for mass worship in plazas open to the sky. Mitla was a shrine, a holy of holies, a place of mystery and peace, and its buildings express this character.

Of the original four groups of low, flat-roofed palaces enclosing plazas, only the central two are in good repair. The one nearest the village has almost been erased, and the highest group of the four was calmly taken over by the friars, who embedded a church and parish house in its heart, using some of the old walls. Fifty years ago, when Eduard Seler and his wife arrived to study the ruins, they found the court of the old palace had long been the priest's stable, and he had just destroyed a whole section of priceless murals to build a pigsty. A few faded fragments remain today, but this part of the ruins is depressing, for the church is unattractive in itself, and its high vertical lines spoil the original scheme of flat terraces descending to the river.

The two central and adjoining plazas which have been preserved are fortunately the most important, especially the temple at the north of the higher one. Here six huge monolithic columns, unique in Middle America, once supported the roof. These round pillars and the tremendously heavy door lintels are of trachyte from a quarry miles away, and they represent a marvel of engineering skill and patient manpower. But the ultimate in patience achieved the stone mosaics which decorate the walls.

These mosaics appear to be friezes carved to make a continuous abstract design in the surface stone, or else small pieces mortared together on top of the facing. Nothing so simple was worthy to decorate the home of the high priest. There are half-worn places where one can see what was actually done. The Zapotecs cut and polished blocks of trachyte about the size and shape of tapestry bricks. On one end, hardly more than an inch and a half in width, they carved a bit of the general design. Then millions of these blocks were fitted together to a hair, without mortar, and set in a facing of hard stucco painted red.

The mosaics thus represent the most arduous sort of jigsaw puzzle, or "cross-stitch in stone," as somebody put it. The labor and calculation involved have been rewarded in terms of durability alone. Since the designs are an integral part of solid stones, they have worn evenly and well, and they have supported the walls stoutly against earthquakes and the buffets of time.

Though the red stucco has all but vanished, so that the white stones no longer stand out against a contrasting background, the mosaics have the purity of a Bach fugue. They are twenty variations of a theme: the stepped spiral that represents the head of the Sky Serpent, Quetzalcoatl. If one feels these designs in terms of counterpoint, they become the expression of the innermost secrets of Zapotec religion and link up with the observatory on Monte Albán. The mathematical relations between the heavenly bodies, which the astronomers worked out so precisely, were developed into an astrological mysticism which linked them with people and the divination of human fate. Thus the mosaics might be taken as symbols of celestial mechanics.

The brilliant Dominican, Fray Francisco de Burgoa, born in Oaxaca almost a century after the Conquest, found Indians who could still tell him a great deal about Mitla of pre-Spanish days. The high priest, Uija-tao (Great Prophet), lived in the northern palace with its mosaics. He was never seen by the commoners, who would be struck dead if they caught sight of this incarnation of Quetzalcoatl. Kings and other high personages visited him to receive oracles and commands, and they reached his rooms through concealed back passages, so that they themselves were not observed. The high priest sat on a high throne with a cushion of jaguar skin stuffed with down, and kings and notables took lower seats. The three other palaces around the plaza were reserved for these visitors and for lower priests and assistants; all were clean and luxuriously furnished.

The underground chambers were used for rites and burials. Below the high priest's palace was a shrine with images to which he talked when he was going into his sacred trance. There were separate chambers for the burials of high priests, of kings, and of warriors. The bodies of kings were borne from the capital of Teotitlán del Valle, and later from Zaachila, richly dressed and wearing ornaments of gold and precious stones, with a shield in the left hand and a javelin in the right. In the plaza the people gathered to bewail their king and to listen to a recital of his deeds, and then he was buried in the chamber below the royal palace he had used as a visiting suppliant.

The account of the warriors' chamber included some strange details. Not only was it a sort of Arlington for national heroes, but its doors were opened to people who were tired of life and wished to enter the sacred cave to wander until they found the feasting place of their ancestors. They were immured alive in this chamber, Father Burgoa was told. The general conviction was that this room was the entrance to an underground passage that extended more than thirty leagues. During Father Burgoa's time some venturesome priests volunteered to explore this tunnel, and they found themselves in a passage whose roof was supported by pillars. Holding to a rope they uncoiled as they went farther into the mountain, they encountered foul odors and snakes, and a cold wind that blew out their torches. In a panic of superstitious terror they rushed back and "walled up forever this back door of hell."

Though no trace of long underground passages has been found, all over this end of the valley the myths persist of secret tunnels, and in this region of limestone caves and untouched ruins almost anything may be discovered one day.

The high priest passed on his supreme office to his son or nearest male relative. Though vowed to chastity, he was obliged at certain festivals to become drunk and enjoy maidens brought to him. If one of them bore a son, be became the heir to the Uija-tao. This repeated the tragedy of Quetzalcoatl, tricked by his enemies into drunkenness and venery, so that he had to leave his country and destroy himself. Like his prophetic trances, the priest's intoxication was supposed to put him in communication with the gods. The common people were not allowed intoxicants, which had a ritual significance.

Since the Uija-tao was invisible to the public, like sibyls in other countries, the public rites were carried on by lesser priests, "guardians of the gods" and "sacrificers." They were assisted by their pupils, the *pixana*, the younger sons of lords and caciques.

A certain amount of human sacrifice, followed by ritual eating of parts of the victim's body, was practiced in Middle America and many other parts of the world, but among the Zapotecs it was strictly controlled and infrequent. An eclipse of the sun was a terrifying portent which required the sacrifice of dwarfs, who were thought to be created by the sun as hostages, so to speak.

Zapotec

The Zapotecs sacrificed prisoners of war, as was the general custom. When a very important person was buried a few of his slaves were sometimes beheaded and interred with him to serve him on the three years' journey through the underworld. A black dog was often sent along on this ghostly journey, for only a black dog could swim a certain lake encountered on the way and bear his master safely across to join the gods.

But the Zapotec gods did not often demand extreme offerings. The people honored them with clouds of copal incense, with the sacrifice of fowls or small animals, but most often with blood drawn from their own bodies, from the veins behind the ear or under the tongue. The blood was caught on grass or feathers and offered in penitence.

From a safe hiding place Father Burgoa watched some mountain Zapotecs in the 1650s who were still practicing the old rite deep in the woods. A priest stood before an image of the god in its dark clouds of copal. The penitents brought strips of dried corn-husk tied in pairs to the altar and laid them down as they confessed the sins these represented. Then they let their blood fall on the strips, and the priest offered this sacrifice to the god in a long oration, begging him to forgive his sons so that they might be joyful and hold fiestas in his honor.

Then the priest turned to the penitents, admonishing and absolving them. So much of this ritual was like the Catholic office of confession that Father Burgoa was horrified to hear the priest's final words: "Now you can be happy and sin anew."

This was not cynical paganism, but a profound knowledge of the human heart. Of course people sin anew—all of us do—but being happy about it until the moment of contrition is a Zapotec twist. One feels that modern Zapotecs, too, are free from a chronic sense of guilt, either in the puritan sense or in the technical definition of the psychologist.

Probably the magic calendar, the most all-pervasive part of their religion, preserved them from another destructive habit—

worry. At first glance the pije system would seem to be oppressive in its domination of everybody's daily life, and it contained both astrology and totemism, which seem to us heathenish.

Still, it belonged to a culture so creative and rich even in the material sense that its expression was in the great arts. Middle America did not adopt the magic calendar at the point of a sword; everybody seemed to thrive on it; and the Zapotecs, who invented the pije and have never quite relinquished it, are the soundest and happiest people in Mexico today.

The first secret of the magic calendar is that it gave each individual his own place in the beautiful order of the universe. To simplify a very complicated system, the 260 days of the pije had different names, a number combined with an animal or element, and every Zapotec was named for his birthday. Three Lizard or Seven Deer or Six Wind meant a certain day and was the name of people born on that day. Each person was bound to the earth by his totemic animal, and also bound to heaven by the positions of sun, moon, planets, constellations at his birth.

As we have seen, the astronomy on which Zapotec astrology was based had a finer method of measuring time than the European calendar system, and the mathematics of casting horoscopes must have been a prodigious task. There was a special class of mathematical mages who did this work in the old days, but this esoteric art has vanished. Many Chinantec villages still cherish the magic calendar but probably understand little of its intricacies. Therefore, all over Oaxaca those people who still believe that each child has his own personal totem, or *tona*, have to find out what animal it is by other means than the magic calendar. Uusually they sprinkle ashes around the mat where a newborn baby lies, and by morning find, or think they find, the tracks of a bird or animal which has visited its human twin.

The old astrologers, who interpreted the pije as it applied to each Juan and Maria, told the parents of the newborn child what lay in store for it. But there were always magic operations by which people could fend off predicted evils and attract good fortune. These priests watched over each individual from birth, even deciding his marriage by a calculation based on the name-numbers the couple bore. Aside from arithmetic, these priests were expert personal counselors and no doubt had a steadying effect on character and conduct.

At the time Mitla was built there began a shift in Mexico's center of gravity, a slow and gradual waning of Monte Albán's power and a building up of new forces on the central plateau. It was the age of Quetzalcoatl the god and of Quetzalcoatl the culture hero of the Toltecs. Until quite recently the historians could not make out who the Toltecs were, for the legends described them as a race of demi-gods responsible for all the arts and happiness of the old days. Their wondrous city Tollan, the Indians told Father Sahagún, had palaces of jade and of red and white shell, "where the ears of corn and the squashes grew to the size of a man, where cotton grew in the plant in all colors, and the air was filled with birds of precious plumage."

The archaeologists looked in vain for Tollan, but finally they excavated ruins in the modern town of Tula, Hidalgo, and found a fine ceremonial city which had been razed to the ground, with enough stone carvings and fragments of great buildings which had escaped destruction to give the legends some reality. The history of the Toltecs has now been cleared up, and they prove to owe their education in the arts to the Mixtecs and Mazatecs and others of the old Olmec strain.

The Toltecs were an Otomi tribe who came down from the north about A.D. 700 as wild barbarians and were taken in hand by the highly civilized Olmecas, who had been educating immigrants from Mongolia for centuries and who unfortunately did not stop their tutelage with the Toltecs, but later on taught the Aztecs all too well. Meanwhile, the Toltecs intermarried with these older peoples, and at Tula and also at Teotihuacán, which they destroyed and rebuilt, they created a brilliant era which lasted from about 900 to 1168, when Tula was destroyed in a civil war and the Toltec empire fell to pieces.

The Quetzalcoatl of history was a Toltec king who, in the prevailing convention, was an incarnation of the god. This is confusing enough, but the story of the real king, Topiltzin Ce Acatl, has become so encrusted with legend—and a very moving legend—that it is often accepted as applying to the god himself. As we have seen, Topiltzin's father was ruler of the Toltec empire, and his mother, Chimalma, belonged to the Olmecas.

Shorn of its magic elements, the story of Topiltzin describes a wise and benign king who fully accepted the old culture of his mother's people: the magic calendar, the arts, and the newly introduced working of metals. From 925 to 947 he ruled over Tula, creating a golden age, when his people worshiped Quetzalcoatl, the great god of the Olmecas. However, some of the Toltecs still venerated the god of war, Smoking Mirror, who belonged to their barbarian past, and a religious war flared up between them and the Olmecas living in Tula. Finally Topiltzin and with him many Mixtecs and Mazatecs were defeated and fled to Olmec Land, their ancestral home. The Toltec empire lasted another two centuries, and then a great civil war led to the razing of Tula and the mass emigration of the Olmecas from the central plateau where they had lived so long and whose civilization they had created.

It must be the tragedy of this retreat that enlarged the story of Topiltzin Ce Acatl into the myth of the living Quetzalcoatl who, shamed and defeated by his eternal enemy, the god of war, was forced to leave his great empire and return to the land of his mother's people to destroy himself. The bitter truth of history is expressed in this myth, for the Olmecas who were forced to return to Oaxaca and Puebla never regained the glories of their long centuries on the central mesa.

The culture hero Quetzalcoatl, before he started his retreat, burned his rich palaces in Tula, buried his treasure in secret mountain spots, and sent his precious quetzal birds to safety far away. He crossed the snows of the great volcanoes, where his dwarf, hunchback servants perished of the cold; farther along he met sorcerers to whom he confided the secrets of all the arts, and everywhere on his journey south he performed wonders, setting up many new cities and lingering for a time in the city of Cholula.

Finally he reached the Gulf coast, where he mounted a raft of intertwined snakes and sailed for the ancestral home of his mother, Tlillan-Tlapallan (the poetic word for the coastal part of Olmec Land), where he sacrificed himself. His ashes mounted to the sky as birds, and his heart became the morning star, Venus.

The fact that soon after the retreat and death of the historical Topiltzin-Quetzalcoatl this legend was connected with the young Mixtec king Ocañaña proves that at base it was a migration legend. His people probably belonged to Mixtecs in the first migration from Tula which took place twenty-five years before Ocañaña's birth. The legend kept enlarging after the fall of the Toltec empire in 1168, when the retreating Mixtecs and other Olmecas did linger in Cholula and other cities on their slow retreat back to Olmec Land.

The Quetzalcoatl cult was in reality a very deep one which summed up and restated all the elements basic to Indian religion from the earliest days: the earth jaguar; the god Xaquia of Teotitlán del Valle, the Bird of Heaven whose plumage was the rays of the sun; Cocijo, lord of wind, rain, lightning; Venus, star of dawn and herald of the sun. As Eduard Seler pointed out, it is the Zapotec language which spells out the history of these transformations in words that telescope centuries of development. The Zapotecs had a supreme, abstract god, Pije-Tao, the god without end and without beginning, the essence of creation. *Pij* means wind, breath, soul, and *tao* means great, powerful. If translated into the Nahuat language of the central plateau, Pije-Tao would mean Quetzalcoatl, the wind god who after death became the lord of the dawn. Thus there was a profound unity in Middle

American religion, and from age to age this unity was symbolized in different gods, of whom Quetzalcoatl was the last and greatest.

The Zapotecs and Maya worshiped another blended god called Heart of the Land in Oaxaca, and Votan by the Maya. On the mysterious Bazan Stone of Monte Albán with its tantalizing glyphs this god is a jaguar linking heaven and earth. In general he symbolized the inner forces of the earth, of night and darkness and the ancestral cave from which oracles came to guide the people.

Perhaps the underground temple of Mitla was one of these shrines. Another was on a small wild island in the lagoon of San Dionisio near Tehuantepec. Here, Father Burgoa relates, the Heart of the Land image was kept in a deep cave, where it gave oracles to a priest. The Mixtecs worshiped Heart of the Land in the form of a great piece of transparant jadeite engraved with a serpent and a bird. This precious symbol was kept in the ceremonial center of Achiutla-Tilantongo, on the top of the mountain. Many pilgrims climbed the steep mountain to the grotto, where a priest gave oracles. Those unable to make the climb, especially women, visited a secondary shrine where the Dominican fortress-convent of Yanhuitlan now stands, directly on the Highway.

When the Spanish came, Fray Benito Fernandez, the great destroyer of Mixtec codices and jewels, seized the precious image of Tilantongo. He thought it was an emerald, and one of the Spanish offered thousands of ducats for it. But he felt that it must be destroyed as a pagan idol, and though he wept at its beauty and value, he ground it to powder, stirred the powder in water, and trod it underfoot.

The Mixtecs had a curious and repulsive god, Xipe Totec, who enjoyed a great vogue all over Middle America. Recently images of Xipe have been found in six Texas sites and in Arkansas near the Oklahoma border, and the cult radiated down into Central America. Xipe was at once lord of spring and patron of jewelers, two aspects with an inner connection.

Since spring brings a fresh coat of green to the earth, Xipe's horrible rite consisted of a priest killing and flaying a human sacrifice and then arraying himself in the flayed skin. By the time the cult was at its height the Mixtecs had learned the secrets of metal coating, putting a fresh skin of gold on copper or cheaper metals. Thus Xipe became god of the goldsmiths, and one of the treasures of Tomb Seven was a solid-gold mask of Xipe Totec wearing the skin of a victim. As Dr. Caso said, he is "the symbol of life concealed by death; life will spring anew from the earth because it has been fed by the flesh and blood of men."

There is a dangerous fallacy in the idea symbolized by Xipe Totec. He was the forerunner of gods who demanded the flesh and blood of thousands on thousands of victims—not to renew life on the earth, but to keep themselves and their people strong—the insatiable gods of the Aztecs.

X

DAYS OF CONFLICT

Just when does a god die? Cocijo was old, nearly two thousand years old, and his vitality was spent. The artists still turned out their Cocijo urns dutifully, mechanically, often making them in molds to supply a wide market. But the god's face was empty; the fluid, living lines had frozen. The artists first of all knew that Cocijo was dead.

The world of which Monte Albán had been the center was dissolving, running off into new channels. Because of pressures from the central plateau and from the Mixtecs, the Zapotecs were forced to expand in order to protect their central valleys. They had to conquer the isthmus in order to hold their trade route to Central America. That meant fighting the Zoque and Huave and driving most of them from the main artery of trade and communications. By 1360 the Zapotecs had uneasy control of the isthmus.

The Mixtecs were pressing toward Monte Albán from the west, and to protect it the Zapotecs reinforced the southern valley and about 1390 moved their capital from Teotitlán del Valle to Zaachila-Yoo, "Home of Cloud Alligator." Here a line of five kings ruled until the coming of the Spanish, and the first three were called Zaachila, Sky Dragon, after the prevailing fashion of making all great leaders incarnations of Quetzalcoatl. When they abandoned their old capital the Zapotecs lost their luck; their peace was ended.

Establishing the capital south of Monte Albán meant that

Zapotec

Zaachila I had to fight the savage Chontal living on the Pacific slope and the more numerous Mixe, who blocked the important trade route along the isthmus. In those days the Mixe were formidable warriors who fought with long flint-tipped lances, and the Zapotecs were still fighting them sporadically when the Spanish arrived.

The great folk hero of the Mixe was Condoy, a real personage about whom a legend has grown. He had no parents but sprang from a great mountain cave, and from him the Mixe race descended. He led the war with the Zapotecs, and when his army was finally surrounded on the bleak heights of Zempoaltepec he set the mountain on fire. Under cover of the smoke he led his army into the great cave where he was born, taking all his people and treasure. He closed the entrance with a huge rock and, as in all such stories, he led the Mixe down a long tunnel to safer lands.

Zaachila II, son of the first known Zapotec king, still fought the Mixe, but his heir, Zaachila III, got into graver troubles. The Mixtecs, forced into unity in order to assault the Zapotecs, made an alliance between their warring kingdoms of Tilantongo and Tututepec which lasted until the Conquest. Moving east, their combined armies invaded the outskirts of Monte Albán at Cuilápam, which they captured. (The town is still Mixtec, on bad terms with neighboring Zapotecs.) About 1420 they climbed Monte Albán, by then abandoned by the Zapotecs, and destroyed its temples and palaces. But they created a great renaissance on the mountain, and the treasures found in Tomb Seven were probably made there or not far away.

With the fall of Monte Albán, the Zapotecs entered a desperate and bitter period in which the god of war and his sons, the Aztecs, prepared Mexico for its ridiculously easy conquest by the Spanish.

It is impossible to follow the bare outline of the struggle between the Oaxaca peoples and the Aztecs without realizing what a pernicious romance William Prescott was tricked into writing—

what one historian calls "Prescott's literary conquest of Mexico." He was tricked in the first place by believing corrupt and incomplete records by the early Spanish, and in the second place by being carried away by his own story—a very pretty, pathetic story, to be sure, but one that belongs on the fiction shelves. In broad terms, his account of the Aztecs is sheer romancing.

The facts are not pretty, but they are clear. We do not know the origin of the Olmec peoples, but the Aztec provenance is definite. The Uto-Aztecan people were Mongoloids from Northeast Asia, part of the great stream of immigrants who crossed Bering Strait and spread down through the Americas. The Uto-Aztecans were cultural sponges, with a tremendous talent for absorbing the local culture of whatever spot they invaded. This race, aggressive and energetic, fanned out into a great variety of tribes: Shoshone, Snake, Ute, Hopi, Pueblo, Yaqui, Huichol, and a score of others.

In the twelfth century the primitive folk who were to become Aztecs arrived in the Valley of Mexico and promptly acquired a burning inferiority complex, which is often followed by an insane drive to dominate the people it knows are superior. One branch of the new arrivals founded Tenochtitlán (now Mexico City) in 1324 and settled on the heights overlooking what was then a large shallow lake.

By this time the great Toltec empire had dissolved, and the Valley of Mexico was in a period of chaos in which various cities and their gods fought for supremacy. The Aztecs enraged their more civilized neighbors by raiding towns and stealing wives, and several towns united to attack them. Many of them were captured and enslaved, but there were always enough unconquered Aztecs in the valley to keep it in turmoil. Meanwhile, they were rapidly absorbing the older culture brought to the area by the Mixtecs and their allies, whose arts were well established in certain towns on the lake, notably Texcoco. An early picture manuscript of about 1300 shows the Mixteca-Puebla men arriving in Texcoco wearing garments of fine woven cloth, while the Texcocans were draped in animal skins. The high culture from the south spread quickly, and the Aztecs, with their aptitude for imitation, soaked up the new ideas. An era of fine craftsmanship and lively trade developed in the valley.

The greatest of the Texcoco kings, Nezahualcoytl (1418–72), was statesman, poet, astronomer, and patron of the arts. For the sake of peace he formed an alliance with the Aztecs under their chief, Itzcoatl, which meant a great step forward for them. They were no longer feudal tributaries of the older towns, but an independent people. Itzcoatl laid out the great city of Tenochtitlán, a Mexican Venice formed of islands of rubble threaded by canals and causeways leading to the mainland. He proceeded to conquer all the valley tribes not subject to Texcoco and went as far as he dared against the great Nezahualcoyotl.

In 1440 he was succeeded by the first Moctezuma, who laid the foundations of the greatest Indian empire of history, a realm which soon stretched down into Central America and which grew with the speed and the terrible vigor of a plague. It is said that this Moctezuma killed a Mixtec king and then married his daughter; certainly it was he who began the wars of conquest against the Mixtecs and Zapotecs.

He coveted the rich Oaxaca valleys for themselves and because they led to Chiapas and Guatemala. His rich merchants, the *pochteca,* were invaluable as scouts and spies, bringing back information about the great realm he was determined to make his own. Gradually his armies moved down the trade routes and brought back tribute from conquered Oaxaca towns—cochineal dye, fine mantles, cacao, gold and jade and precious feathers, and more and more human hearts to burn to keep the bloodthirsty Aztec gods appeased.

Nothing shows more clearly the insecurity which underlay the Aztec drive for conquest than the size of their pantheon. They existed in a state of superstitious fear that mounted into hysteria;

one might call their empire the product of a psychosis. They believed that in capturing a people they captured its gods; in their growing obsession they sent their armies all through Middle America to bring back new deities and fresh droves of prisoners to sacrifice. Finally they had no less than two thousand deities in their pantheon, all of them bloodthirsty and demanding an ever-increasing holocaust of human hearts smoking before the altars. The most insatiable of all their gods was the war lord Huitzilopochtli, to whom countless thousands of Oaxacans were to be sacrificed.

The Aztec strategy was to subdue the Mixteca and then move against the Zapotecs. They needed no pretext for invasion, but early in their spying and scouting period one developed. There were altogether too many Aztec merchants on the main trade road leading down from Cholula, and well inside Zapotec territory a band of them was captured and killed. The Aztecs sent a punitive expedition which stormed the town where this had occurred and took every inhabitant up to Tenochtitlán to be sacrificed. A colony of Aztecs was established on the site, and soon another garrison was established at Tlaxiaco, near Tilantongo.

The Mixtecs fought furiously to defend the Upper Mixteca, often getting help from their allies in Puebla. But Moctezuma I made great inroads in the western valley and finally conquered the southern capital of Tututepec, close to the Pacific. Its inhabitants took refuge in Cuilápam, below Monte Albán.

The next two Aztec kings continued the campaign, fighting their way down the eastward road as far as Tehuantepec, which the Aztecs captured and held for eight years. During this period the religious hysteria in Tenochtitlán was feverish, and the Aztecs constructed a huge temple to the war god Huitzilopochtli and made for it the Stone of Sacrifice, a tremendous stone vessel for the burning of human hearts. The famous Calendar Stone was carved, that twenty-ton symbol of "Mexican civilization," the final travesty of Indian Time.

Zapotec

In the whole line of Aztec monarchs there is only one attractive personality—Cuauhetémoc—and his brief day came after the Spanish Conquest. Meanwhile, the Oaxaca people suffered the depredations of Ahuizotl (1864–1508), a monster of lust and cruelty. He completed the temple to the war god, and at its dedication offered a multitude of victims. His army raided northern Oaxaca and brought back twenty thousand prisoners, every one of whom was sacrificed at the gory ceremonial. The Oaxacans were placed in a double row that stretched endlessly down the steps of the pyramid, and Ahuizotl and his ally, the king of Texcoco, themselves began the horrid rite of snatching out the pulsing hearts of the victims to be burned on the Stone of Sacrifice. Then, in order of rank, lesser notables followed until the business was done.

Ahuizotl carried his conquests into Vera Cruz and down into Guatemala. In spite of stiff resistance from the Mixtec allies in Puebla, he led his armies down to Tehuantepec, which had been recaptured by the Zapotecs. Determined to clear the route to Central America, he made a great campaign, mobilizing a huge army provided with new weapons. In preparation for the thrust, the Aztec women were commanded to fast and the priests to draw sacrificial blood from their own bodies. Finally Zapotecs and Aztecs faced each other across the plains of Tehuantepec, the warriors with faces painted, wearing armor of quilted cotton, carrying bows and arrows and lances edged with flint and obsidian.

Ahuizotl himself commanded the Aztecs, and before the fighting began he made his chiefs swear to die fighting for him. Then he beat a drum as a signal to advance, and they rushed into battle, yelling and clashing their shields. The Zapotecs shouted that the Aztecs would all be killed and never see their homes again. But the Aztecs were victorious, and rather than be wiped out the Zapotecs gave them fortunes in gold, jade, and precious feathers.

Again many thousands of prisoners were marched back to Te-nochtitlán to sate the war god.

By about 1494 the Aztec king had the whole Valley of Oaxaca under his thumb, even the holy city of Mitla. He established a garrison under the shadow of Monte Albán which was to become the City of Oaxaca. There he settled six hundred Aztec families and exacted from the valley a yearly tribute of maize, beans, fine weavings, gold, and cochineal.

The most romantic of the Zapotec kings, Cosijoeza, was then on the precarious throne of Zaachila, which was soon conquered by the Aztecs, but where he probably continued to live. At the moment the Aztecs were not attempting to rule the Oaxaca peoples, merely bleed them to death.

Cosijoeza, in the course of his life, was to conclude unhappy alliances with all his enemies—the Mixtecs, the Aztecs, and finally the Spanish. This does not necessarily mean that he was a weak character; his situation was desperate, and appeasement seemed the only course possible. He began by making an alliance with the Mixtecs to throw the Aztecs out of Oaxaca. The allies raised a huge army of liberation, the Mixtecs contributing twenty-four units to fight under Cosijoeza's command.

Since the Aztecs were intent on conquering all Middle America, they had the habit of leaving rather weak garrisons in captured territory while they moved on to fresh conquests. The combined hosts of Oaxaca thus had no great difficulty in clearing the way to Tehuantepec. There they had a hard fight to expel the Aztec soldiers and their vassals, the Huave, but when this was done they made haste to fortify the town, for they knew that Ahuizotl would soon be upon them. They built an extraordinary fortress on the mountain of Giengola outside Tehuantepec, and much of the fortification is still intact today.

First they surrounded the whole mountain with a stone wall

ten feet high and six feet thick. This was the first line of defense, and at regular intervals they placed piles of huge stones from the river to be used as ammunition. Within this wall and higher up the mountain were two more concentric rings of stout stone. Then at the top of Giengola they built a complete city with pyramids, temples, and palaces, and even a ball court. Their lookouts had perfect command of the flats around Tehuantepec. The allies furnished this city with enough food, water, poisoned arrows, spears, and other weapons to stand a year's siege, and even had a pool dug as a nursery for live fish from the river.

The Zapotecs must have been acknowledged as the stronger partner in the alliance, for when scouts brought word of the Aztec approach, King Cosijoeza posted twenty thousand seasoned Mixtecs at the lower walls and took his own Zapotecs up to the fortress. The Aztec armies arrived tired from their long march, and the Mixtecs took a heavy toll at the first encounter. The survivors determined to lay siege to the fortified city and starve out the Zapotecs. Seven months later the Zapotecs were still safe and well fed; according to the Spanish chroniclers, they salted and ate the flesh of Aztecs captured in night forays down the mountain. Despite reinforcements from home, the Aztecs finally gave up the siege.

Ahuizotl's path to Guatemala was thus blocked, and his armies were sick and demoralized. He offered peace to Cosijoeza, and the chroniclers have it that as a great inducement to a truce he offered the Zapotec king his beautiful daughter, Princess Pelaxilla (Cotton Flake), in marriage. But as they still tell the story in Zaachila, the marriage came about in a different fashion.

King Cosijoeza, his people will tell you, was endowed with magic powers and could travel anywhere he pleased on a cloud. (After all, he was the incarnation of Cloud Alligator, or Quetzalcoatl.) One day he left his cave palace in Zaachila and soared to the Aztec kingdom of Mexico. He saw a lovely girl

bathing in a lagoon and fell in love with her. He proposed marriage, and she promptly accepted. Then she said, "Bathe me!" She
put scented soap on a cloth and put this cloth in a red gourd,
and the young king bathed her, and then she him, and they kissed
like any two young lovers in a sunny lagoon.

Though he was at war with the Aztecs, Cosijoeza told his
white-skinned Cotton Flake that he would send his equerry, Alari,
to Ahuizotl to ask her hand in marriage. She warned the young
king that she was one of three sisters who were so much alike that
Alari must be sure to identify her by the mole on her arm. They
parted; the Zapotec king mounted his cloud and went back to
Zaachila. There he dispatched Alari on his mission.

In Mexico, Alari identified the right princess by her mole, and
she told her father that she wanted to marry Cosijoeza. He was
angry but finally gave his consent. Alari sped back to his king,
and Cosijoeza at once prepared an elaborate entourage, well
guarded, to bring the bride down to Zaachila, sending his own
sedan chair for her. After a fifteen-day fiesta in Tenochtitlán the
bride took leave of her family and was carried all the way to
Zaachila in the chair. The bearers, it is said, fought each other for
the privilege of carrying so lovely a creature.

Runners brought Cosijoeza word that the bridal party was
approaching, and he marshaled all the prettiest girls of his kingdom, each with a bowl and painted calabash such as dancers carry,
and they lined up on either side of the road. As the royal litter
approached, the four most beautiful girls went to meet the princess, dancing before her as the others played their dance rattles.
Cosijoeza came forward to greet his bride and took her into his
palace. Two weeks later there was a fandango that lasted for
eight days. All the girls took part in the celebration; all the people
carried flowers in red gourds, not forgetting to give the bride
the dark violet *flor de borracho,* the herb famous for curing hang-
overs (and still given to country brides to administer to their hus-
bands). The king and queen blessed the people three times, ab-

solved them from their sins, and each celebrant gave the bride a rare feather. Cosijoeza bid his people to dance and enjoy themselves, to guard well their tongues, and to remember that the land belonged to them.

Whether the wedding took place in Zaachila or in Tehuantepec, where Cosijoeza lived much of the time, the legend goes on into sober history. It was a true love match, and Cotton Flake surrendered all Aztec loyalties after the birth of the crown prince Cosijopi and the princess Donaji. Her father, however, had planted her in Oaxaca to act as his spy and ally, and about 1502 confided his plan to reconquer Oaxaca. He determined to send a great force into the Zapotec kingdom on the pretext that they were on their way to replenish the weakened Aztec garrisons in Guatemala and Nicaragua. Once inside Oaxaca, they would set fire to the Zapotec strongholds and murder Cosijoeza.

Cotton Flake immediately warned her husband of this plot, and when the Aztec armies arrived they were graciously given permission to pass through Zapotec territory on their way south— and were escorted to the southern exit by a tremendous force of armed Zapotecs. Soon after this fiasco Ahuizotl died and was succeeded by Moctezuma II, the ill-fated king the Conquistadores were to defeat.

The royal Zapotec pair enjoyed a fairly serene life, bringing up their children in Tehuantepec. But Prince Cosijopi, "Wind of Lightning," had been born under the direst auspices of storms and distressed skies, and the Zapotec high priests, casting his horoscope, could see nothing but disaster for him and his kingdom. He began his career as king of Tehuantepec while his father went back to Zaachila to cope with troubles in the central valleys.

The old king continued the Aztec truce which gave him control of the isthmus and the Valley of Oaxaca. But he handled his other allies the Mixtecs badly, trying to drive them out of the valleys and giving them only a small foothold in the isthmus. The Mixtecs now turned on the Zapotecs, and there was sporadic fighting until the Spanish arrived. To the old king the news from the north seemed a promise of deliverance.

Wonderful white strangers wearing metal armor and riding animals never before seen had come out of the eastern sea and entered the Aztec capital, in friendly guise at first. But Moctezuma was alarmed and visited the oracle of Heart of the Land at Tilantongo to learn what this invasion portended. The high priest went into his sacred trance and with the voice of the god announced that the Aztecs would not be able to withstand the Spanish. With dreadful speed the prophecy was fulfilled; in three months' fighting the Spanish reduced the Aztec capital and were holding Moctezuma a prisoner.

Whether or not Cosijoeza remembered the old prophecies made by the astronomer-priests all over Middle America that one day white strangers would come to the land as lords and fathers, he had no trouble making his decision. Plainly the strangers had arrived to rid the land of the Aztecs and were to be welcomed as god-sent. All over Mexico the peoples who had suffered outrage from the Aztecs came to the same conclusion, and the tiny forces of Cortés were reinforced by hosts of Indian allies.

At once Cosijoeza sent an embassy to Cortés bearing a rich treasure from valleys and isthmus, offering the allegiance of himself and his son to the King of Spain. Cortés sent a force to take over Oaxaca for Spain and to subdue the Mixtecs, who were furiously up in arms. The Conquistadores forced them to make peace with the Zapotecs, giving each race the lands they then held.

Perhaps as a result of this truce Cosijoeza's daughter, Princess Donaji, married the Mixtec prince of Tilantongo, and the young pair were baptized and christened by the padres as Doña Juana Cortés and Diego de Aguilar. But Donaji was like her mother, Cotton Flake, a loyal Zapotec. Later, when the Mixtecs allied with the Spanish against her people, she warned the Zapotecs of the impending campaign against them. At the time she was being held as a hostage in the Mixtec stronghold of Cuilápam, and when the Mixtecs learned that she had warned her people they murdered her. She is now buried in the old Dominican chapel of Cuilápam, the heroine of all Mexican school children.

Meanwhile, the Oaxaca peoples had discovered how cruelly they had been duped by the Spanish, and war raged all over the land. The serranos, especially, put up such a resistance that Captain Briones, leader of the first expedition to subdue Oaxaca, told his commander that he would rather have fought cannons and Turks and Moors than these Zapotecs. Expedition after expedition retreated, carrying off a fabulous treasure in gold and jewels, and years after the Spanish thought they had Oaxaca "pacified" a guerrilla war would break out in some unexpected spot.

The old Zapotec king died as the battle still raged, and he died knowing that his hope of getting the Spanish to put down the Mixtecs had resulted only in the betrayal of his land and the end of peace. In 1522 the viciously cruel Pedro de Alvarado, whose own soldiers so hated him that they tried to kill him, arrived with a large army to mow down the Mixtecs. They tried to buy him off with gold; he accepted the bribe and went on fighting for more gold. He attacked the towns of the fierce primitive Chontal near the Pacific, and they gave him a head injury and nearly routed his army. Finally he got the Pacific region under his control, butchering the Chontal and Mixtec warriors or taking them as prisoners to be branded like cattle and sold into slavery.

Down in Tehuantepec the young king Cosijopi, paralyzed by his belief in the dire fate predicted by the astrologers at his birth, submitted tamely to Alvarado. He loaded himself with humiliation by being baptized as Don Juan Cortés Cosijopi de Moctezuma and even adopted Spanish clothes. He administered Tehuantepec for the Spanish, who kept reducing his income until he was almost beggared.

In his misery Cosijopi turned to the old gods and spirited in six Zapotec priests, refugees from Mitla. It is said that for some years he managed to keep them hidden in his "palace," where at midnight they performed the rituals of the ancient faith. So far the Spanish had not discovered the powerful Heart of the Land shrine on the desolate island off the lagoons, where faithful Zapotecs still resorted to make their sacrifices and consult the oracle. Cosijopi, too, made his secret pilgrimage, but the high priests seem always to have been gifted with prescience (or perhaps hard sense), and they told him his case was hopeless; he could not withstand the Spanish.

One night Spanish spies discovered the six priests at their midnight rites in Cosijopi's house, sacrificing turkeys to the old gods. Vicar Fray Bernardo de Santa Maria, head of the Church in Tehuantepec, arrested priests and king. He set up a church tribunal to try the pagans, but Cosijopi remembered his royal blood and insisted that only the highest court in the land, the *Real Audencia* in Mexico City, could deal with a king. For a year he spent his strength and what little fortune remained to him in senseless litigation with the Spanish authorities. They sentenced him to lose all his rights and property. He started back for home, and as his feet touched the soil of Oaxaca he was overwhelmed with the tragedy that had ruined his beloved land as well as himself, and died of a cerebral hemorrhage. The six priests went through the horrors of an auto-da-fé and were executed by Spanish carrying the black candles and whips of the Inquisition.

Fray Bernardo learned of the island shrine and went to the cave where the miraculous idol of Heart of the Land had been kept. Some loyal Zapotec had carried the god himself to safety, but the shrine was intact. It was a large square chamber carefully swept, with altars along the sides bearing incense vessels, costly offerings of gold and tropic feathers, sprinkled with freshly drawn blood of petitioners. All but the gold objects were destroyed.

The god had his revenge after all, for Fray Bernardo brooded over the tragedy of the last Zapotec king and the high priests of Mitla. He became convinced that he had done wrong, and died

217

literally of remorse. Others of the Dominican friars who early dominated Oaxaca, building scores of magnificent churches and trying to instruct the people in the new faith, had this same sense of wrongdoing and were filled with pity for the people.

But many of the churchmen were devoured by zeal and sometimes greed, plundering and enslaving the people to build their rich churches, destroying codices and land records, melting down ritual objects of gold and silver, forbidding every evidence of pagan days, even the singing and dancing of a people who had rejoiced in their gods. The *encomenderos*, Spanish nobles who were granted towns and provinces for their private plunder, drove the Indians into the mines and worked them to death on the lands. Cortés chose out of all Mexico the central valleys of Oaxaca as his marquisate and took the title of Marqués del Valle.

Perhaps those thousands of Indians who fled to the remotest parts of the mountains chose well. The Oaxaca people possessed immense vitality, but it is possible to kill a gently bred race quickly. In one generation the reports sent to the King of Spain showed an almost incredible slaughter of the population—by plagues introduced from Europe, by overwork, but mostly by sorrow. Almost every old town was reduced to a fourth of its former size, and others were mere skeletons. Tehuantepec had gone down from twenty thousand people to twelve hundred, and many other famous towns were all but wiped out. The people were drinking, which they had never done before—but they had never been unhappy before.

Four centuries of turmoil, oppression, revolution, religious troubles would, one might think, complete the picture of ruin. But the roots of the ancient world are very deep, and from them have sprung today's Oaxaqueños, who have remembered how to be happy and who cherish their chosen way and their liberty more jealously than any people in Mexico.

It is strange to go today to the hillock above Zaachila where the last five Zapotec kings lived in what must have been a modest state. Below this little eminence are green-and-gold fields bordered with trees, and the dense orchards planted by the Dominicans, with here and there a muffled pyramid. On the hillock there are the foundations of old buildings and the soil is thick with pot-sherds. But only the obscene buzzards come up here to devour pilfered chickens, and occasionally children build a picnic fire on the spot where Cosijoeza welcomed his fair-skinned bride.

When I asked the schoolmaster why the site of the last royal house of the Zapotecs had never been excavated, he said, "Because Zaachila does not want it done."

"But don't you want to see what is buried on the hill?"

He shook his head with a sad little smile. "No, we'd rather leave it as it is."

PART THREE

XI

BENITO JUÁREZ: MEASURE OF A FAITH

The people of Oaxaca, having endured three centuries of alien wastage and oppression, finally produced a man whose courage bridged the gulf between the ancient Indian world and a modern republic of mixed peoples called Mexico. Because of Juárez we can telescope the whole Colonial period into a phrase: this was disaster, but it passed. The classic Indian world was savagely destroyed, but the Indians themselves survived to take their place in the society of nations. Because of Juárez, Mexico's struggle for liberation and reform was enlarged until it became part of the unending, painful progress of mankind toward its own best goals.

This was his faith: that mankind may set itself the highest goals and in time achieve them. Juárez, who started as a village Zapotec, became a Mexican and finally one of those figures that belong to no one nation or period. Because he contained the unfulfilled, Juárez is indestructible. He is timeless and intact because, like Lincoln, to whom he is most often compared, he was so profoundly a man of the people. Both men had to bring their nation through its critical hour, and both drew their strength from an inexhaustible source. Only humanity never gives up its faith in itself, and they were able to tap that reservoir.

In the Sierra de Juárez, in Guelatao where he was born on March 21, 1806, in Ixtlán where he was baptized the next day, Benito is everywhere; the potential is not diminished. The boy is romping out of school now, and it bears the name of the Benito who wept in vain for a school. When he gets older, this serrano will sit with the other town councilmen and debate how liberty and progress can be won for his village. The struggle is endless, and Benito himself has not changed.

He is a compact, sturdy figure, drawn in the few strong lines that make the eternal pureblood Zapotec—high cheekbones, deep, rather long eyes, a wide mouth with a quirk of humor but which expresses more often dignity and resolution. A lock of straight black hair falls over his round, full forehead. Benito Juárez is so perfectly the serrano that he is forever melting into his background of mountains and forest streams. He is anonymous, often invisible.

Two of the favorite stories about Juárez concern his Indian trick of melting back into the race. Actually, it was the Zapotec gift for never being out of place, for when he entered public life he was always amazing foreign observers by his correct and formal dress, his sober manners, his dignity. They realized that "the Zapotec" was not an Indian who somehow managed to look the great gentleman; he *was* a great gentleman. In the same way he could be all Indian.

Once he enlisted in the guerrilla forces fighting for the liberation of Mexico and served as a private for a week before his commander discovered that he was the former governor of Oaxaca. And when in Vera Cruz he came up to the roof of his new boardinghouse asking for water, his landlady, taking him for a *mozo*, barked, "Get it yourself," which he did without a word. By dinnertime she discovered she had been giving orders to the President-in-exile, and fled, crossing herself in terror. These incidents were cherished by his friends, but Juárez found no bizarre humor in them. If the President looked like a mozo and "the Zapotec" looked like a cultivated statesman, it was all one to him. As his biographer[1] put it, Benito Juárez always knew who he was, and in time the world knew.

[1]Ralph Roeder, *Juárez and His Mexico*, 1947.

Benito Juárez: Measure of a Faith

When the twelve-year-old Benito ran away to Oaxaca he was following a well-beaten path. The only way for young serranos to get an education was to go to the city as domestic servants, and at that time almost all the household staffs in Oaxaca were from the Ixtlán neighborhood. He soon became the chore boy and godson of Don Antonio Salanueva, a bookbinder and lay brother of the Third Order of St. Francis, who hoped to develop his lively charge into a great churchman. Benito entered the only real school the city offered, the seminary for the training of priests.

Just a month before, in September 1821, Mexico had won its spurious freedom from the long rule of Spain. Independence ended a decade of struggle by its heroes, Hidalgo and Morelos, without realizing their aims. Revolution had diminished to a series of deals which created the Mexican Empire, which was soon replaced by a republic of sorts, and so for another half century the process continued through two regencies, two empires, several dictatorships, and seventy-four changes of government. Benito Juárez, who was to give the only meaning to this turmoil, began his education in the wrong place, for the seminary students, as the "Marmalade Battalion" in exquisite purple uniforms, had fought in vain to keep Morelos from capturing the city.

Juárez had no desire to take holy orders, and when the liberal Institute of Arts and Sciences was founded he gladly transferred to it and studied law. In these formative years his timing was slow. He became a lawyer in his late twenties, with a large practice because he took cases only for the poor. In his late thirties he married Margarita Mazza, whose family were of Italian origin and solidly established in the city. In Margarita and their children Juárez centered his happiness and whatever personal ambitions he possessed. It was an ideal marriage.

In 1847 he was elected governor of Oaxaca and gave his state an administration which has remained a model. Soon after his election his neighbors, the serranos, arrived with ceremonial gifts of fowls and corn, in the old Zapotec fashion. Their spokesman said, "You know what we need and will give it to us." They all spread their blankets in the governor's mansion that night and returned to the sierra with a peso apiece as a token of what Juárez wanted to do for them and all the people. He built schools, he subsidized the Institute and created two branches in the back country, he fostered the education of women. Knowing that poverty was the base of all troubles, he tried to lift the level of life in Oaxaca, introducing better farming methods, creating public works, reviving industries. He found the state bankrupt and left it solvent.

Mexico was suffering the shock of losing the war with the United States, and with it Texas, California, Arizona, and New Mexico. It suffered even more the japeries of "His Most Serene Highness" Antonio López de Santa Anna, who nine times made himself dictator of the country. Tired of being bounced out of his sinecure, he decided to eliminate potential rivals. He exiled two liberals, the social reformer, Melchor Ocampo, and Benito Juárez. Juárez was put on a packet bound for England, but he got off at Havana and joined his fellow exile in New Orleans.

Here a group of political émigrés were plotting the downfall of Santa Anna. They lived in a mean boardinghouse and kept themselves alive with odd jobs. Juárez worked in a cigar factory or a printing shop, kept up his study of constitutional law, and learned much from Ocampo, who had lived abroad and absorbed the revolutionary ferment of the times. On the whole, the two years of companionship with this group of liberal leaders were valuable training in the arts of politics and of exile; Juárez was to need both.

Meanwhile, the liberals in Mexico were preparing a coup d'état, and in 1855 Juárez slipped across the border and joined them. The liberals captured the country, and Santa Anna was exiled to Havana, his fine feathers clipped forever. Juárez became Minister of Justice and Public Education in the new liberal cabinet and at once published his famous "Ley Juárez," which abolished the legal immunities of the clergy and the army and made the law apply equally to everybody. But the time was not ripe for genuine reform, and his colleagues were already making innumerable compromises. Juárez could always be governor of Oaxaca, so he went home to pick up his model administration again.

He could feel a storm building up, a reaction against the liberal victory, the Ley Juárez, and the new constitution modeled on that of the United States, including its faults. In this coming storm the states must hold firm, and he put his own house in order. Then he returned to the capital and its twilight reforms. He was given two cabinet posts, the tactical one as President of the Supreme Court, obliged by law to become Chief Executive in an emergency.

The reaction very soon forced out the liberal President, and Juárez became his legal successor. But the conservatives had their own puppet President and managed to get physical possession of the capital. Mexico was plunged into civil war. There was nothing for Juárez and his cabinet to do but move the government elsewhere.

From 1857 to 1860, while civil war raged through the country, the duly elected liberal government remained in Vera Cruz. The usurping conservatives had the army, most of the money resources, the support of the Church and the rich landowners, and the recognition of the European nations. The liberals were backed by the United States, the people of Mexico, and the league of state governors, who helped maintain an army of liberation. Their greatest asset was Juárez himself, using law as dynamite to blast away the obstacles to a free Mexico. His great Reform Laws nationalized church property and gave the state control of marriage and education. The laws meant, he wrote a friend, "the absolute independence of the civil power, and religious liberty. For me these were the capital points to be won in this revolution."

The revolution was succeeding, too, in the field of battle. Late in 1860 Juárez and his family were at the opera when a courier rushed to his box with the news of a decisive victory. He rose, and in a trembling voice read the dispatch to the audience. Everybody burst into the "Marseillaise" and cheers of thanksgiving. The long exile was over.

Forty years after Mexico was liberated from Spain it won a government determined to function for all the people. That year of 1861 was a fateful one, the year of the comet, of the Civil War in the United States, of Napoleon III's resolution to gain control of Spanish America. Juárez's triumphal return to the capital was, as he well knew, an acceptance of the defeat implicit in his victory.

The nation was not only bankrupt, it was overwhelmingly in debt to the European powers. No choice was possible, and Juárez suspended payment on the foreign debt service. At once France and Britain severed relations with Mexico, and the fantastic chapter of Intervention began.

Napoleon now had an excuse to realize his design and take over Spanish America. With Spain and England he hatched the scheme to put Maximilian of Austria on a Mexican throne. Juárez and Lincoln watched this outrageous plot develop and were equally powerless to deal with it. Juárez had inherited a nation in chaos; Lincoln was struggling with the Civil War. He was Mexico's steadfast champion and did what he could. His policy of "strict neutrality" was more than that; he never recognized any but the Juárez government. The United States could not help Mexico fight Europe, but at least the record is clean.

A year after the ovation in Vera Cruz at the liberal victory, the port was bombarded by Spanish warships. President Juárez made a characteristic gesture: he bought a house in Mexico City, which he knew would soon be a battlefield. It was an act of faith in the destiny of Mexico, and it was followed by a miracle. Somehow he persuaded England and Spain, whose forces were already on Mexican soil, to withdraw from the war. Now Mexico had only the French to fight, but that "only" was terrifying enough.

Many of the streets in Mexico today are named for the days of great victories over the French. The most glorious was the "Cinco de Mayo" when the Mexicans captured the great city of Puebla. But they lost it again, and so the war moved from city to city, with French reinforcements constantly pouring in. Napoleon was engrossed in his great adventure and was grooming Maximilian and Carlota for their entrance as unsuspecting puppets into a country they were assured was longing for their arrival.

The French forces reached Mexico City before them, in June 1863. Juárez, who always gauged the odds, had already retired north with his cabinet and his family. The French kept pushing him farther and farther north, until he finally reached the Rio Grande, and there he stayed, refusing to abandon Mexican soil, even to attend friendly parties to which Americans across the river invited him. He literally would not desert his country, and this had the dynamic power of a symbol.

Since the country now knew who Benito Juárez was, it did not matter so much where he was. The French were in virtual control of the country and their Emperor was about to arrive, but Juárez's comment on calamity diminished it. "*No tenga cuidado.*" That was all—don't worry.

On the voyage to Mexico, Maximilian interrupted serious work on a manual of etiquette for his new court and wrote Juárez a letter. The charming Hapsburg wanted everybody to love him and thought that Juárez, whom he much admired, would love him, too, if only they could meet and have a pleasant talk. He urged the President to come to Mexico City for a chat.

When this preposterous letter arrived, Juárez sat down after midnight, when the pressure of work was less, and wrote a stern, rather paternal answer. He tried to explain Mexico to Maximilian, to show him that he was the dupe of the powers, and ended:

"It is given to men, sir, to attack the rights of others, to take their property, to attempt the lives of those who defend their liberty . . . but there is one thing that is beyond the reach of perversity, and that is the tremendous verdict of history."

Zapotec

As the French armies moved north, Juárez sent his family for safety to New York City. Margarita was the other half of his soul, and he worried about her health, undermined by her concern for him. But instead, fate struck at his sons. First his beloved Pepito died, then Antonio. There was only one cure for the father: the sufferings of his country.

All through the Civil War, Juárez acted as Lincoln's discreet ally, refusing to admit Confederate agents, allowing Union troops to pass across Mexican soil. He asked nothing in return. "It is enough for us," he wrote his family, "that the North destroy slavery and do not recognize Maximilian." More could not be expected by a realist. But the spring of 1865 the French occupied the state of Oaxaca and held it for a year; the French were everywhere, and in desperation Juárez appealed to General Grant for aid. It was promised, and at that moment Lincoln was assassinated. The American foreign legion never materialized, though many demobilized Union soldiers tried to enlist in the Mexican Army.

Secretary of State William Seward limited military aid to smuggling arms across the border. For the sake of the United States quite as much as Mexico, he exerted diplomatic pressure on Napoleon at the critical moment when he was casting up the accounts of the Mexican fantasia and finding the cost too high.

Under the brilliant leadership of General Porfirio Díaz the Mexican armies fought stubbornly, and just as stubbornly Napoleon made a last desperate drive to realize on his investment. Early in 1867 the French forces were withdrawn and the country was rapidly liberated. Maximilian stood siege for a month at Querétaro, then was captured and condemned to death by a military court. His last days before the execution retrieved him as a man. He had come to Mexico expecting to be loved by everybody, but in the end it was Maximilian who loved Mexico. "May my blood be the last to be shed," he wrote Juárez, and in that spirit Juárez accepted the inevitable sacrifice, which cost him much anguish.

Benito Juárez: Measure of a Faith

The little Indian, "the Zapotec," had measured his faith against a threat which involved both Americas. In his single person he had embodied the Monroe Doctrine and kept the republics safe from the imperialism of European powers. When he issued his first proclamation of a liberated Mexico, he rephrased the Doctrine in a sentence which has the quality of a homely maxim: "Among nations, as among individuals, respect for the rights of others is peace."

All along his triumphal progress back to the capital the slogan was repeated on banners strung on arches of flowers, painted on the walls, reiterated on placards: *The People to Juárez*. It was a cry of gratitude to the man who had liberated Mexico from invasion, a tribute to his steadfast faith, but much more. It was the serranos again, telling him, "You know what we need and will give it to us."

That victorious journey back to Mexico City had its ironies, like the one six years before, when he returned from Vera Cruz as the beloved leader of the nation, only to be confronted by a new crisis. This time the danger did not stem from Europe, but from the reactionary forces in Mexico itself, embodied in Porfirio Díaz. The popular hero of the war, Díaz expected the presidency as his reward for liberating the country.

The duel between the Mixtec and the Zapotec, between the incipient dictator and the inveterate democrat, began at once. Juárez called for an election, and defeated the general. Sore in his defeat, Díaz retired to his Oaxaca farm, biding his time. Juárez celebrated his victory by giving the people free and compulsory elementary education. For the next five years, literally to the night of his death, he labored to fulfill the trust expressed in that cry, "The People to Juárez." He did not trust Díaz, who would reverse the phrase into "The People for Díaz," and in the duel between these prepositions the whole modern history of Mexico would be written.

There was time, still, for friendship with the people beyond

Mexican borders. William Seward paid a visit to Mexico and in a public speech declared that Benito Juárez was the greatest man he had ever known. This was so startling, coming from a close associate of Lincoln, that Seward was asked to confirm his statement. "Yes," he said, "this is my mature and considered opinion." Napoleon and the French Empire collapsed, and Juárez was widely praised for playing a crucial role in this downfall. But he was more interested in the new French Republic and the struggles of "the glorious Garibaldi." A force of Mexican veterans was sent to fight with him "the sacred cause of the universal republic."

As long as Juárez lived he fought for the universal republic. But his sturdy Indian health was failing, and he had to call on his last reserves of strength to run against Díaz in the next election. Again he defeated the man he could not trust with Mexico's cloudy destinies; but death cut short the battle. On the morning of July 18, 1872, he called in his doctor, and by midnight he was dead. In the hours between he had a busy day, and nobody but he and the doctor knew he was dying of angina pectoris, in excruciating pain.

The "little Indian" went through long conferences with this minister or that, his mind perfectly clear, and at night he took to his bed, with the exhausted doctor napping beside him. Thus he was spared a deathbed scene and a final word.

The final word lay, and still lies, in the people of Mexico.

Just as Oaxaca produced the two men who embodied Mexico's eternal duel between the cynic and the idealist in public affairs, this state, in the general strike of 1952, illuminated in glaring outline the dilemma in which the republic has lived since the days of Juárez. The issue between dictator and democrat is of course universal, but it happens to be sharp in Mexico because of the tragic heritage of Colonial days and the confusions of its racial strains. In Oaxaca it is especially vivid because nobody has forgotten the struggle between Juárez and Díaz.

Juárez, who managed to function for all the people even

through Mexico's gravest crisis, was really carrying over into national affairs the spirit of the old Zapotec town government. This spirit is deeply inbred in the Oaxaca people, just as the tradition of the New England town meeting still lives in our own country. Thus Oaxaca often becomes the touchstone of national issues.

Díaz, who enjoyed Mexico as his personal fief for thirty years and had nothing vital to leave behind him, should by now be as dead as the dodo. But there is definitely a Díaz cult in Oaxaca. In the tense days before the general strike one could hardly walk down the portales past the politicos idling over their beer and dominoes without hearing Díaz defended and praised. This showed a filial spirit; the politicos are his spiritual heirs.

Mexico is a seesaw between democracy and dictatorship. Juárez followed Santa Anna; Díaz bred the Revolution of 1910, which tried to give the country back to the people. Then the seesaw swung back to monolithic power which gives the illusion of stability. Nowadays the dictatorship is not personal, it is the extreme of one-party power. The Partido Revolucionario Institutional, the PRI, has outgrown popular control. It always elects its man because, as the Mexicans themselves will frankly admit, ballot counting has gone out of fashion.

In 1950 the PRI nominated Manuel Mayoral Herédia for governor of Oaxaca, and the opposition candidate was realistic enough to withdraw from the farce of a campaign. The party was also able to put its men into a good many town governments as presidente and secretary, and in Tammany fashion controlled pockets of the state. But Oaxaca is regarded as a ticklish proposition by the PRI because its people have the inconvenient habit of exercising popular control.

The personal tragedy of the new governor was that he never realized that he might have won acceptance. He alienated the people only because he regarded himself as an alien. He was born in an unpopular part of the state which has a scattering of gangsters, and his whole adult life was spent outside Oaxaca, rising on the party escalator. After he took office Herédia made no attempt to get acquainted with his people but spent most of his time in Mexico City. When in town he lived literally barricaded in a walled villa guarded by soldiers and never appeared without his personal bodyguard of *pistoleros*.

The new governor was afraid of the people. He expected them to hate him for what he was about to do. Somehow the whole picture recalled the early days after the Conquest, when encomenderos from Spain were given areas to exploit for themselves. Herédia arrived like an alien of Colonial days whose sole interest was to increase the yield of tribute.

Since the people were already staggering under taxes, the tribute could be increased only by grinding them down toward the Colonial level. Herédia vetoed Sunday-afternoon concerts by the State Band; he disrupted the School of Fine Arts, supported by state funds. He curbed fiestas, and at Christmas a year after his induction the calendas were pitiful indeed.

The breaking point came with his Ley Fiscal, which levied new state taxes up to 20 per cent, not on luxuries alone, but on the very substance of living, even food. The legislature obediently passed the governor's bill, which was to go into effect early in 1952. Revenue agents went through homes appraising stoves, refrigerators, pet dogs, books, beds. "Let them sleep on petates," was the attitude. The stallkeepers in the market, the merchants great and small, everybody who had more than a charcoal brazier and a dirt floor was to be penalized.

In Oaxaca there are two chambers of commerce, one for larger concerns, and the "Little Chamber" for market people and the owners of small stores and businesses. Having protested the law in vain, these chambers resolved on a state-wide strike. Five years before, Oaxaca had rid itself of an unpopular governor by a bloodless nine-day strike. A stoppage of all trade would mean a severe sacrifice for everybody, but fundamentals were at stake. When government became predatory, it was time for the people to defend themselves.

The market buzzed with talk of the coming strike, and on Saturdays, when distant vendors and customers came for the big market, the word was spread. A network of careful preparation covered the state. The most amazing change came over the people; they were no longer relaxed and happy. Everybody was bitterly intent on the coming crisis, exactly as people are in the first days of a war.

The governor, too, was mobilizing. He was much in Mexico City, laying plans for the struggle which the PRI especially dreaded in a presidential election year. The general strike was called for Friday, March 21, the birthday of Benito Juárez and a national holiday. The PRI recruited its strikebreakers with heavy manpower levies on party presidentes and caciques. The *rurales*, the country constabulary, were alerted, and thousands of *cuerudos* were summoned from the governor's part of the state. These "Leather Jackets," so called because they wear deerskin coats in cold weather, have a sinister reputation in Oaxaca.

Besides these party stalwarts a good many innocent campesinos and village idlers were tricked into joining the governor's war party. The mobilization was carried out so secretly that only later was it apparent that the state machine planned to provoke a civil war in Oaxaca that would drown the real issues in confusion and bloodshed. Enlisting campesinos from the central valleys was part of the strategy of confusion.

"Friday is the birthday of our beloved Juárez," these simple peasants were told. "Come to the city as our guests. There will be food and lodging and all the mezcal you can drink. And since you'll want to fire off a few salutes to Benito, bring along your guns."

All these men, innocent and otherwise, were spirited to the outskirts of the capital the day before the strike began and were housed in great empty barracks well supplied with food and drink.

Zapotec

El Pueblo Oaxaqueño, the Oaxaca People, celebrated Juárez's day by a complete stoppage of public functions. As on any national holiday, every place of business was closed, but ordinarily the streets would have been thronged with people in their holiday best. That day they stayed indoors, with the gates padlocked and the shutters closed, and every family had laid in supplies for a long siege. This was merely to show the solidarity of the citizens; nobody expected trouble. The Defense Committee of the state chambers of commerce was in full charge of the demonstration; the police and the local military garrison were on sympathy strike. The soldiers were in barracks, and the police were confined to quarters.

In this rather deathly quiet the governor and his party returned from the sierra town of Guelatao, Juárez's birthplace, where fulsome speeches had been made in honor of Mexico's lawgiver. Herédia at once went into conference with the Defense Committee. By then it was evening, and an unforeseen element had invaded the orderly picture—that floating group of boys and young men, to be found in any city, which craves excitement and which by self-infection may turn into a mob.

By dark a large crowd of youths milled about the Zócalo, armed with clubs and stones and slogans of hate against the government. The next step was to throw stones through the windows of the Government Palace at the foot of the Zócalo, and soon there was no pane unbroken.

The governor got into a panic. He knew it was useless to appeal to the police or the garrison, who were avowedly on the side of the strikers. For six months Herédia had been fighting tooth and nail for his fiscal law; now he dropped it like a hot coal. He told the Defense Committee he was abrogating the tax law and ordered notices to this effect printed and posted all over the city. The general strike had won its announced purpose in its first day. The tax law was dead, and so far there had been no demand that the governor resign.

236

Benito Juárez: Measure of a Faith

Until nearly midnight the Halloween band of marauders was quiet. Then it went to the administration newspaper and wrecked offices and plant. Filled now with destructive fury, the youthful mob poured down the streets to the governor's walled mansion and began throwing stones. Without warning, Herédia's pistoleros fired down round after round into the crowd. A moment later the street was littered with dead and wounded, and the survivors were on the run.

Red Cross ambulances finally picked up two dead boys and twenty wounded. But in the interval, everybody was convinced, the governor's guards had taken several bodies and rushed them away in jeeps, to hide them in deserted arroyos or dump them in the River Atoyac. In the next days family after family reported sons who had been in the riot and had not come home. They never came home. Sometimes their bodies were found; often they remained hidden. All over the state there were tragedies of this sort.

For all of that Saturday the bodies of the two victims which had been recovered lay on open biers in the arcade of the Government Palace, with a crude sign near them saying, "Herédia, here's your work." And the people filed grimly past in endless procession. The night before these young men had been hotheads helping to wreck the orderly process of the general strike; now they were martyrs. Now the strike was going on with a new demand: the resignation of the governor. One realized that the picture of Oaxaca as a peaceful, pleasant state had been incomplete; it had lacked the dimension of rage, the potential of revolution. That contemptuous, bitter sign, "Herédia, aquí tu obra," the shattered windows of the palace behind the humble biers—this was the dark side of popular revolt.

On Sunday, Oaxaca buried its martyrs after a service in the little market church of San Juan de Dios; a vast concourse of mourners followed the cortege to the cemetery. Then every household tied a streamer of black crape over the doorway; every household except those belonging to the bureaucracy.

Zapotec

There was a nightmare feeling in Oaxaca that night; the massing of powers getting ready to spring at each other. Hundreds of campesinos had trudged into the city with their families to help the strike, but many others had been intercepted by posses organized by the PRI and turned back home. There was rough work on the roads leading to the city. The Leather Jackets were still being held in leash outside the capital, but the 12th Motorized Cavalry had arrived with its tanks and machine guns, the symbol of federal intervention in the Oaxaca crisis. One remembered that the President was a *compadre* of the governor; this was his personal reinforcement.

After that warm gesture of the townswomen feeding the enemy, which for the moment made Oaxaca seem itself, the ugly feeling closed down once more. At two in the morning the federal soldiers were ordered to clear the Zócalo and make the whole center of town a military zone. The weary people sleeping under the trees picked up their children and took refuge by the Church of Soledad, and there in the big atrium and in the church itself they spent the next days, praying constantly, standing by for a call from the strike leaders.

The governor's civil war began Monday noon. The Leather Jackets came into the city, roaring drunk and well armed. They staggered around the Zócalo two or three thousand strong, yelling, "Viva Herédia, death to the traitors!" Then they went to the plaza formed by the cathedral and the Institute, where the strikers were waiting for them. It was the strategy of serrano warfare during the Conquest all over again. The strikers were armed only with stones and brickbats, but they were stationed on higher ground than the enemy. The roofs of the sacristy and the other buildings lining the plaza were massed solid with defenders. They let the Leather Jackets begin hostilities, then they discharged a rapid barrage of stones. The only casualties were among the invaders, and only one was seriously injured.

For the 12th Motorized Cavalry abruptly terminated the governor's war. Its men fired their machine guns into the air, and both sides evacuated the field. It was a magnificent victory for the Republic of Mexico.

For two weeks the general strike, the general paralysis, was maintained. That is a long time for people to go without markets or newspapers or supplies of drugs—or the offices of the postman and the garbage collector. The city reeked, but it was quiet. Open warfare went on in the country districts, where the Leather Jackets were at work, so terrorizing the people that sometimes whole villages fled to the mountains. The valley towns around the capital loyally sent in supplies of food, which seeped to the people through a sort of white market. In towns with a local PRI government there were attempts to load camions with supplies for the governor's forces, and more than once this resulted in a dead PRI presidente.

The general strike reached every corner of the state, but it was bigger than Oaxaca. It was a fuse touching off latent charges of rebellion all over the republic. Other states like Puebla and Tamaulipas had already had their troubles with predatory government, and the liberal newspapers in Mexico City warned that there was a lesson in these state rebellions. The thirty thousand Oaxaqueños in the capital reinforced these warnings with huge demonstrations. All over Mexico the universities and secondary schools went on sympathy strike with Oaxaca.

In a year when the PRI must elect a President, these nationwide warnings were alarming enough. The Oaxaca challenge of course ended in a deal, as political conflicts generally do. The strike was called off, and the governor agreed to resign after the July election. But the Institute, of which Benito Juárez had been director just a century before, remained closed until the *Te Deum* roared in the cathedral across the way to celebrate the final departure of Mayoral Herédia late in July.

In the testing of forces between which Mexico has been torn

since its independence was won from Spain, Oaxaca presented an amazing strength, which was the power of unity and the acceptance of sacrifice. The real triumph of the general strike was the fact that all the people, from the humblest to the highest, recognized the basic issue. Benito Juárez had made this issue, the winning of genuine democracy, clear to the nation and clearest of all to his own *tierra*, Oaxaca. If ever there is a national fight for government of, by, and for the people, Oaxaca will be in the vanguard.

During the dragging days of the strike there was a picture which makes the truest symbol of its meaning. On the hill above the city the Juárez Monument stands on the most dramatic site in the whole state. There, on the natural belvedere which commands the union of the central valleys, looking across to Monte Albán, the bronze figure stands with the right arm raised, as if in exhortation.

Around the base of the monument, every day of the strike, a little group of men were on watch. No enemy bands could approach the city without being visible from this perfect lookout. They were guarding the city, guarding their rights as free men. Now and then one of them would glance up at the quiet figure of "the Zapotec." He too was keeping his eternal vigil.

XII

REMEMBERED GODS

When Dr. Caso first lowered himself into Tomb Seven he found the floor littered with bits of turquoise and mother-of-pearl which had once formed a mosaic on wood or leather. The matrix had been consumed by time, and the pattern could not be restored.

In Oaxaca today the ancient religion has been fragmented in much the same way. The Spanish friars managed to destroy the matrix which held many elements in a pattern, but they could not destroy the elements themselves. Many of them could be absorbed into the new religion; long familiar to the Indians were the rites of fasting, confession and absolution, the celibacy of priests, baptism, and the symbol of the cross. But others stand out as curious survivals, simply fragments of a religion as definite as Buddhism or Christianity, a faith that once held Middle America together through long centuries.

The Oaxaca peoples are extremely devout, and most of them have poured their devotion into the Catholic faith—but still with the old pagan attitudes, for the Christian saints are only a new generation of gods. Sometimes magic will be brought into the church; often saints are invoked by a witch doctor performing a cure. The old gods are not quite forgotten, nor are the new ones quite accepted, to the exclusion of each other. The Zapotecs are especially skillful at carrying water on both shoulders; they want all the supernatural help they can get.

Mitla is a curious example of the rather furtive bargaining that

241

goes on with the powers. Its people are sophisticated; both men and women are notable traders and move about a great deal; the town is a mecca for tourists—and yet it is far more pagan than many remote mountain villages. The Mitla people have never taken the new religion deeply to heart; there is only the one church, the ugly interruption in the ruins. They revere the temples as the home of all dead souls, and their lives are threaded through with magic.

The first day I visited the church I stopped at a side altar where there was a Madonna dressed in dingy pink satin and lace. She looked neglected but was carrying what appeared to be an elegant gold mesh bag. On closer inspection it turned out to be a bag-shaped honeycomb. Some beekeeper was practicing sympathetic magic in the ugly old church.

Then on the Feast of San Pablo, the town's patron, I climbed to the little chapel which is built on a ruined pyramid. This chapel contains nothing at all but three crosses mounted on rough stands. Before the central cross was a curious little arrangement of pebbles: more magic, possibly black magic.

The three crosses are one of the mysteries of Southern Mexico. All through Oaxaca and Chiapas three thin crosses stand on the tops of lonely mountains. The women of Yalalag have from time immemorial worn three silver crosses joined together with a bar so that the whole design forms a fourth cross. The first friars in Oaxaca found them wearing these crosses and began to wonder if earlier missionaries, perhaps St. Thomas himself, had not been there before them.

It is safe to say that the Indians of Southern Mexico usually regard the cross in their ancient way rather than in the Christian fashion. The crucifix bearing the figure of Christ is of course a church symbol. But in general the cross means space–time, the core of the old religion based on the magic calendar. In the minds of the simpler people much of the old significance has been lost, but it remains a potent symbol. It is used in curing and all sorts of magic rites; the mountain people put it over their doors; the vallistas set a cross at the entrance to their village, and passers-by leave little offerings of flowers or certain magic herbs below it. Fords and crossroads, regarded as magic by primitive people all over the earth, will be guarded by a cross which has nothing to do with the crucifix of the Church.

But the three crosses remain a mystery with too many explanations. Some people tell you that they represent Quetzalcoatl's journeys over the earth, and the Yalalag cross with its design suggesting the four cardinal points means that he will return. Others say that the triple crosses represent the Trinity, or the three Marys. In the ceremonial city of Chamula in Chiapas, where rumor insists that a crucified Indian is buried, three crosses guard the entrance to the village, and the people will fend off questions by explaining that one is to keep the devil out; the second, sorcerers; and the third, *ladinos*, strangers of white blood.

With self-isolated Maya we come close to understanding the power, if not the symbolism, of the triple cross. All the ancients of Middle America worshiped the cross, but the Maya especially treated it as a god, and the famous Palenque cross, so like India's tree of heaven, expresses this worship. It survives widely among the Maya today. As for three crosses, they are used in secret magic of the most solemn sort.

The explorer Frans Blom and Oliver La Farge[1] once found a Maya shaman laying a curse with three crosses. As in Oaxaca, when a witch doctor lays a spell he must be intoxicated, or drugged with a narcotic mushroom. This goes back to classic days when the high priest became intoxicated before he went into his sacred trance. So this Maya shaman began his black magic by drinking *aguardiente*.

He then set up three crosses deep in the woods, the largest one in the center, and in a hole before each he placed offerings of food and wine. Then he knelt and prayed, calling aloud the name of the

[1] *Tribes and Temples*, Blom and La Farge, 1927.

man whose soul he wanted to capture. He repeated this rite for eight days, then he sprinkled some of the food and wine on the crosses and in the four cardinal directions. He now laid his curse: "I am going to capture a soul now, gods of the earth, and our mothers of the earth." He invoked all the Great Men and Great Women, most of them Christian saints; he called on the southwest wind and other powers.

This macabre rite only raises another question: Why did he call on the southwest wind? Why is the observatory on Monte Albán pointed southwest? It happens to point straight at Tahiti and the Marquesas; but there we must leave the matter.

The cross seems to us an abstraction, but in Southern Mexico it still is anthropomorphic, a wonder-working god. And because it is also a Christian symbol its pagan worshipers can safely invoke it. As for the gods in the guise of jaguars, dragons, serpents, they still walk their ancient realm in the twilight of confused but passionately devout minds. As we have seen, the Olmec jaguar evolved into the rain god Cocijo (or Chac among the Maya) and finally into the celestial dragon Quetzalcoatl. This long evolution is going on today among the mountain peoples of Oaxaca who worship a water serpent. Like the cross, this seems a harmless superstition, but it is fundamental.

When Howard Leigh recovered the Zapotec name of the jaguar god, Béeze, he also found that this god was the lord of riches. Nothing could be more natural. In Southern Mexico the Old God of the sun died at a very early period and was replaced by the rain god, for the simple reason that the sun shines every day, but a delay in the rains means famine and death. Thus water is another word for wealth. And among the mountain peoples whose eroded lands have less and less water the cult of the water serpent is essential.

The highland Zapotecs of the Yalalag region and their neighbors, the Mixe, believe that the giver of water and life is a horned water serpent (in other words, a water dragon) who lives in mountain springs. Men will not swim in these pools for fear of the serpent. During the spring sowing the people place in these magic pools a few seeds of everything they have planted, along with the wonder-working double ears of corn from the last harvest. If the rain god is kind they return at harvesttime with thank offerings sprinkled with the blood of fowls.

Anyone who has watched the approach of the Oaxaca rainy season knows that winds and lightning are the heralds of the rains. The Mixe of a region quite near Mitla make special offerings to the gods of winds and lightnings, aspects of the ancient Cocijo. Before they plant they sacrifice a turkey in the center of the field, sprinkle its blood over a pile of tortillas and tamales, and pray to the gods for a rich field of corn.

In another Mixe village the farmer observes a period of celibacy before he plants, and prays in the church before the seed is sown. He takes to his field thirteen perfect ears of corn (perhaps a memory of the magic number thirteen in the old calendar) and any double-pointed ones saved from the last harvest, sprinkles them with the blood of a turkey he has sacrificed, and buries them in his field. Then he passes the severed head of the turkey over the spot in a counterclockwise motion. When the new corn begins to tassle out he takes up the buried ears and they are made into tortillas and tamales. He sprinkles the blood of a new sacrifice on the young leaves and takes some of them as an offering to the summit of Zempoaltepec, the holy mount of the Mixe. Leaves sprinkled with sacrificial blood were the usual offering in pagan days.

The Mixe think that the Water Serpent causes floods in the rivers, and in a tempest of rain he can be seen emerging from the clouds—which is close to the old conceptions of Cocijo, god of rain, wind, and lightning. He lives, too, in curious little dwarfs, *chaneques*, who carry lightning in their hands and dwell in caves or behind waterfalls, where they hide loot stolen from people. These imps, mischievous and busy as gremlins, are a great worry all over Oaxaca.

245

Zapotec

Perhaps no god or godkins have as long a lineage as the chaneques, for they are old men with baby faces, and very strong—in other words, they belong to the very ancient cult of the baby jaguar which spread all over the Olmec region. The Mazatecs and Zapotecs of Olmec Land are afraid of these imps, who are only two feet tall but can seize a grown man and throw him flat. When a chaneque has put his spell on a person death will follow unless a special cure is followed. Worst of all, they are amorous, forever plaguing pretty girls and even carrying them off.

Since the chaneques can, in an amiable mood, provide rains, and since they are the masters of game and fish, prudent hunters placate them before starting out. Quite near the city of Oaxaca there is a mountain village called Cuatro Venados, where the chaneque cult is all-important. When a baby is born an egg is buried near it to keep the dwarf god away. The people have built several shrines for the chaneques on the slopes near the village, and at the chief one, the Casa de Chaneque, the men leave offerings of cigarettes, food, and candles before they go hunting.

These imps are clearly jaguar cubs in the best Olmec tradition, and the jaguar himself is still regarded with uncanny terror, especially on either side of the isthmus, where he lives as king of tropical beasts. Any living jaguar was supposed to be supernatural and almost impossible to kill; an early friar tells of some Indians who encountered a tigre in the forest. Instead of trying to shoot him with their bows and arrows, they fell on their knees and began confessing their sins, whereupon the beast devoured them. The friars never quite managed to kill jaguar worship, and the isthmus men still perform a jaguar dance.

The magic calendar and the totem cult which was part and parcel of it are divorced today. The tona cult flourishes all over Oaxaca, but the calendar itself, which required mathematical wizards to interpret it, is very nearly forgotten.

Several Chinantec villages still use the pije calendar of eighteen months of twenty days, with the five "indifferent" days placed somewhere in the year. It is remarkable that even this much should survive in a world counting time by twelve months. The Chinantecs do not use the calendar for divination, but as a farmers' almanac, a function which it had, too, in ancient times. They regulate their planting and reaping by the old system. The pije day names have been lost, but two of the month names have an ancient meaning. The name for our June is *mo hi na*, "at noon, when the sun is at its zenith, he stands still for a moment"—a description of Midsummer Day. The winter-solstice month is *hi ta nyi*, "a spike thrusts itself into the face of the sun, preventing it from falling further."

When a Mazatec *brujo*, magician, practices divination he throws kernels of corn over twenty cards bearing animal pictures, and it is believed that these occult cards preserve the animal names of the twenty days of the old month. In the Zapotec town of Ocotlán there were, not long ago, several deeply respected old men who had some memory of the pije and were in charge of the fiesta calendar. They were called *gulaanis*, phonetically the same word as *colanjis*, the priests of the Classic age who had special charge of the pije and divination.

Most of the Oaxaca tribes still practice augury, often by casting corn on a mat and observing the pattern in which it falls. The Zapotec brujo can foretell events by observing the flight of birds or their songs. He finds a stolen animal by suspending a basket by a cross made of twigs, or more often nowadays by scissors. Then he pronounces the names of suspected thieves, and at the name of the guilty man the basket falls. In Mitla the curandera tending a sick person will kill a chicken on a cross she draws on the ground, and if it dies with its head to the east the patient will recover. All over Polynesia and Middle America east is the direction of life; souls travel westward at death.

Since the elaborate calendar which linked a newborn child with its animal or bird tona is forgotten, all sorts of devices must be

Zapotec

used to find what creature is the spiritual twin of the new child. One is the counting-out method. As birth approaches, the father keeps naming over animals and birds, and the creature he names at the moment of his wife's delivery is the tona of the child.

In Ocotlán there is a rather dreadful technique. The newborn child is left utterly alone in the hut the first night after it is born. Around the mat on which it lies the parents have sprinkled ashes, and at dawn they examine these ashes to find the prints of any creature which has been near the baby during the night. The tona is supposed to be anxious to greet its human twin, and if it cannot visit the hut it will hover nearby. When parents hear the insistent cry of a bird or some animal in the mountains, they recognize that the tona is announcing itself.

From then on the individual is bound to his tona: hawk or newt, jaguar, snake, eagle, or other creature. The Chinantecs believe that people are born with two souls, and one enters into the tona. All the simpler peoples of Oaxaca think that any harm suffered by the tona is reflected in the person linked to him. Before he dies his tona gives him warning so that he can prepare for the end.

It is hard to find much sympathy for this animism now that it is divorced from the old pantheism in which all living creatures had their place. No doubt psychologists would say that the tona cult is a healthy projection and acceptance of man's animal side. Certainly the Oaxaqueños live on close terms with the creatures about them and will not harm their individual or tribal totem; the Huave will not kill alligators, and the Zapotecs venerate as a kind of race totem the eagle and the zapote tree for which they are said to be named. But this does not prevent Juan, whose tona is a lizard, from shooting his neighbor's twin, a buzzard. The whole picture is confused and fortunately fading out.

In the same way modern medicine will someday replace the dubious offices of the curandera and the brujo. Meanwhile, even in the cities where doctors are at hand, ignorant souls will resort to the magic healers. Often they are helped, for the Indians of both Americas know their herbs and gave modern medicine quinine, digitalis, and many other essential drugs. A witch brew may happen to be extremely good medicine. Moreover, the Indians were early in recognizing psychosomatic illness and have just as effective cures for it as our expensive specialists. Such illness is called *espanto*, fright caused by a shock of some kind. Like sickness in general, it is often supposed to be the work of witchcraft and is treated by countermagic.

In Mitla the curandera has the patient ill from espanto lie on a cross she makes on the ground, surrounded by offerings of copal incense, eggs, and other magic elements. The egg is the symbol of strength. The curandera returns to her own house, where she makes another cross on the ground decorated with flowers. She beats the ground with a stick, calling to the soul which left the patient at the moment of shock and which must be recaptured. She keeps calling at the cross and at the four corners of the room (the magic cardinal points again), "Come, get up!"

In other regions the straying soul must be caught in a big olla at the spot where the patient suffered shock, and restored to him. The isthmus curanderas work on an opposite principle; instead of the espanto driving away the soul, the fright is in the patient and must be blown away. The witch doctor makes the sign of the cross over the patient, blowing hard, and places a handful of earth on his body at the four cardinal points. An incantation is pronounced, urging the espanto to leave the patient and fall into the sea or the wilderness. If this cure does not work, the patient rides through town, followed by a crowd, and every now and then he tells what caused the fright.

Colds, lung troubles, and rheumatism caused by evil airs, *aire*, are treated with a more familiar therapy of alcohol rubs, hot cloths, and massage, accompanied by the special rite of "sucking out the poison." Sometimes the curandera puts her mouth to the afflicted spot and sucks hard, or she may merely put her lips close to the patient and make a curious humming sound.

Zapotec

The Mixe often treat disease at a distance from the patient by sacrificing a turkey in a magic cave or lighting a bonfire on their sacred mountain Zempoaltepec. The Mazatecs have the most elaborate cures of all. The brujo eats a narcotic mushroom, then he arranges a great variety of wonder-working elements like cacao, eggs, copal on a table. He prays to the Christian saints, burns pagan copal, throws forty-eight kernels of corn on a mat to diagnose the disease, and prepares a medicine bundle with the elements on the table, which include a prayer written on bark paper with a guacamayo feather. This bundle is buried near the sick person, who may also be given herbs which the brujo has taken to the church and rubbed over the images of saints.

One of the commonest sights in the Oaxaca churches is the touching of flowers or herbs to the image of a saint. This device for absorbing the magic power of the saint may be practiced by ordinary people, not brujos alone. The herbs or flowers are then placed on the home altar ready for emergencies, like our first-aid shelf in the bathroom. For one never knows when a child or pretty girl may not be visited with the evil eye from the glance of an admiring stranger, or the father come home from the fields with an espanto because some witch has turned into a ball of fire rolling down the slope.

Because so much illness is caused by witchcraft, the Mitla people are cautious in giving advice when a neighbor is ill. If the patient died they might then be accused of having laid an evil spell on him. They are sensitive on this point because their fellow Zapotecs in Yalalag think that Mitla people are apt to be brujos. Fifty years ago they thought that *all* Mitla people were brujos; nowadays if anybody falls ill in Yalalag when a Mitla coffee trader is there, he is blamed.

The towns have a good deal of contact since both are trading centers clearing each other's products for their neighborhoods and since Yalalag people often pass through Mitla on their way to the city. The people of both these towns are as charming as possible, and yet they have an inscrutable, veiled manner. Tourists never guess what troubles these people have with witches in general and with each other.

For instance, Yalalag people think that cats and buzzards are as a rule witches in disguise, and Mitla is full of cats and buzzards. If Yalalag travelers, who usually make the long journey to the city afoot, must spend the night in Mitla, they will not go indoors, but sleep near the temple ruins, which protect all Zapotecs. Mitla traders are necessary in Yalalag, but people are criticized for trading with them or giving them shelter.

Naturally Yalalag has brujos of its own. The most famous witch doctor, who has now passed to his reward, was Maestro Antonio Allende. He possessed a stone "with a prayer inside." Whoever could see through the stone and read the prayer, as Allende did, could turn himself into any animal he pleased. The old maestro's stone is now in the safekeeping of a prominent citizen, but nobody can read the magic prayer.

The way for ordinary people, usually ugly old women, to turn themselves into witches is to jump three times over a bowl of water, muttering certain spells. Or they resort to a witches' sabbath at the cross guarding the entrance to a cemetery. There they take off their heads and put them in some safe spot while they romp as pigs, dogs, or monkeys for the rest of the night. They run between the legs of late wayfarers, tripping them up; they cause magic fires in forests, which consume no trees. The village dogs always recognize them as witches and set up a lugubrious howl. Others, in the guise of sirens, lure men into pools or lead them far from home.

The Oaxaca practice of leaving the human head behind while these japeries are enjoyed sometimes leads to complications. The valley people tell of a crone who returned from her frolic dangerously close to dawn, the zero hour for witchery. In her haste she clapped on a man's head. At home she went to bed with her rebozo over her face, pretending to be sick. But her husband pulled the rebozo back, found his wife wearing a mustache, and beat her until she confessed.

Oaxaca witches are legion; a lexicon of words is necessary to name the varieties. They are annoying but as a rule harmless or even useful in keeping men home at night. And there are many remedies. A needle or a sharp-pointed stick will immobilize a witch; a coyote tail disconcerts him. Men have often gotten rid of a were-pig or were-dog by switching huaraches, wearing the left one on the right foot. More religious ones have found rosaries, scapularies, and crosses a good protection.

However, there is a creature which is not a witch but a human vampire, the *nawal*, which sucks the blood of sleeping persons and injures the child in the womb. In the hot country the nawal takes the form of a were-jaguar in the direct service of the devil, and the isthmus people are terrified of him.

An odd twist in the interweaving of old and new beliefs is the notion that the devil, who was well known in Oaxaca before the friars came, has living as well as dead slaves. This grew out of the idea that hell is not "somewhere else" but all around. A man who has made a losing bargain with Satan may vanish, but he is not dead. His old neighbors see him sometimes from a distance, toiling away in some bleak barranca or tending the devil's sheep on an inaccessible slope of mountain.

People driving down the Highway between Tlacolula and Mitla will see at the left a cliff on which some ancient hand outlined a horse in white paint. The legend of the Little White Horse, as gathered by Wilfrido Cruz from Tlacolula patriarchs, tells of a man enslaved by the devil about two centuries ago. This unsavory character, whose Zapotec name means "Crow," was an easy target for Old Scratch, who bewitched Crow's sheep so that they all died. At the psychological moment, when Crow was in despair, the devil came riding up on a white horse (and it is interesting that Satan was elegantly dressed as a charro, like the unpopular Spanish). The usual bargain was made, and Crow, after an interval of prosperity, vanished into the hell which in Zapotec fantasy is just around the next mountain. The infernal rider on the white horse still haunts the neighborhood but has found no victims of late years.

The Zapotec idea of heaven was much like the one brought by the Dominicans: a happy place in the sky. But the Zapotecs emphasize endless leisure as the chief delight of heaven. "In glory we do not work," they say. And there is always plenty to eat.

Many Oaxaca people still regard death as the beginning of an actual three-year journey to the next world. The Mixe have even remembered, for more than four centuries, the pagan version of the soul's search for his final home. He comes to a huge lake which he cannot cross, but a black dog appears to ferry him to the other side. A white dog cannot do this. The Mixe, during the nine-day wake while the soul is still lingering at home, provision him for the journey with baskets of tortillas and gourds of the local drink, *tepache*. Small pots are "freed" for the soul's use by having holes made in their sides, like the offerings in Monte Albán graves from the earliest periods.

The Mazatecs give a dead man the seeds of a certain plant to use as money in the next world. Some Tehuantepec folk bury their dead in special sandals made with very thick soles so that they can cross a certain river with a bed of sharp stones which they will encounter on their journey. The Mixtecs and certain Zapotecs believe that placing the body on a cross outlined in lime will shorten the time the soul must spend in lonely travel. Though the funeral is held the day after a person dies, all over Oaxaca the family and friends spend nine successive evenings eating and drinking with the dead soul in a sort of bon voyage ceremony, and sometimes these wakes are gay. They are always festive when children die, since they go straight to heaven.

The souls, of course, return on the Day of the Dead, first the children, greeted with firecrackers and regaled with wondrous

cakes and toys, then the adults, for whom a banquet is spread, as
it is all over Mexico. It is the familiar ceremony, with variations
peculiar to Oaxaca. Here the family do not eat the festive foods
after they have been offered to the souls, as is the common custom.
In Yalalag the souls take the delicious smells and tastes of the
offerings away with them, mounted on grasshopper wings. The
same town observes a novena before the Day of the Dead, ending
in a procession to the cemetery, where the leader, in true Zapotec
fashion, makes a long speech to the souls, thanking them for their
help in the past year and assuring them that their families will
always love and honor them.

Though the souls are "in glory" they still have human feelings,
and on their annual visit they are treated with great consideration.
Their favorite food and drink are offered, the songs they liked
best are sung for them, and the children are kept on their best be-
havior, as if honored guests were in the house. In Oaxaca there is a
charming tradition of hospitality to souls who have no families
to entertain them; the candles are lit and the offerings spread for
them, so that no soul will feel lonely and neglected during this
general reunion.

To the Oaxaqueños the tangible world is saturated with the
supernatural. They live close to their animals and close to their
witches and *santos;* there are no compartments dividing animal,
human, and spirit beings from each other. This mingling of the
three kingdoms is childlike; children and Indians live in a rich
fantasy world with an armadillo or a shining angel on the same
level with people.

In this fairy-tale atmosphere saints have moods, and a butterfly circles around a man's head to tell him that his best friend is
dying. Who knows whether a pig is merely a porker or somebody's tona, or even a witch? Santiago has his vanity and needs to
be placated with new silver spurs. Certainly Soledad was pleased,
like any beautiful woman, when the sailors gave her pearls.

Remembered Gods

Strangers are often jolted by the extreme informality of the simpler Oaxaca people with their santos. Each image is at once a god and a human being gifted with magic powers. Favorite santos are friends; they are almost members of the family. One will see a recently bereaved woman at the Feast of Guadalupe weeping aloud, "*Ay, Lupe, Lupe, chula!*" Only a deeply religious person could call the greatest Lady of Mexico by a nickname and add the slang endearment "sweetie." But God Himself is often called Tata, a child's word like Daddy.

It is impossible for most Mexican Indians, and certainly for the Oaxaca people, to regard the deities of the Church as distant, inscrutable beings. In some areas they are still on probation as aliens who may turn out to possess power. Some primitive Mixtec-Negro people on the Pacific once made a procession with a santo, hoping to be given rains. When no rains resulted the image was dumped ignominiously outside the church and the people paraded with an idol. Even in the city one will sometimes hear a saint berated for failing to respond to prayers and offerings.

The habit of taking mysteries literally makes church festivals strange and moving. There are the Christmas calendas with their living pictures of the Nativity. In some villages the Feast of the Assumption is celebrated, with complete piety, by sending a firework-rigged dummy of the Virgin Mary to heaven on a rocket. The drama of Holy Week is presented in the villages and the simpler city churches as a communal passion play.

It is a time of silence in which the people sincerely grieve for Jesucristo. From Thursday noon until Easter Sunday all church bells are mute; the images along the nave are swathed in purple. The Host is removed from the altar and the people do not genuflect when they enter the church. Cristo is not there, he is dead. There is a symbolic suspension of all life, as in the ancient days before the beginning of a new fifty-two-year cycle.

On Holy Thursday we went to the little valley town of Tlacochahuaya, not far from the city, but with an air of remoteness and innocence. It was an important seat of the early Dominicans, and here Fray Juan de Córdoba wrote the first dictionary and grammar of the Zapotec language. The order built an enormous church in a huge atrium where one misses the usual Indian laurels. But the church itself is enchanting, for it was built and decorated by the local Zapotecs. The façade is ornamented with sculptures which in candor and gaiety recall the Romanesque churches of Southern France. Inside, walls and ceiling are painted in red and blue floral scrolls, with cherubs, stars, and great festoons of colored feathers.

At noon the church was thronged with people in their holiday best; the little boys wore bright satin shirts with a gaudy silk kerchief tied over one shoulder. But there was a strange tension in the church, and one realized that all these people were playing their parts in a mounting drama. They were immobile, utterly silent, and their stillness had an emotional quality which was impressive.

At intervals there were sounds expressing the silence, the unearthly wail of the ancient chirimía, and the dry clacking of the *matraca* in the tower. This giant rattle which replaces the bells at this solemn season has a ghostly sound, a tone of utter deadness.

Presently a group of village elders emerged from a side chapel carrying the great coffin in which the Cristo was to lie after the hours on the cross. It was gaily painted like the church in bright colors on a base of white. They set it down to the left of the altar in a bank of fresh flowers and tall candlesticks with tapers of pure beeswax. Above the coffin was a row of cone-shaped pots sown with new grass. During Holy Week one sees these charming offerings everywhere, a symbol of spring and resurrection.

The preparation of the coffin was one episode in the communal drama. That night, all over Oaxaca, village elders would enact the Last Supper, and during the hour of Gethsemane there would be the ceremony of *tinieblas*, darkness, the people kneeling with lighted candles, which one after another would be extinguished until the church was dark.

On Good Friday the villagers enact the trial of Christ, the betrayal by Judas, and the procession to Calvary. In many towns the Crucifixion itself is dramatized; a young man is tied to a cross and hangs for an hour above the lamenting throng. Literal crucifixions have occurred in Oaxaca and the neighboring state Chiapas. Only a few years ago the Chontal near the Pacific crucified a volunteer zealot named Di Gabrielli. The most famous case in Chiapas occurred in 1868, when the Indians of Chamula chose for crucifixion a young man called Domingo Gomez Checheb. There are persistent rumors that the body of this man is hidden in the Chamula church and that Indians from far and wide make secret pilgrimages to it. The church is kept locked, and only favored people are ever allowed inside.

Token crucifixions still take place in two Oaxaca City churches. One is in the oldest part of town in a run-down section near the railroad station. Santa Maria del Marquesado, which belonged to Cortés's private estate, is a small charming church set far back from the street with an avenue of superb laurels leading to it. Along this mall on Good Friday we found a double row of stalls for food and refrescos, for the church was crowded all day with people from the city and from neighboring towns. Here at high noon a young man was hung on a cross while the people knelt and wept. Then all afternoon there was a black gauze curtain stretched before the altar, and behind it was the dim figure of the crucifix flanked by kneeling Marys. This dark curtain was a touch of artistry, as if it veiled an agony too great to witness.

The tragedy is cut short in Mexico, and the Resurrection is celebrated the next day, the Saturday of Glory. At nine in the morning the Mass of Glory is held in the cathedral, and the people swarm the streets in their new clothes. The Zócalo is decked with fresh green boughs, and the band arrives at eleven to play its gayest tunes. At noon Judas is burned before the cathedral. He is a giant figure of papier-mâché, dressed in a black business suit and derby, and looking remarkably like a fat politico. When the fuse is lit he whirls round and round with giant crackers snorting, then suddenly catches fire. With a final blast his head explodes and the crowds cheer and hoot. The boys rush across the street to kick the framework apart and find souvenirs to carry home.

The mystery of the Passion is dissolved in the normal magic of spring; the annual death and resurrection of nature have been celebrated. But there is a larger cycle in Oaxaca that with certain church festivals brings back the ancient days.

When we left the church in Tlacochahuaya we walked over to the town hall, where an old stone has been embedded in a front wall. It is an ancient bas-relief of a jaguar, like the one in Teotitlán across the valley, but much finer. As we stood there studying it, an old man came out of the cabildo and joined us. We all looked at the jaguar for a long time, and when the chirimía wailed from the church tower it seemed that a moment of mourning had come for all the great symbols, for the jaguar god, for the Cristo, symbols which may suffer a token death but are indestructible.

XIII

THE PRIMITIVE WORLD NEXT DOOR

There is no global Big Ben. Time ticks away at very different speeds in New York and Oaxaca, and a visit to the neighboring state of Chiapas dispels any notion that absolute time exists for people as it does for planets. In this fantastic region on the edge of Guatemala the pulse is so slow that one can feel the sort of time paleolithic man knew, time so sluggish, registering so little change, that millenniums are the yardstick.

Something about the primeval mountains of Chiapas and the incredible motley of tribes around San Cristóbal Las Casas halfway across the state upsets one's personal metronome. It is rather like the protest of the eardrums at sudden changes in altitude. Many Americans who drive to Las Casas have this rather uncomfortable sensation of falling backward too fast through time.

The experience is acute because you are busily ticking off modern time on the Inter-American Highway, and since the Mexican engineers who built it are masters of the mountain curve, you are moving about a mile a minute. A few hours of this and your body is saturated with the sense of swift forward motion. At Las Casas you come to a sudden stop; you are plunged into a human pool where time has stagnated. The people are still living in primitive time, thousands of years back. They are not really our contemporaries; they are still back in prehistory.

In a more tangible fashion Chiapas seems foreign because it was long a part of Guatemala and has been a Mexican state for less than a century. On its eastern fringe the Old Maya built Palenque and other noble cities which they abandoned thirteen centuries ago. This wholesale migration of a great culture explains the contrast between Oaxaca and Chiapas. In Oaxaca one has the sense of living in an ancient classic culture which is still ingrained in the people. But the Chiapanecos in the center of the state are not Maya, but marginal tribes which probably came from Mongolia over Bering Strait and had little or nothing to do in ancient times with the Maya. What one finds in Las Casas is not the backwash of greater days, but a pocket of peoples who have scarcely left the primitive level of the Ice Age.

Thus the journey to Las Casas becomes a recapitulation of history, of legend, and of that tremendous shadowy migration from North Asia which peopled the Americas. The present tense, expressed in geography, of which one encounters a rich array on this drive, also contains the past. As for the future, so large an element of any region in the United States, it has not been born.

The geography of this route is full of contrasts. We crossed the familiar golden Valley of Oaxaca and climbed into the maze of the Sierra Madre, this winter still faintly green because of the generous rains of the last season. But when we circled down to the isthmus a vicious norther was blowing the sandy soil into dust clouds and whipping the gorgeous blouses of the tehuanas as they fought their way to market.

The opulent isthmus was taking a beating, but the Huave fishermen on the Pacific lagoons were suffering much more. We thought about them as we crossed the flat monotonous stretch between the Sierra Madre, which here runs close to the Pacific, and the treeless, comfortless sandspits where the Huave live. Like the Monterey cypress, they have survived by clinging to the westernmost edge of the continent. Driven up the Pacific from Peru, these refugees enjoyed what comforts the mainland could afford them until the armies of King Zaachila I drove them into the Pacific. Only brave and hardy souls could conceive of living on sand bars with no vegetation and swarms of insect pests. When a norther blows they cannot go out to fish, and the wind catches the coarse sand and pebbles and flings them like a discharge of birdshot. No doubt the Huave feel safe now; nobody covets their land.

As we climb slowly out of the sand flats there are miles of pale green sugar cane and charming old *fincas* with comfortable colonial houses, and refineries waiting for the new crop. This is a fertile stretch, but we are coming now to a region where even fact becomes fable, the least-known part of all Mexico. This is the wholly negative triangle of Oaxaca at its union with Vera Cruz and Chiapas, unexplored, undesirable, uninhabitable. But this last negative is followed by a question mark.

This is the watershed of the Sierra Madre, a mass of naked indigo peaks where storm clouds hover all the year round and torrents of rain descend to feed the great rivers which flow into the Gulf. In this fearsome wilderness a plane crashed some years ago, and rescue parties traveled for days into the big triangle. Finally they reached a dark impenetrable forest, and then they began to be afraid. For there was no living thing in the forest, not a bird or a snake, a complete taboo against life. The search parties could not go on without game to shoot, and were forced, to their great relief, to retreat.

But nearer the Highway there are sections of this mysterious triangle which abound in game—deer, jaguars, armadillos, curassows, wild boars—and conceivably people could live in these bleak mountains. If so, they are completely estranged from the rest of their kind, but in this part of the world anything is possible. There may be remnants of an extremely ancient migration who have been hiding in these mountains literally for thousands of years, or the descendants of some of those terrified Oaxaqueños who fled from the Spanish and have become retrograde. Either theory would explain the descriptions of the creatures that the people of this thinly settled region claim to have encountered.

Zapotec

The Zoque of the two villages called Chimalapa may be turn-ing fact into fable. These hamlets, San Miguel Chimalapa and Santa Maria Chimalapa, are the last outposts of the familiar world, and their people claim that now and then they find strange crea-tures raiding their garden patches, or a hunter encounters them in the mountain wastes. Their story is that these are the de-scendants of refugees from the Conquistadores who used magic to turn themselves into binquizacs, sons of the devil. Not quite human any more, they have forgotten their language and de-veloped animal keenness of smell and lightning agility in climb-ing and running. They are timorous creatures, and the sign of the cross drives them into headlong flight.

One is more apt to believe there is something behind these tales because the neighborhood also makes a great mystery about the Andes Road, which is simply a fact told with bated breath. At Zinatepec, just before the Highway enters Chiapas, the ranch-ers like to tell of going up into the mountains and finding ruined buildings and traces of dead cities, covered now with vegetation. On these sites fruit trees are growing, planted by unknown hands, garden flowers bloom, and there are old plantings of coffee and cacao struggling against the tide of wild growth. All through this region the people insist that there are traces of an ancient highland road and that villages of living people are strung along it to keep strangers away and help those of their own blood on their journey.

These local spellbinders would have a far more wonderful tale to tell about the Andes Road if they knew its history. It was one of the great trade and pilgrimage routes of the world, as venerable as the Icknield Way or the Silk Road through the Himalayas. The highland trail is an alternate route of the ancient trade artery between Mexico and Central and South America, and we are spinning down the main stem, the coastal branch. But long ago, because the coast route might be flooded or held by hostile tribes, a path was cut through the mountains.

The Primitive World Next Door

Don Leopoldo Torres and two or three of his sons once decided to take this mountain trail to the fair of San Esquipulas in Guatemala, as many pilgrims and traders have done until quite recently. Unlike their ancestors, who were their own pack animals, they took along burros to carry their piles of serapes.

"It was hard going at first," Don Leopoldo told me. "In the old days there were more villages, but now we had to walk twenty days before we reached the first one. After that there were more people, and they were glad to see us. It is a secret way, and only friendly people know how to get to San Esquipul across the mountains."

In the Classic era there were doubtless comfortable towns and perhaps cities along the highland route, which must have been used a good deal by traders, envoys, and pilgrims, since the Zapotecs did not control the coastal plains until late in the day. The last thing needed in southern Mexico is more likely sites to excavate, but both the highland and the coast branches of the Andes Road should yield high dividends and possibly help explain the mystery of Middle American culture. In its entirety this route went all the way from Teotihuacán on the central plateau to Peru.

Our modern section of this venerable highway takes us up the jagged Chiapas mountains and into the state capital, Tuxtla Gutiérrez. The city has an implausible air, the shabby gentility of Spanish Colonial overlaid with false touches from earliest Hollywood and latest Maya. With its plaster "steles" inspired by the recently excavated site of Bonampak, which had the tallest ones ever found, Tuxtla is trying hard for the tourist trade. But the next morning's market with its lusty Zoque provides the normal pandemonium.

The world beyond Tuxtla drops people altogether; it belongs to nature in a superb mood. There is the fine rush of the Grijalva River, silver on the green plain, and a really big river full of water in the dry season is an experience in this semi-arid land.

Zapotec

The mountains are more beautiful than those in Oaxaca because they are still clothed in virgin forest, a treasury of precious woods which is already in danger of despoilment by wreckers like those of our Jay Gould days. In Oaxaca countless generations of charcoal burners and corn planters have destroyed most of the virgin stands, but nobody lives in these Chiapas mountains. There is no human vestige but the Highway itself, opening up vistas of range on range of forested peaks and steep ravines which stretch as far as the eye can follow—the world primeval.

We felt that this magnificent world had been created not long since, that a vast brooding spirit like one of William Blake's supernal creatures was still there, diffused in the crystal air. It was like surprising the act of Creation on the fifth day, before people came into the world.

With no real break, humanity evolved out of the forests. Little solitary farms appeared on the rock bastions plunging from the mountainsides and offering a level space for a cornfield; farther along there were small villages in the upland valleys. These habitations were still part of primordial nature; the small *chozas* grew out of the soil, square mud-and-wattle huts with steep four-sided roofs of thatch coming together in a sharp crest, toy copies of the mountains.

There was something inexpressibly remote about these little settlements, and as we began passing people trudging down the road to Las Casas they rushed away in terror, and the women covered their faces.

All over Mexico there is a sight so familiar that it is often used as the national symbol—an Indian, in white field pajamas, big straw sombrero, and huaraches, trotting along beside a laden burro. There was no element of this stock picture in Chiapas. There one seldom sees burros, and instead the more prosperous folk use little scrubby horses. And despite the bitter cold of these uplands there is not a pair of long trousers to be seen. The men of Chiapas go bare to mid-thigh, displaying magnificent legs of deep mahogany. Their chief garment is a *chamarra*, simply a length of homespun wool with a hole for the head, often belted and tied at the sides to form a drafty tunic. Under this, depending on the tribe, they wear white cotton shorts or curious diapers, and the more civilized Chamula add a long-sleeved white shirt.

The Chamula also wear their own parody of the Mexican sombrero, a straw hat with a pointed crown and a brim sharply rolled up at the sides. They are shod in a neoclassic sandal with a heelpiece which mounts higher up the ankle and calf in direct proportion to the man's position in tribal life. The other tribes go barefoot, but their hats are the sensation of Chiapas.

The Chiapas man's hat is a small, utterly silly affair. It is often of double-woven straw with a round crown coming to a point, embellished with a tassel of shocking-pink wool and further embellished with a cascade of narrow silk ribbons in rainbow colors. The hat varies with tribe and village; some have flat crowns and are small enough for a tiny child. All hats are tilted at a rakish angle, partly for swank, partly to shield the eyes from the sun, so the angles change with the time of day.

The handsome and clothes-conscious Tzotzil, to whom the Chamula belong, sport other accessories—a leather pouch like a boy's schoolbag hung over one shoulder, and a versatile triangle of black-and-white cotton with more tassels of shocking-pink wool. Sometimes they tie the scarf around the neck, on hot noons they shift it to the waist, and when the sky is overcast, which means piercingly cold weather, they prudently wear it turbanwise under their foolish hats. Only men of the most indisputable masculinity would be seen dead in such costumes, but the whole rakish outfit is becoming, and the Chiapanecos know it. Bachelors advertise their charms by displaying the most and brightest ribbons and tassels.

As one might expect, the female of the species is a drab little biddy-hen. Her clothing has no style, and her features are unformed and blobby, quite unlike those of her savagely handsome husband. It evidently takes long evolution to produce females with allure. Let the anthropologists explain the puzzle, but in the remote Oaxaca highlands there is this same type of flat-faced cave woman whose husband may have well-cut features. Quite possibly these Oaxaca people who live on the badlands between the valleys and the true sierra stem, like many Chiapanecos, from the earliest streams of migrants such as Australoids. And since women in general stick closer to the primitive racial pattern than men, they are more apt to remind us of our remoter ancestors, who were certainly not comely.

For fiestas the women wear gorgeous huipiles of soft white cotton woven on the old saddleback loom (as are all Chiapas garments), with inwoven or embroidered decoration in brilliant colors. But everyday wear is simply a length of homespun for skirt and for blouse a chamarra shorter than the man's, or else the *quexquemetl*, two oblongs of cloth joined diagonally so as to form points. The Chamula women weave lengths of white cotton with a narrow pinkish-red stripe, suggesting dish towels, and use them for blouses, carrying bags, and headdresses. The universal Mexican rebozo is absent, as is the gift of wearing the simplest garments with an air.

The Colonial town of San Cristóbal Las Casas is exquisitely set in a wide green bowl ringed with mountains. It lies well over seven thousand feet high, and since the sky is often overcast it is a byword among travelers for biting cold. This exotic little city of twenty-five thousand was founded in 1528 as a Spanish outpost and named for its patron, St. Christopher, and for Fray Bartolomé de las Casas, Bishop of Chiapas and a true friend of the Indians.

There is a curious footnote to history here. When Cortés came to this region he had among his forces a troop of submissive Aztecs and another of his allies, the Tlaxacalans, who had helped him defeat the detested Aztecs. He gave both groups lands in the new town, and there their descendants remain today, living in separate barrios. The Aztecs are the weavers and dyers of Las Casas, for each quarter has its craft. In Cerillo they are iron-workers; in Guadalupe they make wooden toys; in San Ramón, pottery; and in Santa Lucía, the fireworks for fiestas. Another barrio is the home of Quiché Indians whose ancestors fled here from Guatemala three centuries ago.

It is significant that the city is thus divided into groups, for the general atmosphere is one of disunion and chill, very evident to anyone coming from the friendly warmth of Oaxaca. We missed the outpouring of devotion the Zapotecs give their santos. The churches of Las Casas are often fine, and Santo Domingo is splendid; but they are cold and lonely. The people do not come in from dawn to dark, as the Oaxaqueños do, to offer flowers and golden candlelight and the loving murmur of prayers to their holy ones.

The market, too, raised steeply above the street, seemed to us a poor affair, poor in goods and in spirit. The townspeople scuttled up the stone steps to buy their provisions, not stopping for friendly chats. As for the Indians, they knew just enough pidgin Spanish to learn the price of thread or salt, but they did not even talk to each other, and we began to think that the urge for byplay and joking, or even simple conversation, must have developed late in human evolution and that these splintered tribes had not yet reached the stage of verbalizing for the fun of it.

One enjoyed the frivolous hats the men wore above their thundercloud sullen faces, the peppermint-striped chamarras of the Chamula, and the sight of a tiny Tzotzil, dressed just like his father, being yanked by the scruff of his little red girdle to be given the breast. One puzzled mostly at this grab bag of racial odds and ends. There were Negroid and Mongoloid types rather like those carved on the Dancers stones of Monte Albán. But there were others—and I was never able to identify their race—who whirled my thoughts back twenty thousand years.

Zapotec

First, in the market press, I was hurtled against an ancient crone about four feet high, and I'm afraid I gasped when I saw her face, a child's drawing of a witch. Then I began to see pairs —father and son—and finally a family plodded down the street, and I knew where I was. I was in the Museum of Natural History, looking at a life group of extinct people.

There they came, the vanished Australoids, first the man, leaning on his staff, then the woman with her baby, then the older children. They were squat, humped little people with prognathous jaws thrust far forward, extremely narrow foreheads, wild black hair, and the squint eyes of paleolithic man. They were naked except for a garment of rough wool worn like an animal skin.

They plodded forward, heads bent to the ground, and there was something so invincibly patient—as the woolly mammoth was patient—in their gait that for the moment I saw that long trek the length of Asia and North America that had ended for them in Chiapas. I felt that this very family had made that most toilsome migration of all human history. It seemed impossible that people could live in Chiapas two hundred centuries or more and still look like Stone Age man.

But there they were, a proof of human tenacity and refusal to change except at the pace of the slow old clock which ticked in centuries instead of minutes. After all, it took Stone Age man 100,000 years to make improvements in his tools, and by that measure this family coming to market was speeding up evolution.

Until somebody corrects me, I shall continue to think them survivals of the once widespread Australoids, like their distant kinsmen, the Vedda of India and the Ainu of Japan. Long ago the Australoids began boiling over from an original center, probably in India, some of them going down over now sunken land links to become the blackfellows of Australia, others working north through Asia and crossing the ice cap that covered what is now Bering Sea. Over a period of from 25,000 to 15,000 B.C. there were successive waves of these migrants, and scientists can trace their passage south along our Pacific coast by the great heaps of oyster and abalone shells they left behind.

Slowly, leaving contingents all along the trail, the Australoids worked their way to South America. They may have left a group which developed into today's Chontal of Oaxaca, who suggest a common ancestry with the blackfellows of Australia. Possibly they were not the first immigrants to the Americas, but they became citizens before the last great ice cap had begun its retreat. And now, in Las Casas, they were still indomitably on the march.

After the excitement of encountering the primitives, the Bloms remind one that Chiapas is also Maya country. The home of the archaeologist-explorer Frans Blom and his gifted wife Gertrud Duby is a charming old villa on the edge of a ravine, where one is welcomed with a roaring fire and animated talk over coffee and cake. It is also a museum of Maya past and present which will be presented to the nation upon Blom's death; a library, a collection of tribal objects, and documentary films to supplement Gertrud Duby's eloquent photographs.

Frans Blom is a lean, blue-eyed Dane who came to the Maya country in 1918 and has stayed ever since, becoming an authority on the ancient civilizations and filling in blank spaces on the maps. He has written *The Conquest of Yucatan*, an easy and entertaining book about the Maya, and in collaboration with Oliver La Farge the valuable *Tribes and Temples*. One wishes he would write more, but much of his time is still spent in the saddle exploring highland and jungle for traces of the Maya.

All students of these wonderful people turn into mild fanatics on the subject, and Blom is no exception. He reveres and loves all Maya, even their poor relations, and those for whom he feels the most affection are the weird Lacandones, a hundred-odd vanishing people who live in the jungles near Guatemala. Once he found them starving from crop failures and sent a runner back to the nearest settlement to alert the government. When food was dropped by a plane, Blom became the white god of the Lacondones, and the bond between them is so deep that almost every year the Bloms make the difficult trip to the snake-infested swamps where the Lacondones, still speaking the pure Maya tongue and worshiping the ancient gods, are living out their span.

It is a wonder that anyone found these people. They live in an unexplored region of dense jungle threaded by lakes, where the growth is so thick that on their first journey it took the Bloms fifty-five days to travel fifty miles, literally cutting their way through the jungle with machetes. Since then the interest in this handful of unreconstructed pagans has become so intense that a group of Mexican anthropologists are planning to build an air strip in the jungle and begin excavations of a site which appears to be ancient and promising.

The living Lacondones are apparently the residue of humble Maya who stayed behind when most of their people emigrated to Yucatan in the seventh century. They live by fishing, shooting wild game with the bow and arrow, and raising corn. They have domesticated the wild pig of the region but have not managed to exterminate the dangerous snakes around them. Living all these centuries without the slightest contact with the outside world, they offer a perfect museum exhibit of the Old Maya gone retrograde. The men have two or three wives, who nurse each other's babies with complete impartiality. Men and women dress exactly alike in a single rough cotton garment and leave their straight black hair long and unkempt. They continue to worship the rain god and offer the first ears of the corn crop ground into meal and set afloat in a gourd in a stream or lake. Their creation myths are rich and fascinating, and they believe that in the end the world will be eaten up "by the big jaguar."

Blom can take one outside his house and point to Maya sites, as yet quite unexplored, all around the mountains near Las Casas. He has learned to be patient about the delay in excavation, which is a slow and expensive business in a country which offers an *embarras de richesses.* A story is told about Frans Blom attending an archaeologists' meeting in Mexico City, when a project was discussed for building a museum which would house all the country's ancient treasures under one roof.

"Under one roof?" Blom asked.

"Yes," a savant answered. "How large do you think it should be?"

"Oh," said Blom negligently, "about the size of the Mexican sky."

There is another sort of excavation which Blom finds just as fascinating, and that is digging into the customs and folklore of the Chiapas people to find links with the past. But Blom the archaeologist is always getting derailed by Blom the good neighbor. Having worked out my theory about Esquipulas as the site of an ancient pilgrimage fair quite independently, I was naturally delighted to have Blom confirm it. But he ruined my picture of modern pilgrimages to San Esquipulas, the great healer of afflictions, particularly blindness.

"This cult has been blinding hundreds of people," he said. "A while back the state of Chiapas asked me to investigate the terrible epidemic of onchocercosis, the blindness caused by an insect bite. They were sure that this disease was connected with the pilgrimages. Following a hunch, I avoided the main highways and worked along the old trade road across the mountains. Finally I located three villages where the parasite was rampant. The upshot is that pilgrimages to San Esquipulas are now strictly forbidden. I had to have an operation to save my own eyes."

It was Blom and La Farge who in 1925 alerted the scientific world to the strange monuments they found in La Venta in Tabasco, and thus started what Blom calls "the Olmec craze." He made a wry face when I mentioned the word "Olmec," which is anathema to all Maya devotees, who feel that their people alone were responsible for the great days of Middle America.

"I find the first colossal head," he complained good-naturedly, "and suddenly everybody goes wild about this mysterious culture. It's Olmec this and Olmec that, but it doesn't get us anywhere."

No, it doesn't get us anywhere fast enough to satisfy the itch to know, right away, the solution of the greatest mystery in the New World. Perhaps our modern clocks are running too fast, and we must listen to the slow tick of mid-America, where such momentous advances in man's consciousness took place so long ago.

XIV

INDIAN TIME

One of the curious things that happens to a newcomer in Oaxaca is the realization that the Indians live in a time scheme completely different from our familiar one. This does not mean simply that they do without clocks and regulate the day's activities by the position of the sun. It means that there is a conception, an attitude, even a way of life that can be summed up as Indian Time.

We are all vividly conscious of time in the sense of having just so much of it to spend before the next appointment and before the final appointment with death. But what do we know about the great abstraction Time? Perhaps it does not exist at all. Perhaps it is only something we have evolved to measure things that interest us, the life of living creatures and of solar systems. The central clock ticks in the veins of men, with the pulse. Moths and kittens carry a smaller timepiece, and so we pity them; the California redwoods, with their mighty life span, are envied as closer to a godlike immortality. All we can do is to measure the life of everything from the moth to Mars, and know that Time is relative.

But we have a very definite conception of time as experienced by human beings, and it happens to be completely different from the Indian picture. To us Anglo-Saxons time is horizontal, and in movement. It is a stream moving out of the past through the present into the future, and the human game is to rush with time as far

273

into the future as possible. It is a one-way current which inevitably carries us toward death. All who embark on the stream of time face in the same direction: toward the future and toward death.

This conception is intolerable; we all secretly hate and fear time. Since there is no way of reversing the current, we have invented all sorts of devices for concealing the dreadful nature of time as the force impelling us toward death. We Americans are especially busy at these desperate games. Since we have "so little time," we chop it up into small rations and admire the man who "packs a tremendous amount into a day." We dramatize our duel with time; we are avid to possess as much of the future as possible, to "get ahead fast." The strongest swimmer "gets somewhere" and the drifter is left in a backwater. The past is dead, it is "behind" us. Our language is full of phrases revealing our intense consciousness of time as a rapidly moving stream whose destination is extinction.

Horrible as it is, we think this is the only possible description of time. But the Indians have lived for thousands of years by almost the opposite conception, which was the core of Middle American religion.

To the Indians, time is vertical, and it does not move "somewhere." It moves no more than the vast Pacific, which has its waves, tides, currents, but stays within its given space. Time cannot move because it is also space—an idea very difficult for us to grasp. It gives the Indian a relation to the three tenses that is different from ours. We live in a very narrow present, since time is moving us out of a past which is immediately dead into a future which is the next tick of the clock. The Indian lives in a present which contains all the time there is.

To the Zapotec the past is not something behind him, but around him, because he lives in an ocean, not a stream. The past is part of the present, which is a depth, an amassed fortune of experience. The future, too, is part of today because amassed experience has given him the faith that it exists as part of the vast ocean of time.

The Zapotecs do not divide time into tenses—and tensions—as we do. They do not think of their racial past as something "over and done with." They are notoriously hazy about dates and sequences, at telling a chronological story with one thing happening after another, unless there is a cause-and-effect connection. A Zapotec may relate an incident which occurred a century ago as if it had happened in his own lifetime, and in his vertical time system this is correct. Experience, like faith, lives in today, which is the three tenses merged in space-time.

Despite the confusion of Christian ideas mixed with pagan faiths, the modern Zapotec has held onto the general attitude which was the heart of the classic religion. Instead of fearing time, he worships it as a divine gift. Because he is mortal there is fear in his attitude toward the future, but this is fear in the religious sense.

The Old Zapotecs, in fact, had such a terrifying conception of time that only a powerful faith could balance it. They believed that time shared human mortality and that only the kindness of the gods could keep it going. The Middle American clock stopped dead at the end of the fifty-two-year calendar round. This period was about the span of human life as well as the interval necessary for the pije to fall in with the solar calendar. Thus we may take it that time was regarded as human and mortal, and became god-like only through periodic renewal. The Middle American religion hinged on the necessity for the resurrection of time.

Every half century the Middle Americans faced the possibility of universal death. In this atomic age we are beginning to understand this terror all too well, but our situation is worse because the threat is chronic, and we have no religious conviction that life will continue. The Middle Americans believed that by prayer and sacrifice throughout the cycle they must keep their gods kindly disposed; and at the crucial moment of decision all mankind must pray together for its clock to start ticking again. The choice was total extinction or total worship.

Perhaps no religion has ever had such a powerful driving force. A man may accept his own mortality, but he cannot bear to think that his sons and grandsons will not follow him. Therefore, each individual was impelled to live aright in the sight of the gods, for the life of all humanity depended on him. It seems a big burden for one soul to carry, but the core of Indian thought is that the individual is the race and vice versa, and thus all burdens and blessings are shared.

Christian mysticism contains this realization that all men are members of each other, as every vital religion must. There is no escaping human interdependence. In the closed world of Middle America the unifying and disciplinary force of the effort to keep time going could operate in a remarkably effective way. Today human survival is a global matter, and half the globe is supposed to hope that the other half will be extinguished.

Here again our conception of time plays a pernicious role. We are so obsessed with the idea of time as a rapidly moving stream that the Western world is trying to swim with frantic haste to beat the other half of the world into the future. Thus our duel with the world behind the Iron Curtain becomes more a matter of competing schedules than of clashing faiths. Both halves of the globe are becoming totalitarian because both are in a race against time.

We cannot switch our whole concept of life in midstream and suddenly believe, with the Indian, that one must not struggle against time since it is the element in which we live. And yet there is something in Middle American history which ties in with today's crisis: peace is the first necessity; it is the only condition in which people can slowly learn to live as brothers.

We think that it is impossible to establish peace until people are better human beings, and that there will not be time enough for humanity to improve before the atom and hydrogen bombs extinguish us altogether. Indirectly we blame the shortness of time for our dilemma. The Indian would say that we have all the time there is, and that people are, and probably will continue to be, very much the same.

Middle America, with all its varied peoples, managed to live in a state of peace. We have only a vague idea how the Zapotecs managed to maintain their thousand-year truce or to get it started. But evidently they began with religion, for Monte Albán is the expression of space-time. They kept their warriors trained and armed against possible aggressors, but most of their energies were directed to spreading their religion and its culture among a widening circle of neighbors and maintaining a lively trade with them.

There was one other method which the followers of the magic calendar used to preserve a condition of peace, a method with which few Americans can feel sympathy. That was the doctrine that each man's fate, his name, and his animal totem were determined by his position in time, his birthday. It seems impossible to us that this idea should keep people happy and contented, but because of the whole cultural context it kept them not so much static as stable. They learned to accept fate, to be themselves, to be content with being themselves. When one says that this attitude was the source of Benito Juárez's strength, as it has been of the Zapotec race in general, one begins to get a glimmering of what Indian Time is. It is not necessarily connected with a religious cult, but it contains the essence of religion: that the individual must first of all be at peace with himself and with the mysterious forces which brought him into being, and then he is ready to live quietly with his fellows. The man who said, "Respect for the rights of others is peace," lived in Indian Time.

In Oaxaca even an American, as full of anxiety about the future as any other, can feel what Indian Time is. Perhaps it is the simplest of all pictures, a man with a wooden plow following his oxen home at sunset. Who can place this picture in our sort of

Zapotec

time? It is timeless, the tiller of earth going home after his day in the sun. This man with his earth-stained plow is one with his race and one with the everlasting forces of nature. The rhythm of labor and rest, of planting and reaping, of prayer and fiesta, this is the pulse of time in Oaxaca.

ACKNOWLEDGMENTS

The writer wishes to thank Mr. E. R. Frissell and Mr. Howard Leigh of Mitla for allowing her many fruitful excursions through their fine collections of Zapotec art. She is indebted to Mr. and Mrs. Frans Blom of San Cristóbal Las Casas for a glimpse of their Maya world.

Librarians can never be thanked enough for shortening the task of research. Señora Jovita Zubaran of the Benjamin Franklin Library in Mexico City, Dr. Jorge F. Ituribbaria of the Oaxaca State Library, and Mr. Sylvester Vigilanti and Mr. Ivor Avellino of that wonderful Room 300 in the New York Public Library have been resourceful in suggesting material.

Very special thanks are due to Dr. Alfonso Caso for finding time in his busy life to illuminate many problems about ancient Oaxaca, to present the writer with special material, and, best of all, to show her through his superb collection of Zapotec pieces under study in Coyoacán.

Mr. Walter A. Fairservis, Jr., of the American Museum of Natural History generously cleared up a basic question about the beginnings of Middle American culture.

And finally, the writer is under the greatest obligation to Dr. Gordon F. Ekholm of the Museum for patiently going over the chapters on Oaxaca's prehistory and correcting the worst blunders.

In expressing her thanks to these archaeologists the writer must absolve them from any responsibility for the speculations she has allowed herself in trying to suggest a solution to the mystery of ancient Middle America.